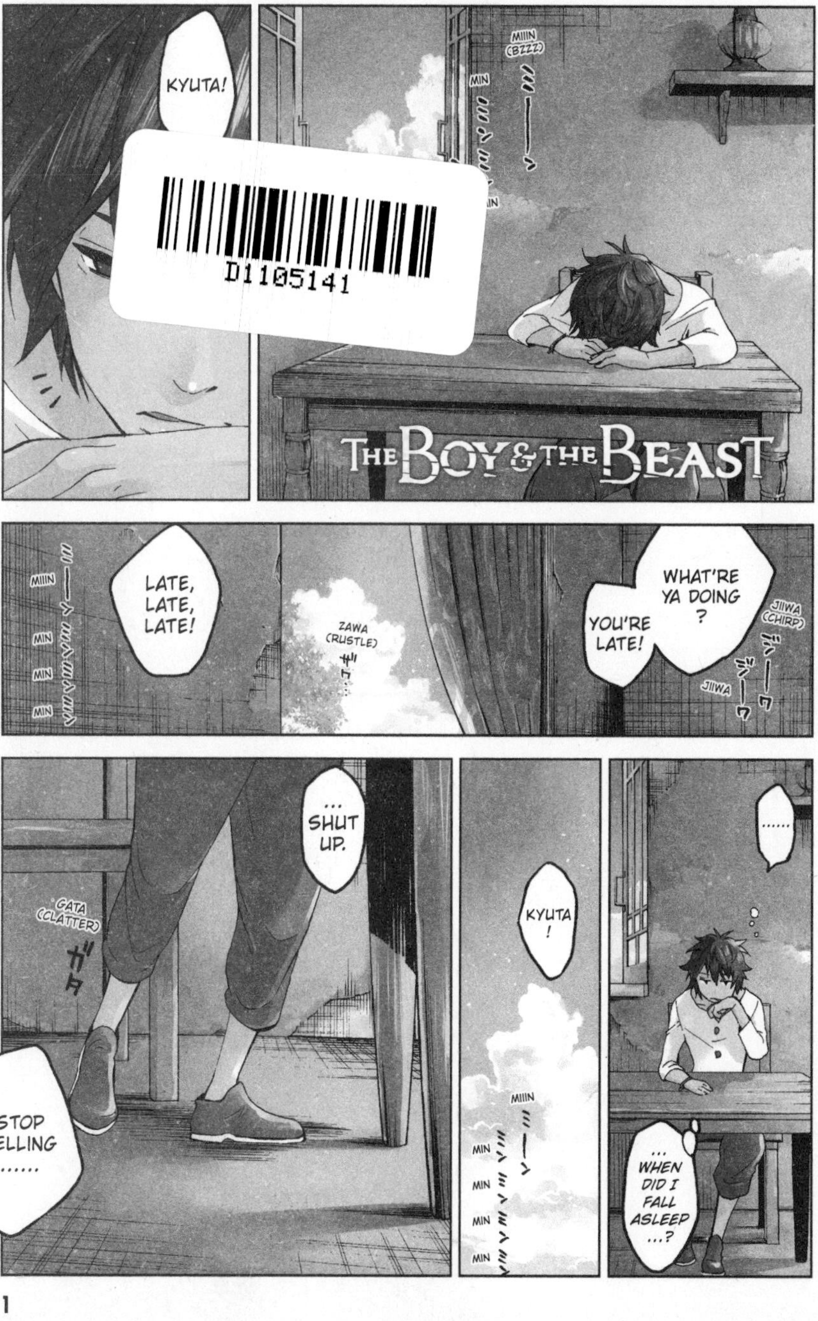
MIIN (BZZZ)
MIN
MIN
THE BOY & THE BEAST
KYUTA!
WHAT'RE YA DOING?
YOU'RE LATE!
JIIWA (CHIRP)
JIIWA
ZAWA (RUSTLE)
LATE, LATE, LATE!
MIIN
MIN
MIN
MIN
......
... WHEN DID I FALL ASLEEP ...?
KYUTA!
MIIN
MIN
MIN
MIN
MIN
... SHUT UP.
GATA (CLATTER)
STOP YELLING ......

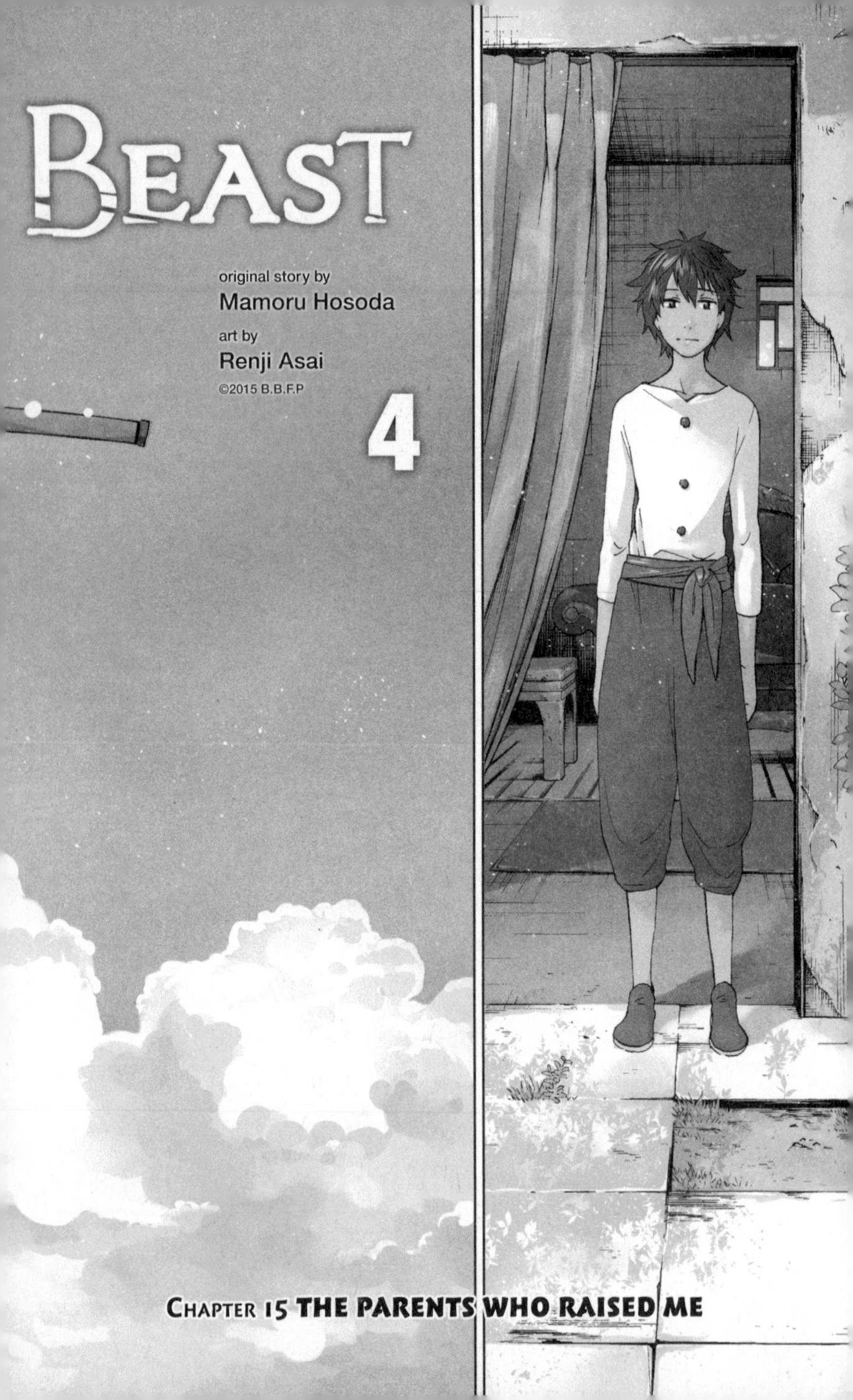
BEAST
original story by
Mamoru Hosoda
art by
Renji Asai
©2015 B.B.F.P
4
CHAPTER 15 THE PARENTS WHO RAISED ME

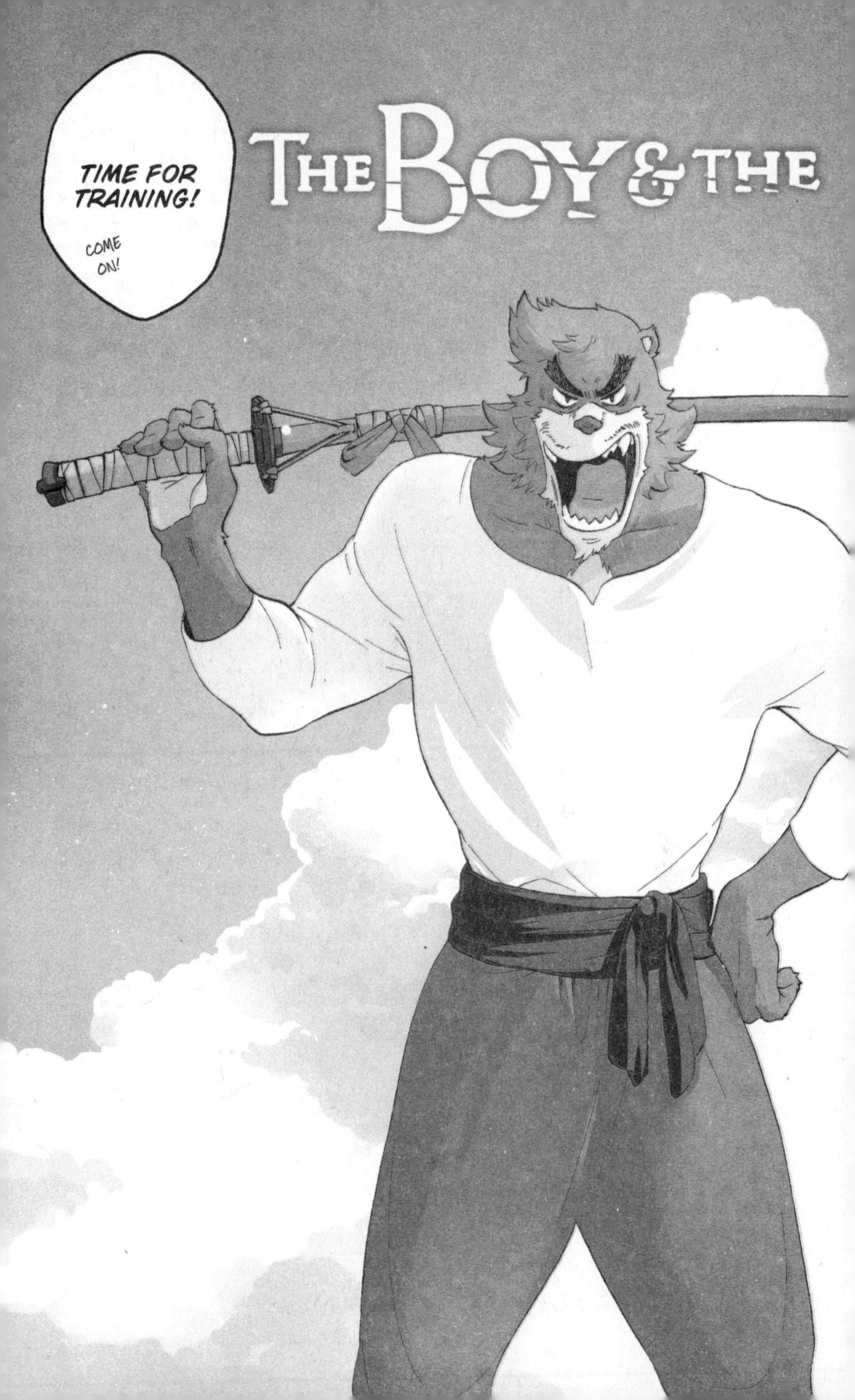
TIME FOR TRAINING!
COME ON!
THE BOY & THE

THE BOY & THE BEAST

original story by
Mamoru Hosoda

art by
Renji Asai

4

CONTENTS

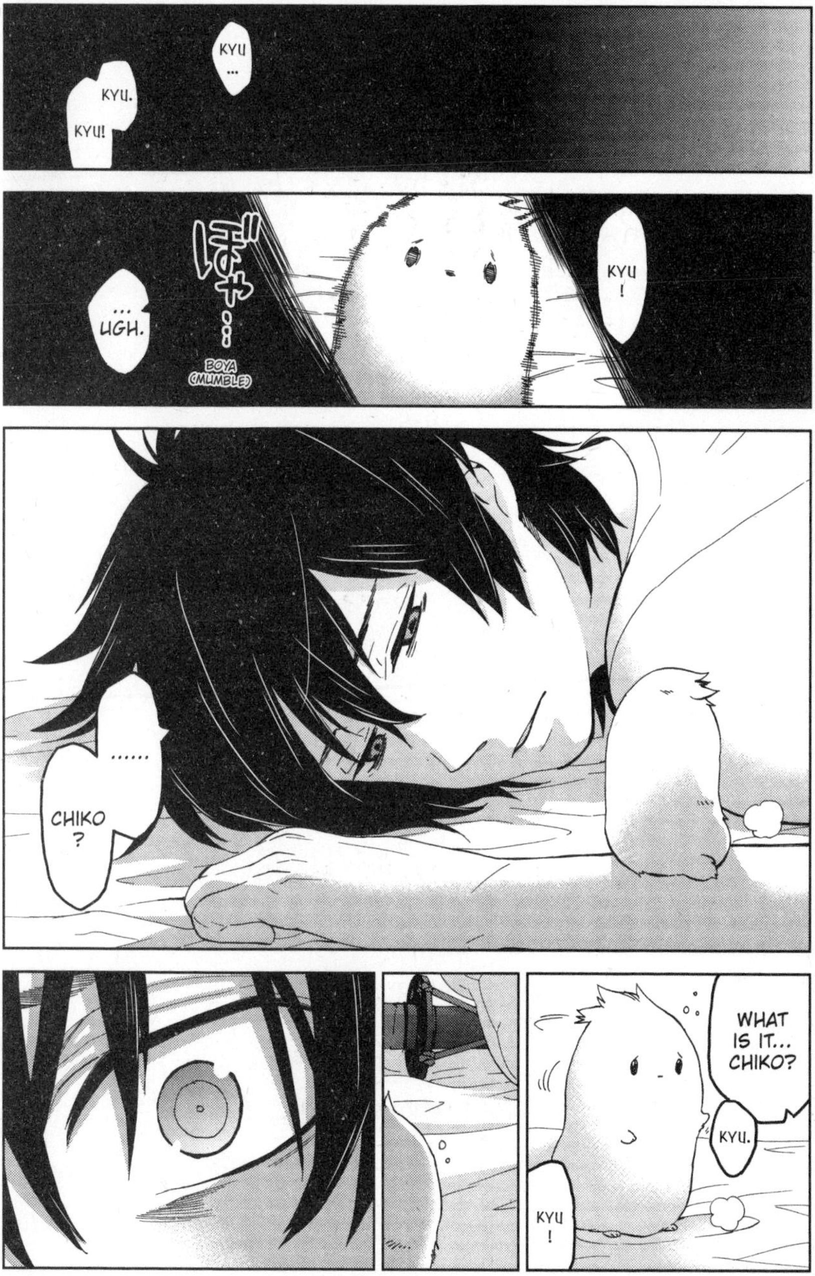
KYU ...
KYU.
KYU!
KYU !
ぼや…
BOYA (MUMBLE)
... UGH.
...... CHIKO ?
WHAT IS IT... CHIKO?
KYU.
KYU !

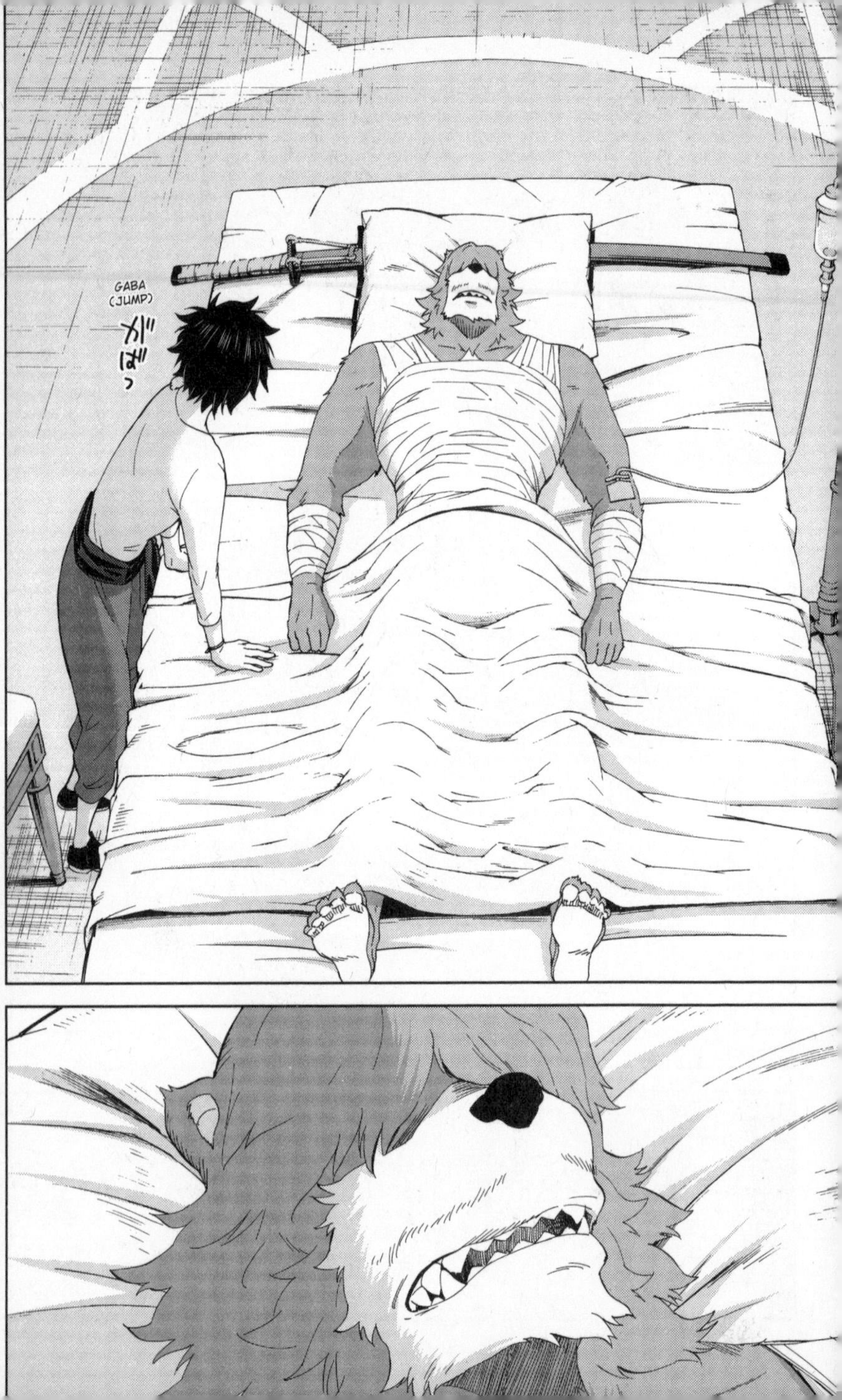
GABA (JUMP)
ガバっ

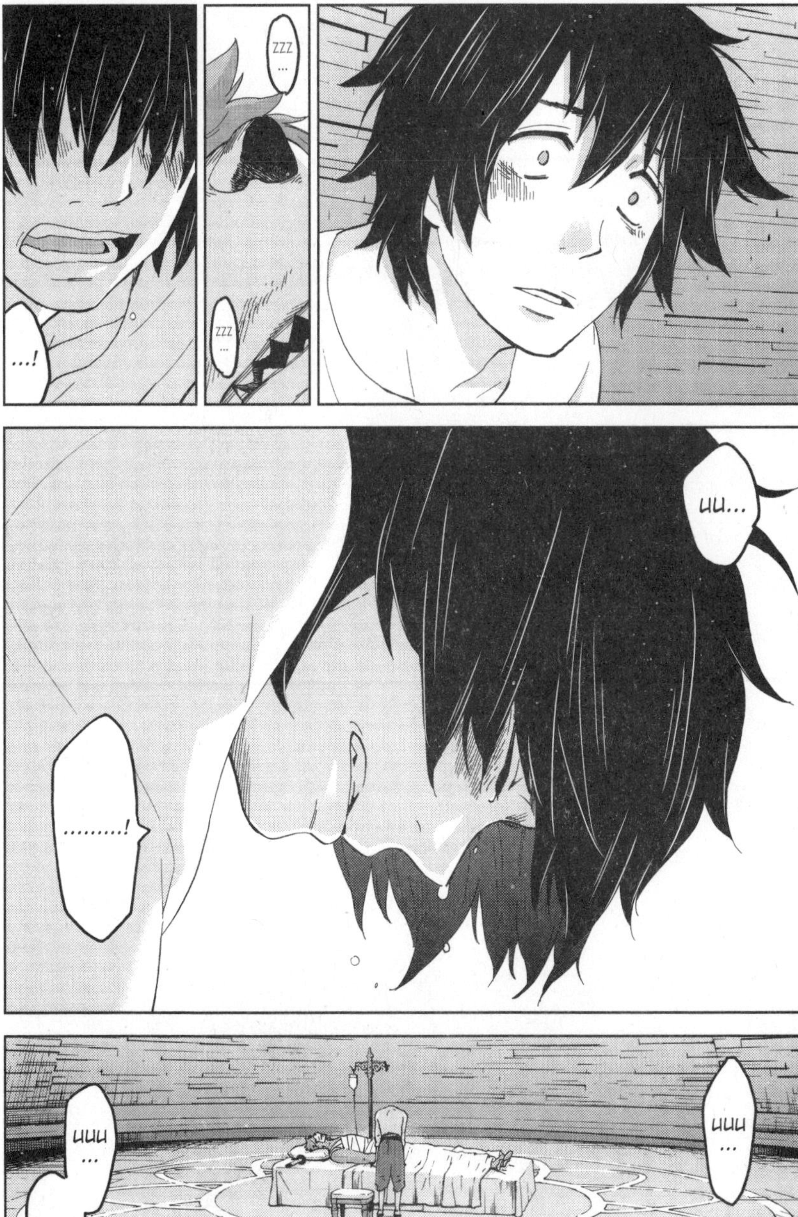
ZZZ
...
ZZZ
...
...!
uu...
.........!
uuu
...
uuu
...
......

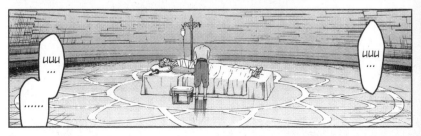

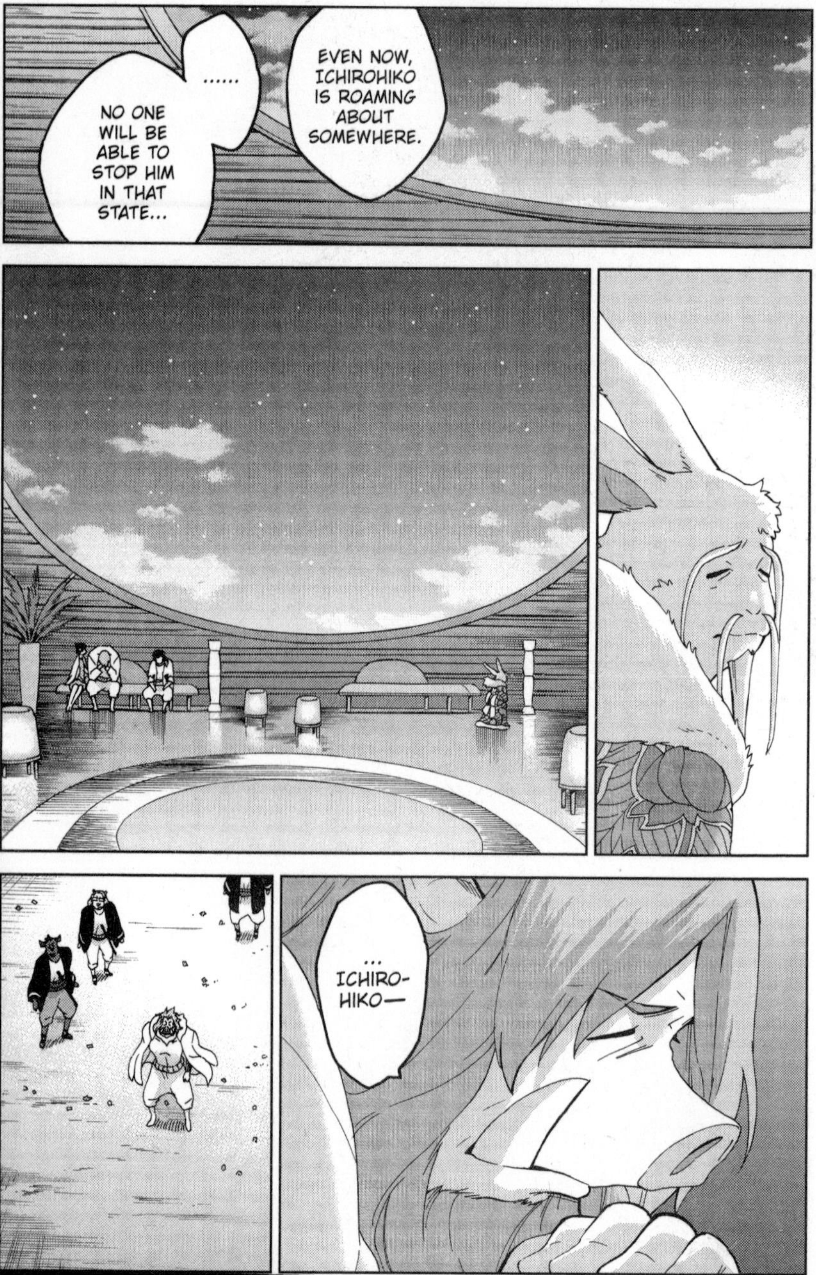
EVEN NOW, ICHIROHIKO IS ROAMING ABOUT SOMEWHERE.
......
NO ONE WILL BE ABLE TO STOP HIM IN THAT STATE...
... ICHIRO-HIKO—

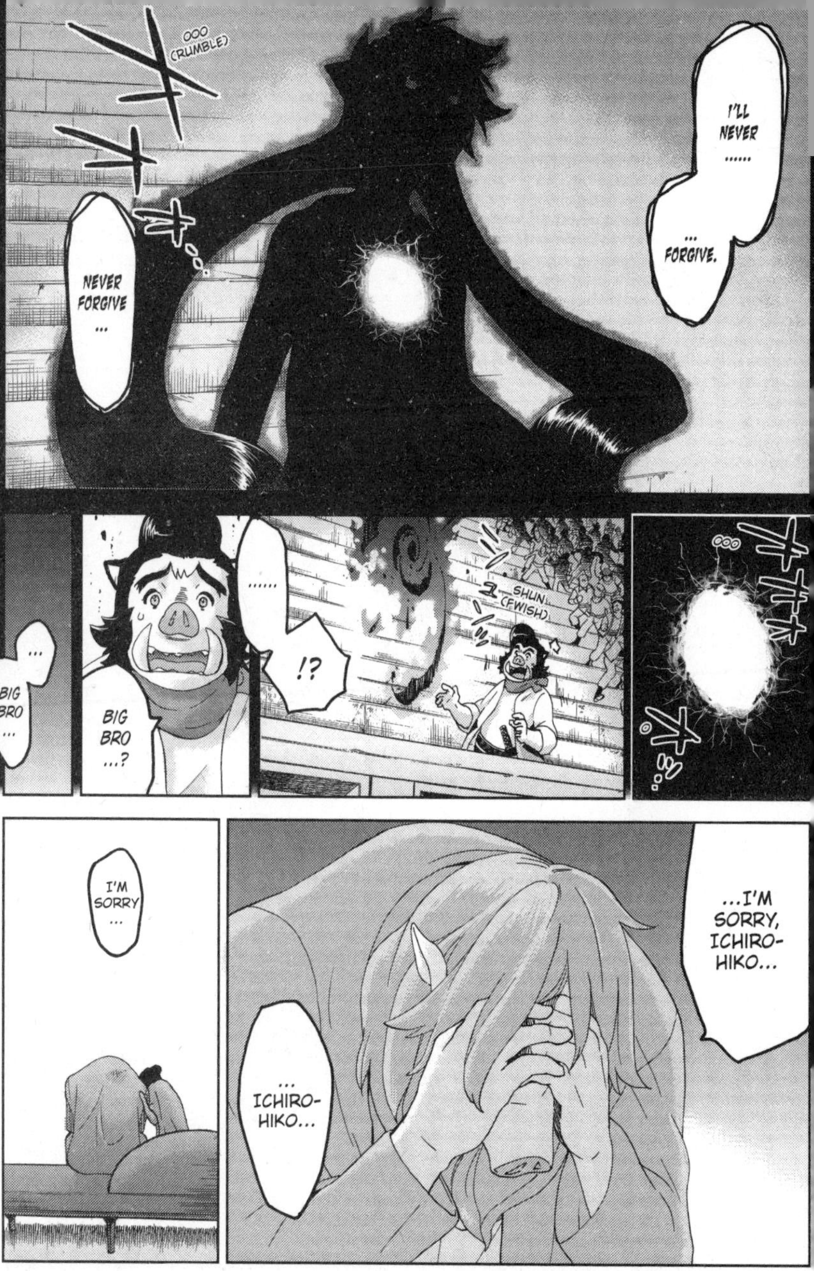
I'LL NEVER ......
... FORGIVE.
OOO (RUMBLE)
NEVER FORGIVE ...
OOO
SHUN (FWISH)
!?
......
BIG BRO ...?
... BIG BRO ...
...I'M SORRY, ICHIRO-HIKO...
... ICHIRO-HIKO...
I'M SORRY ...

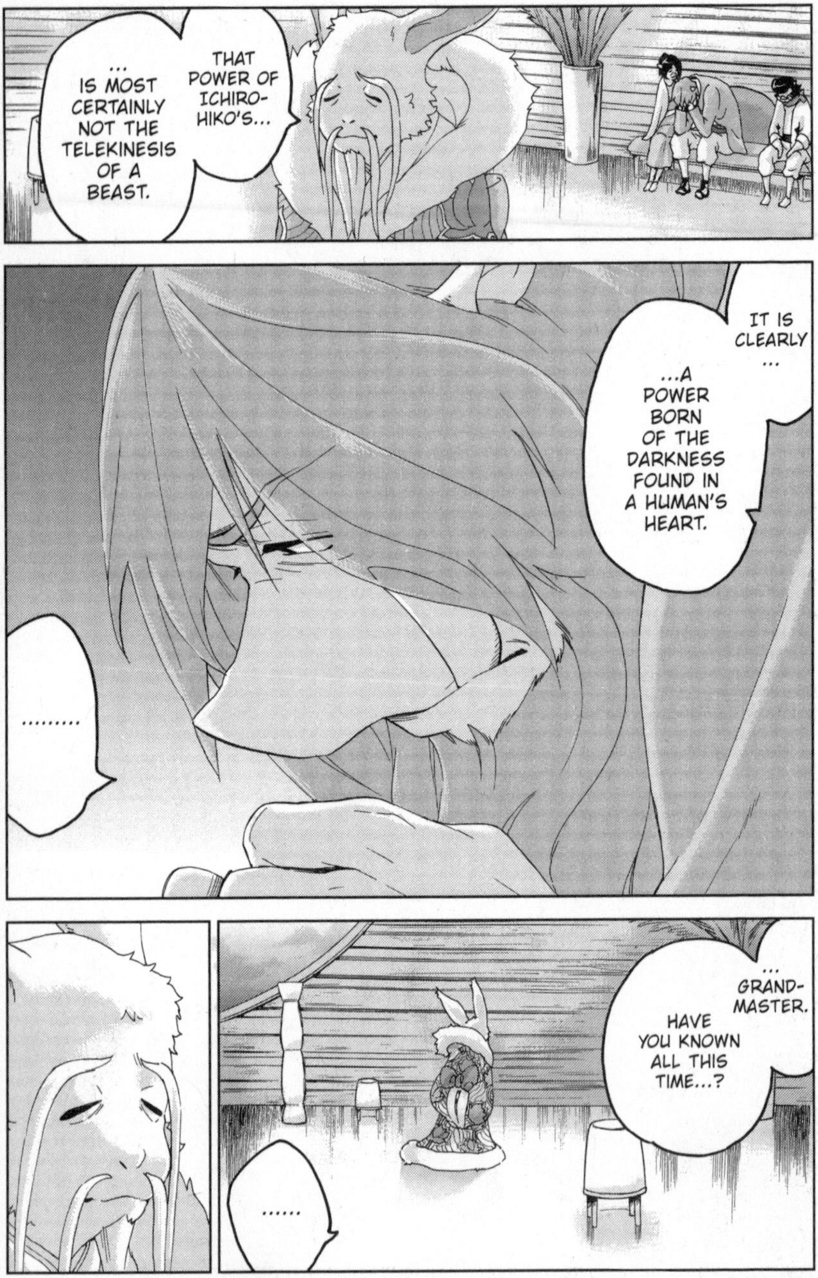
THAT POWER OF ICHIRO-HIKO'S...
... IS MOST CERTAINLY NOT THE TELEKINESIS OF A BEAST.
IT IS CLEARLY ...
...A POWER BORN OF THE DARKNESS FOUND IN A HUMAN'S HEART.
....
... GRAND-MASTER.
HAVE YOU KNOWN ALL THIS TIME...?
......

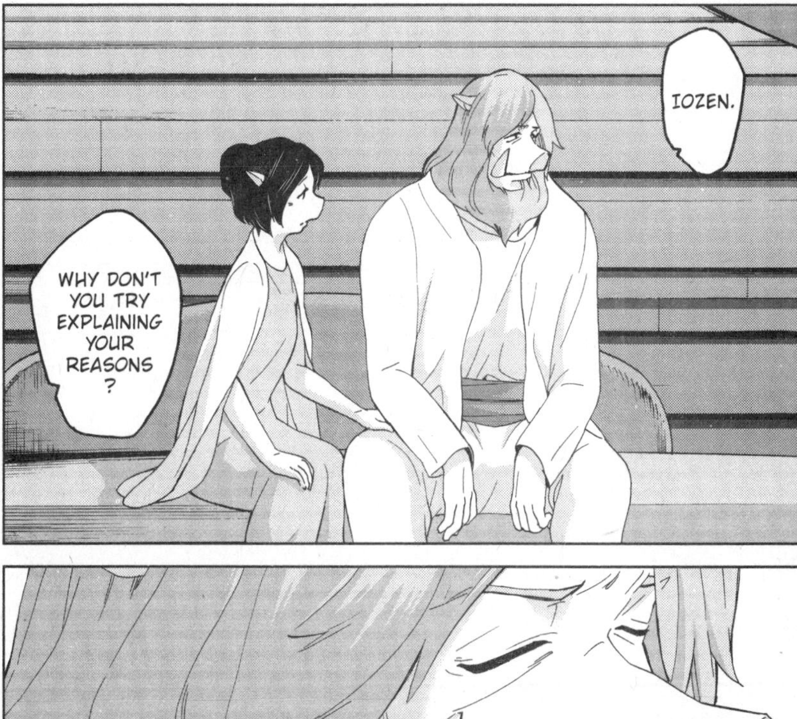
IOZEN.
WHY DON'T YOU TRY EXPLAINING YOUR REASONS?

SIGNS: STUDY ABROAD BY THE STATION / CONVERSATIONAL ENGLISH NAVA / TOKAI BANK

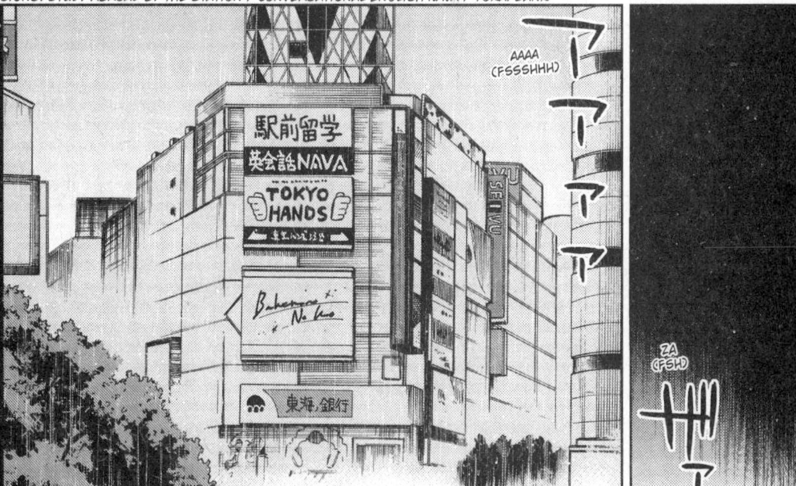
AAAA (FSSSHHH)
駅前留学
英会話NAVA
TOKYO HANDS
SEIYU
東海銀行
ZA (FSH)

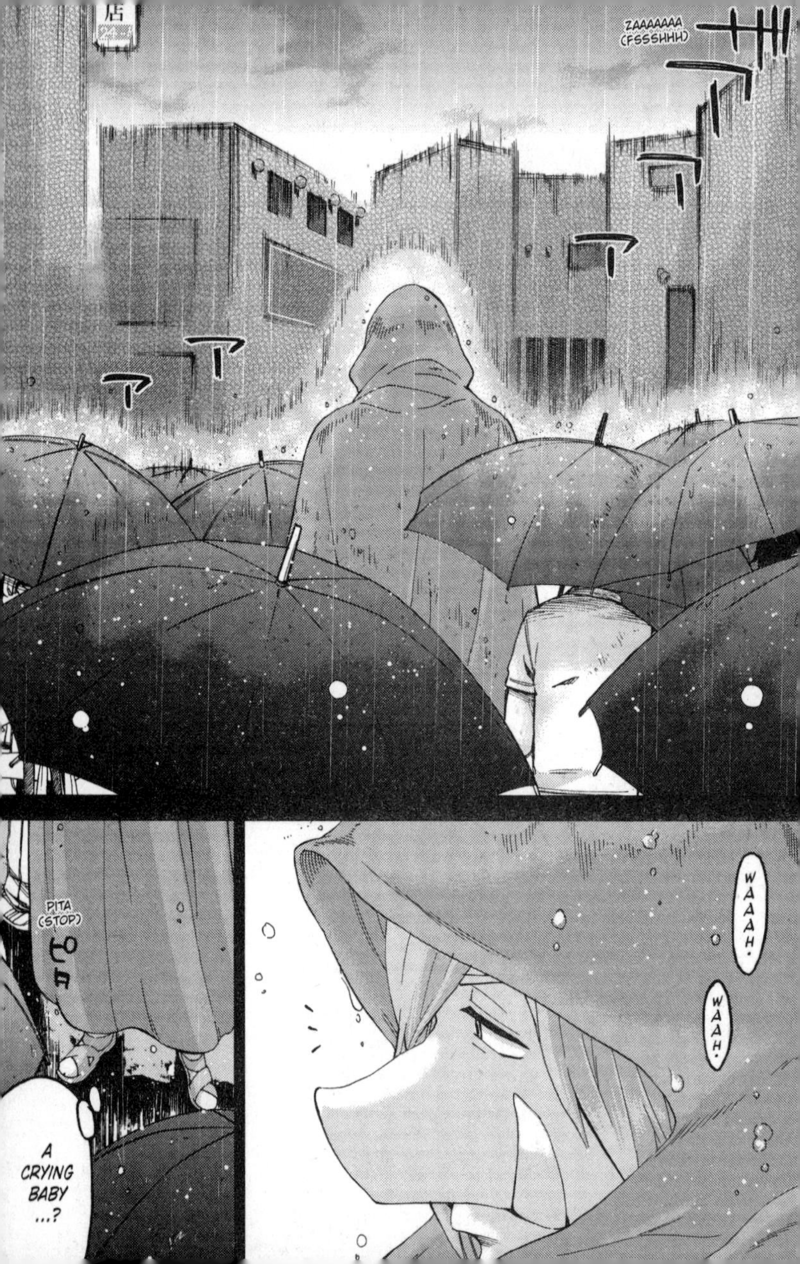

店
ZAAAAAAA (FSSSHHH)
WAAAAH.
WAAH.
PITA (STOP)
A CRYING BABY ...?

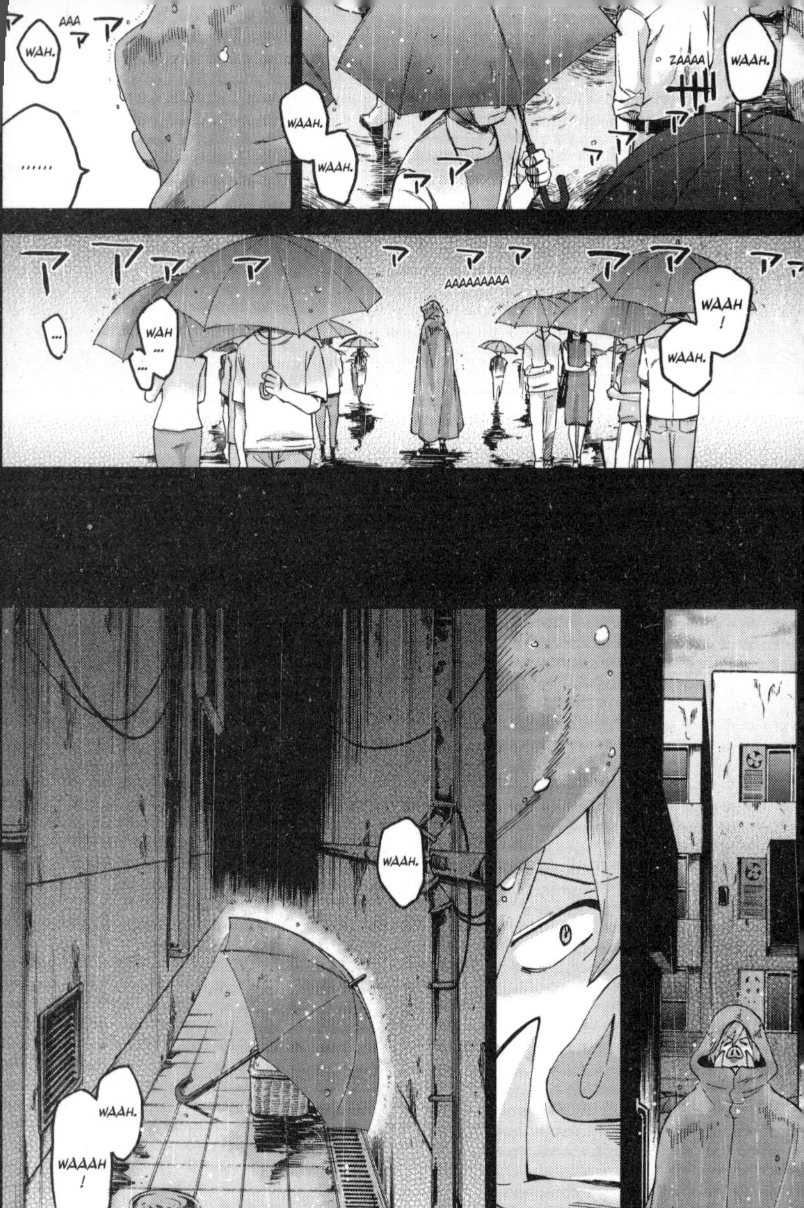
WAAH.
ZAAAA
WAAH.
WAAH.
WAH.
AAA
......
WAAH!
WAAH.
AAAAAAAAA
WAH...
...
...
WAAH.
WAAH.
WAAAH!

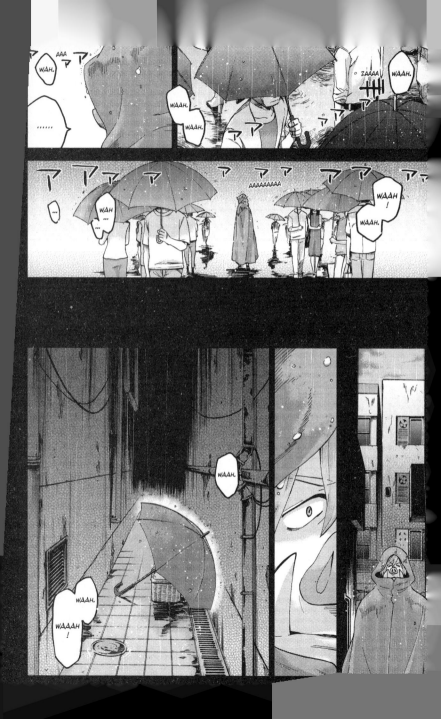

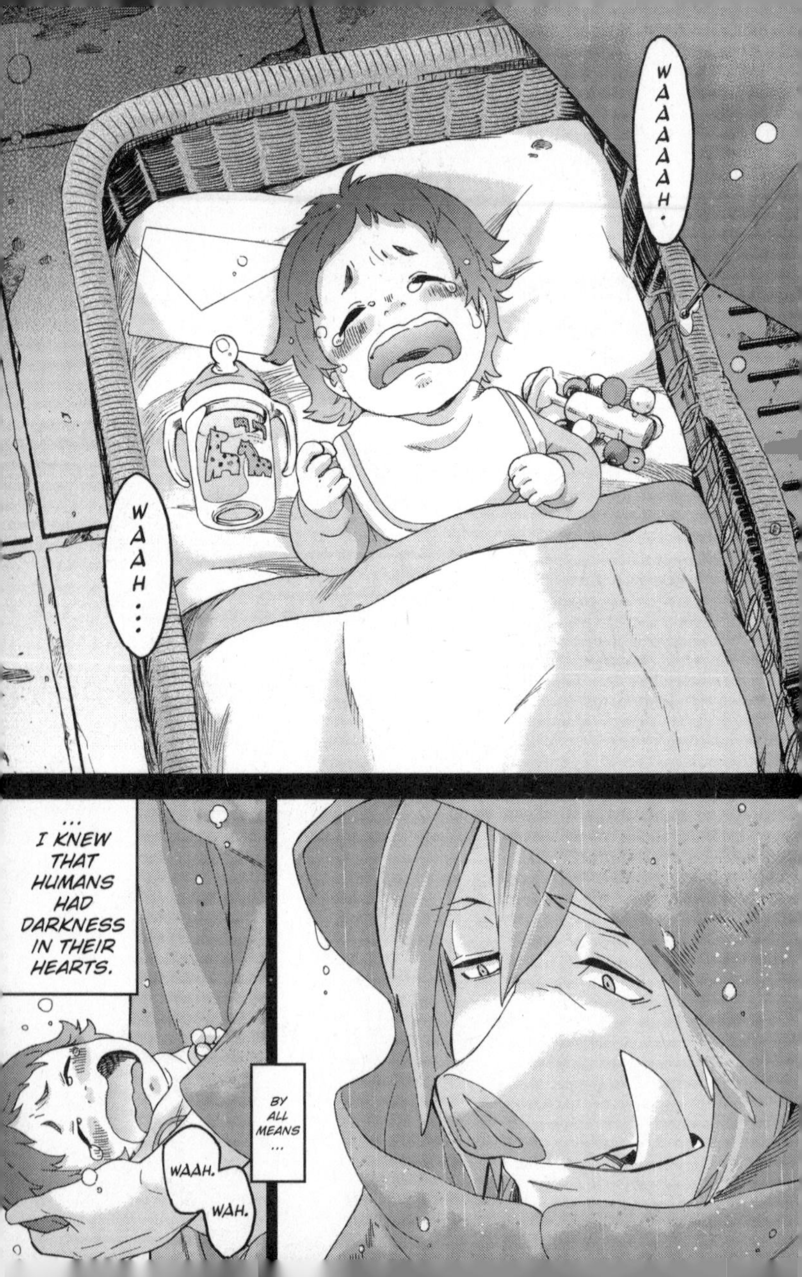
WAAAAAAH.
WAAAH...
... I KNEW THAT HUMANS HAD DARKNESS IN THEIR HEARTS.
BY ALL MEANS ...
WAAH.
WAH.

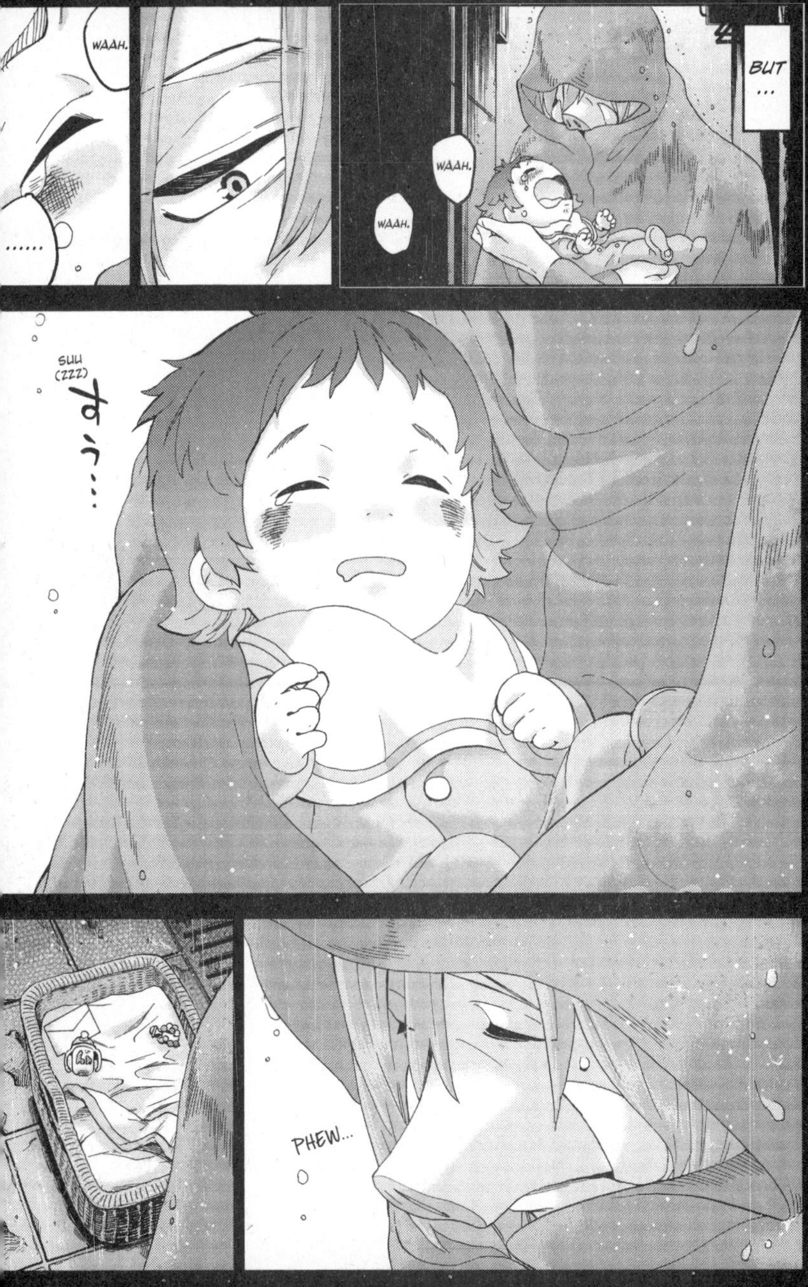
BUT...
WAAH.
WAAH.
WAAH.
......
SUU (ZZZ)
すぅ…
PHEW...

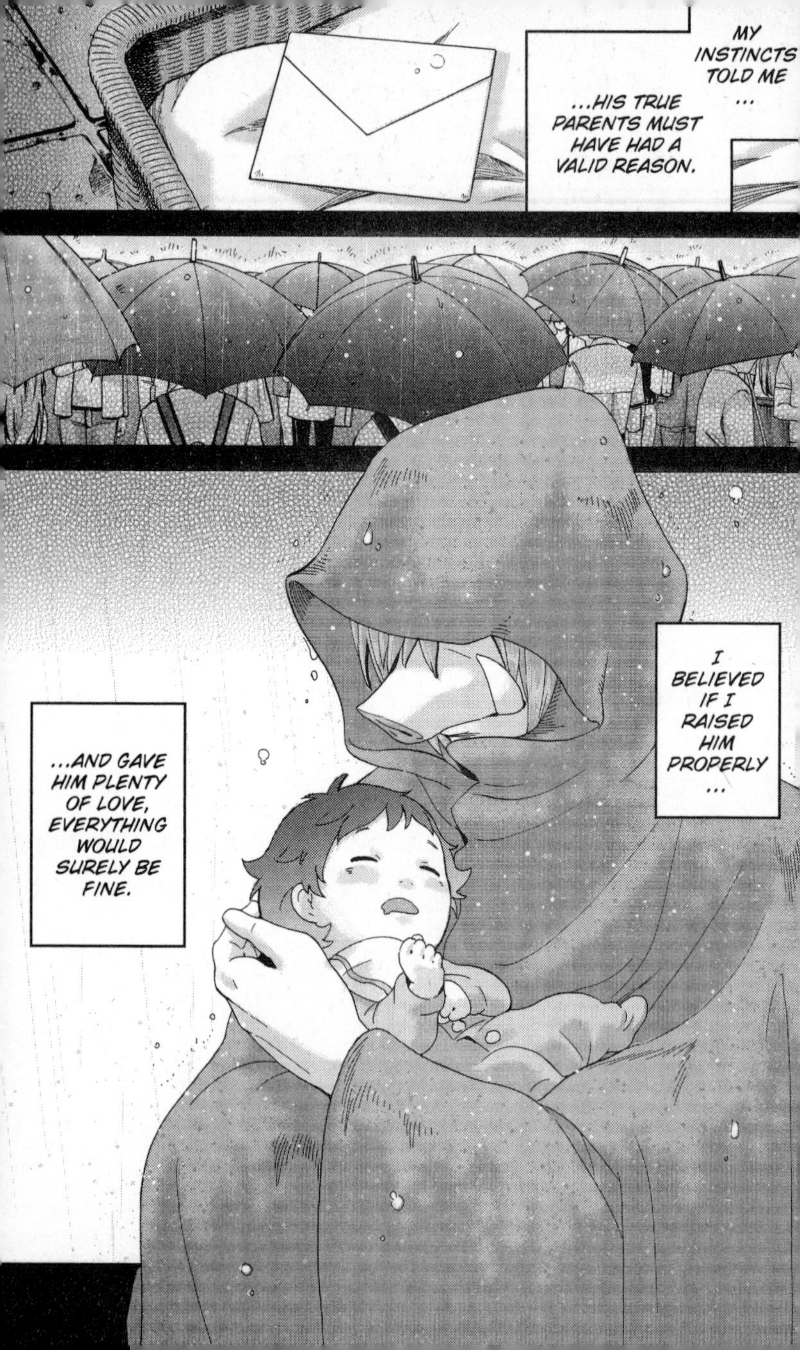
MY INSTINCTS TOLD ME ...
...HIS TRUE PARENTS MUST HAVE HAD A VALID REASON.
I BELIEVED IF I RAISED HIM PROPERLY ...
...AND GAVE HIM PLENTY OF LOVE, EVERYTHING WOULD SURELY BE FINE.

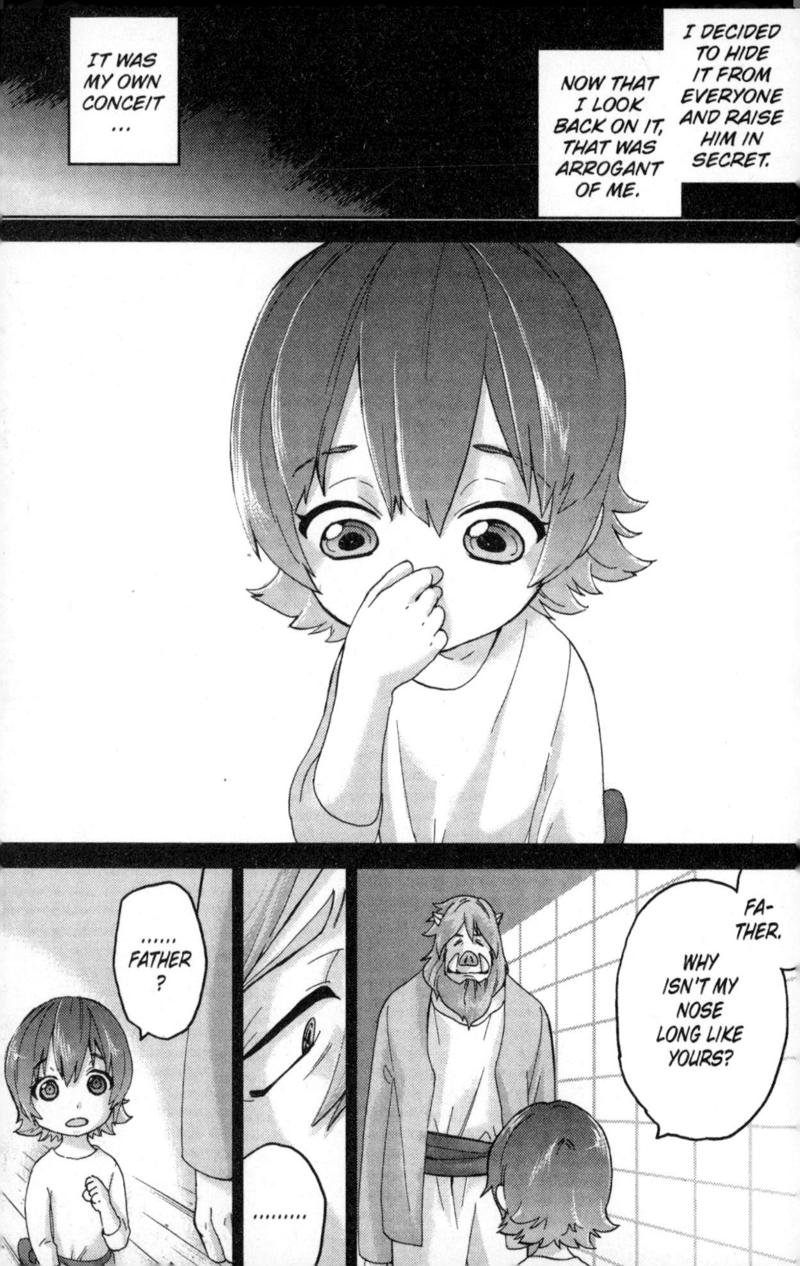
I DECIDED TO HIDE IT FROM EVERYONE AND RAISE HIM IN SECRET.
NOW THAT I LOOK BACK ON IT, THAT WAS ARROGANT OF ME.
IT WAS MY OWN CONCEIT ...
FA- THER.
WHY ISN'T MY NOSE LONG LIKE YOURS?
....
...... FATHER ?

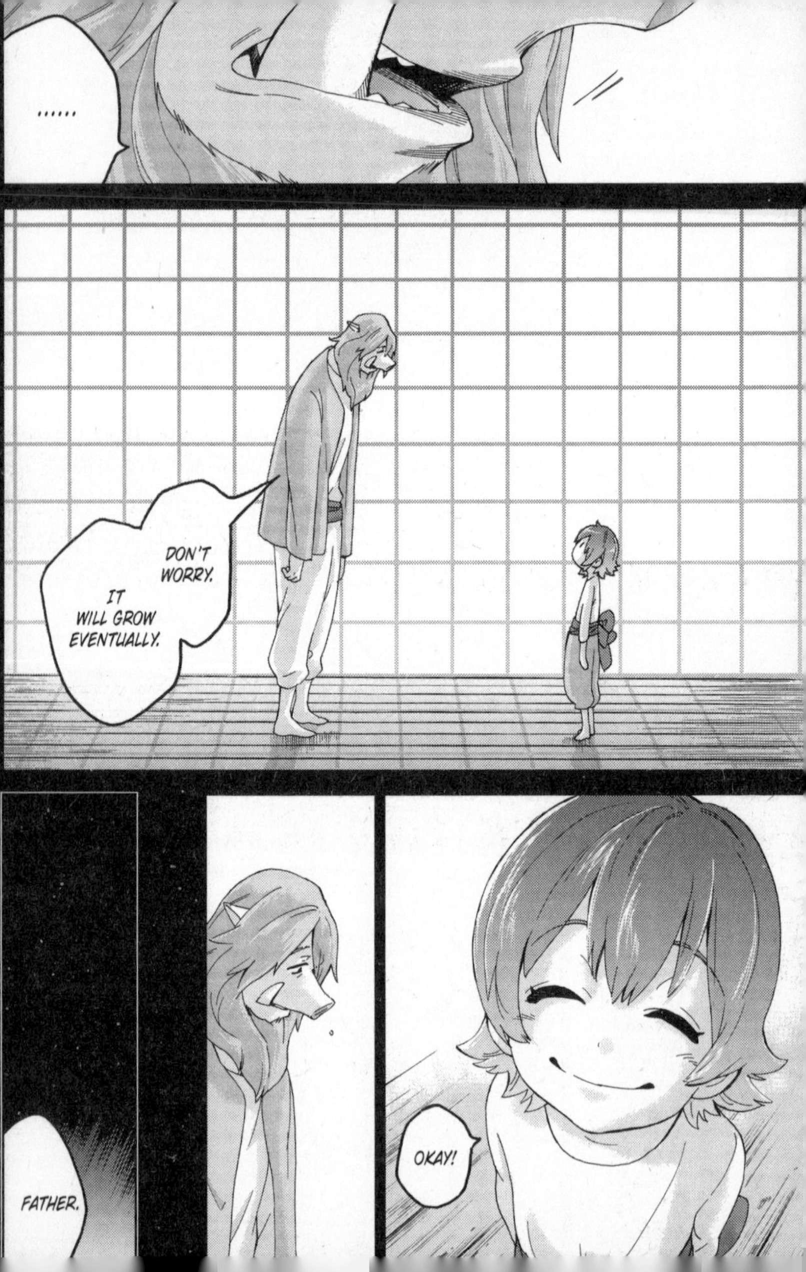
......
DON'T WORRY.
IT WILL GROW EVENTUALLY.
OKAY!
FATHER.

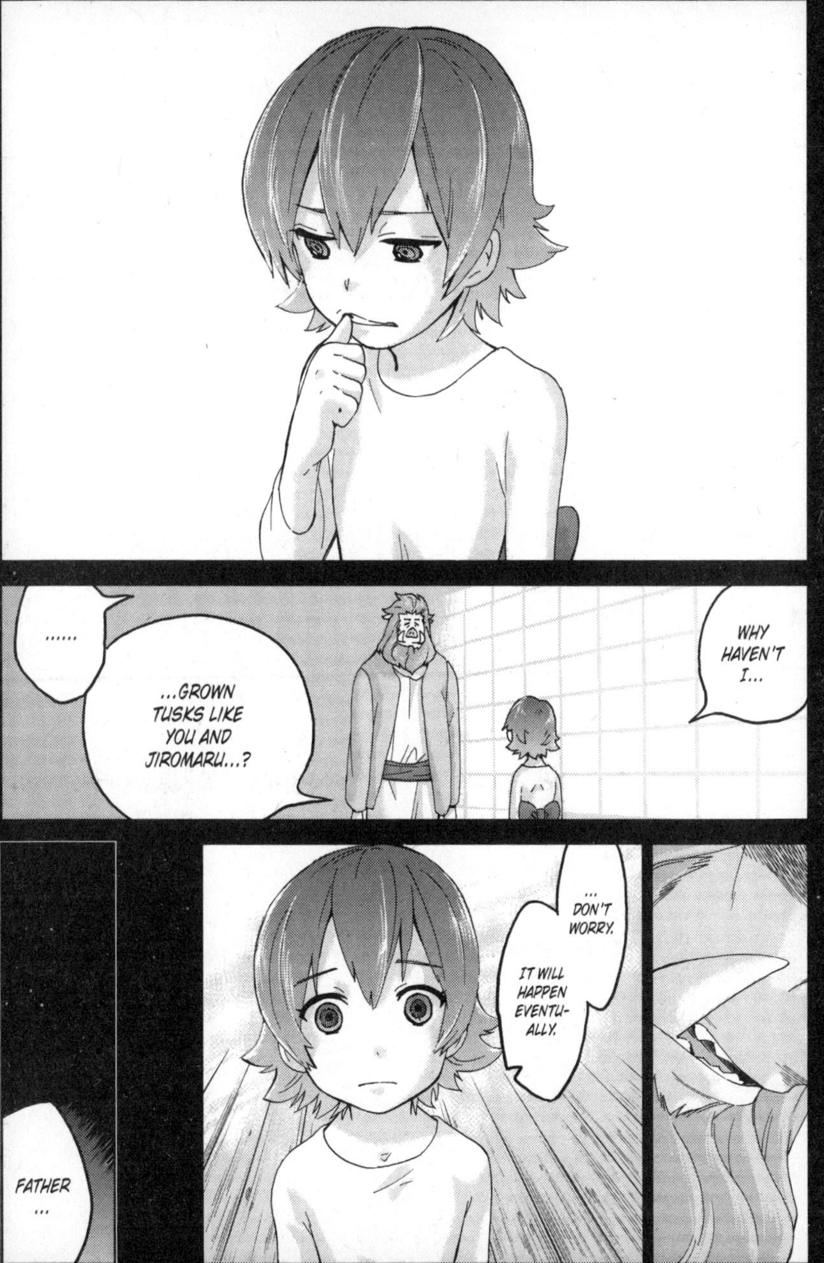
WHY HAVEN'T I...
...GROWN TUSKS LIKE YOU AND JIROMARU...?
......
... DON'T WORRY.
IT WILL HAPPEN EVENTU-ALLY.
FATHER ...

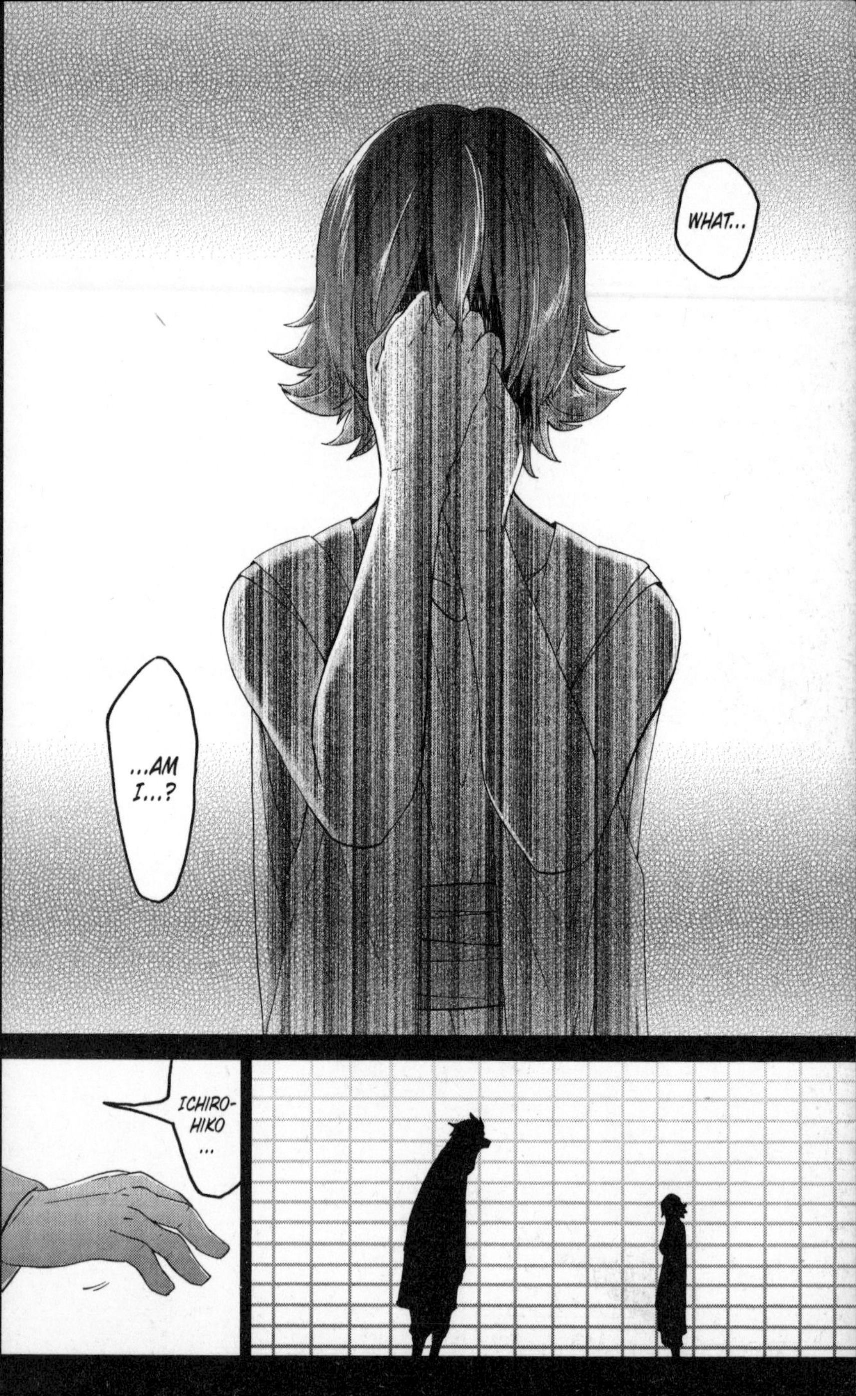
WHAT...
...AM I...?
ICHIRO-HIKO ...

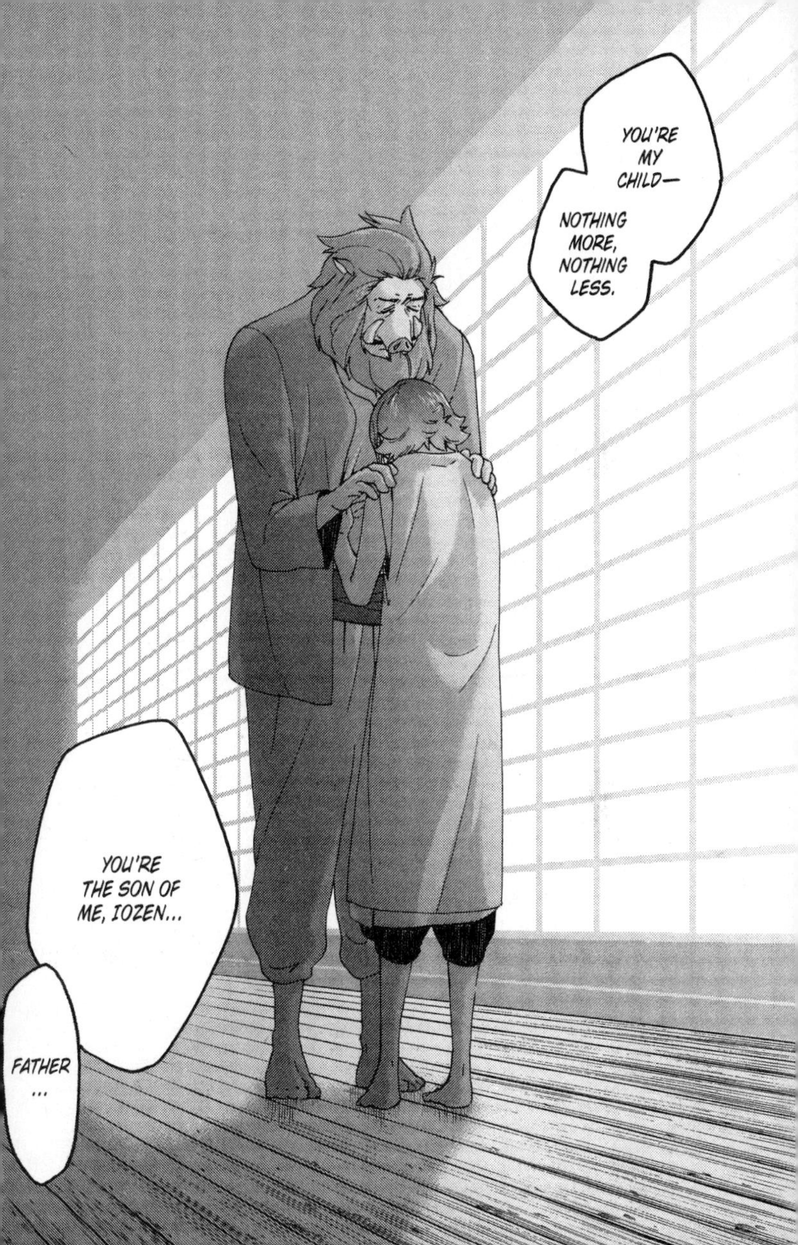
YOU'RE MY CHILD—
NOTHING MORE, NOTHING LESS.
YOU'RE THE SON OF ME, IOZEN...
FATHER ...

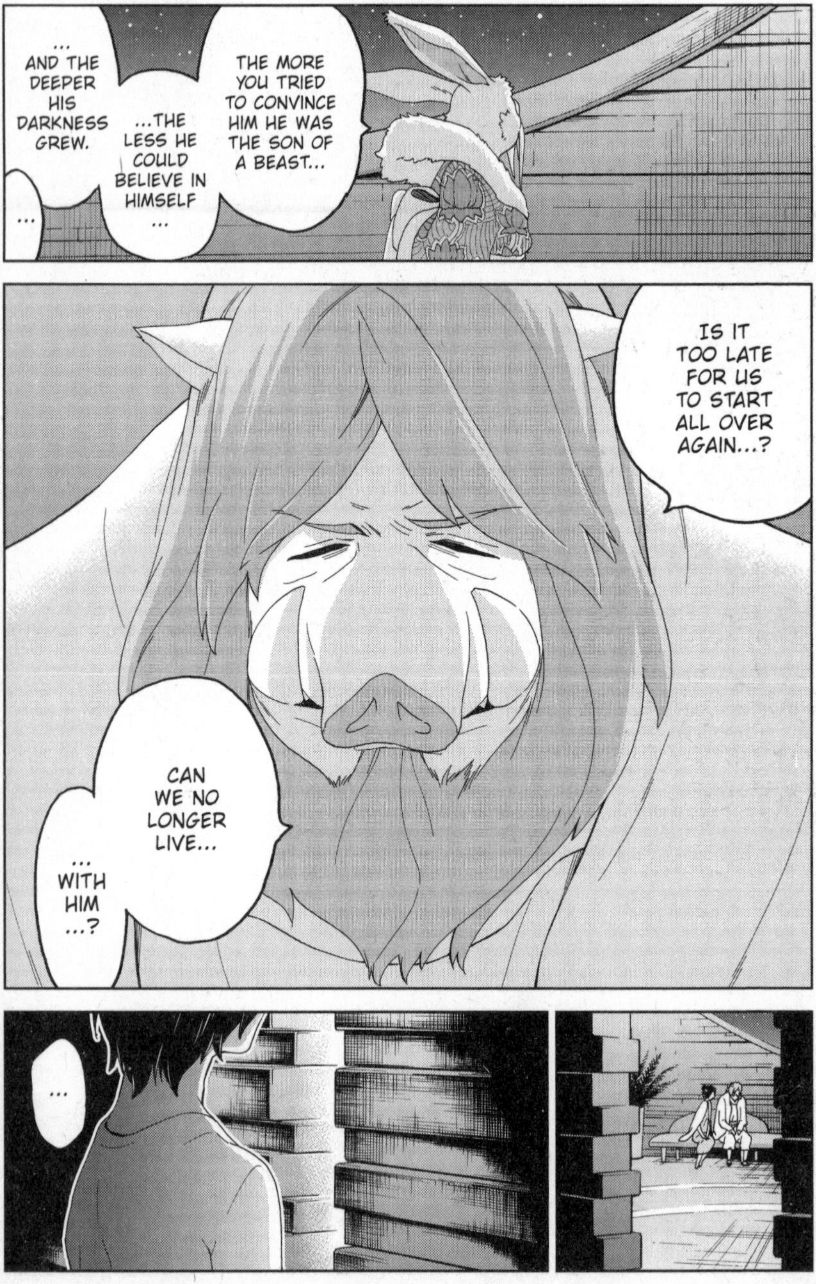
THE MORE YOU TRIED TO CONVINCE HIM HE WAS THE SON OF A BEAST...
...THE LESS HE COULD BELIEVE IN HIMSELF ...
... AND THE DEEPER HIS DARKNESS GREW.
...
IS IT TOO LATE FOR US TO START ALL OVER AGAIN...?
CAN WE NO LONGER LIVE...
... WITH HIM ...?
...

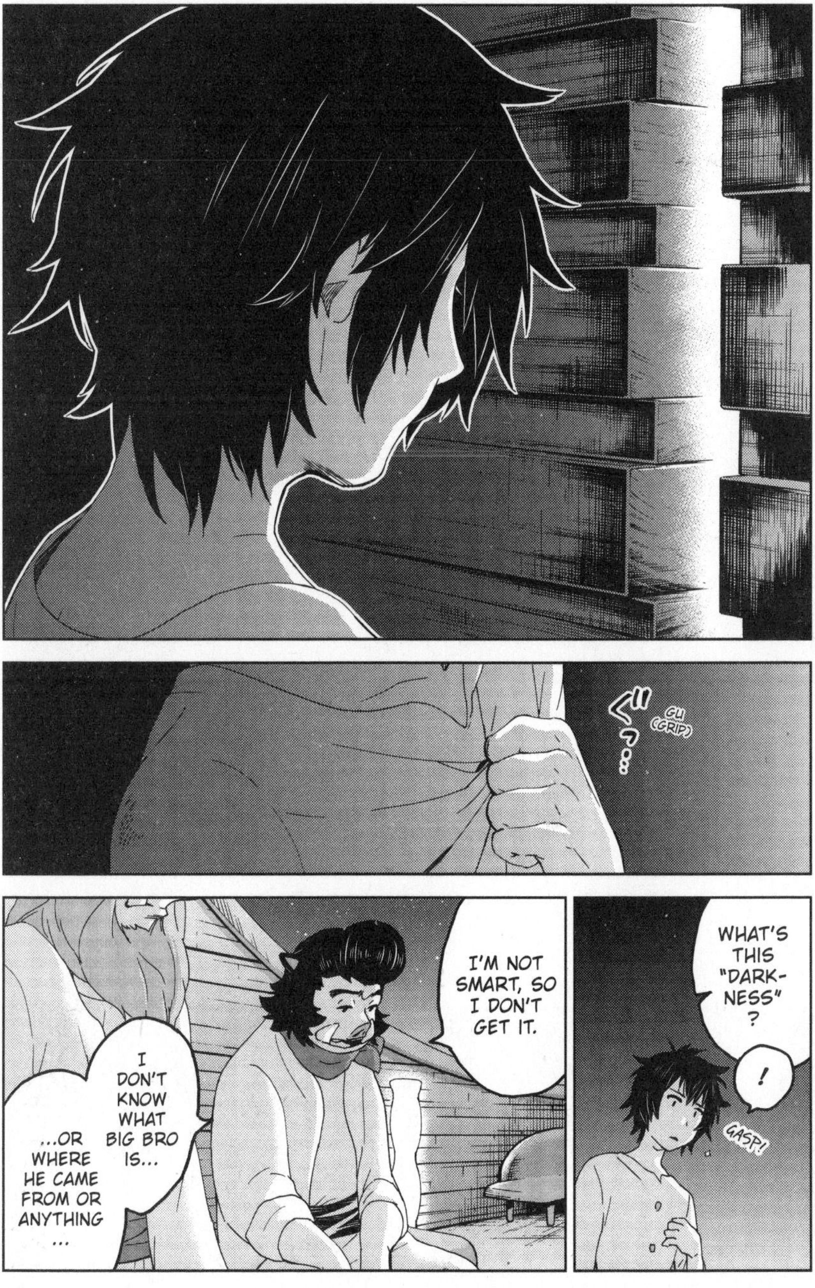
ぐっ…
GU (GRIP)
WHAT'S THIS "DARKNESS"?
!
GASP!
I'M NOT SMART, SO I DON'T GET IT.
I DON'T KNOW WHAT BIG BRO IS...
...OR WHERE HE CAME FROM OR ANYTHING...

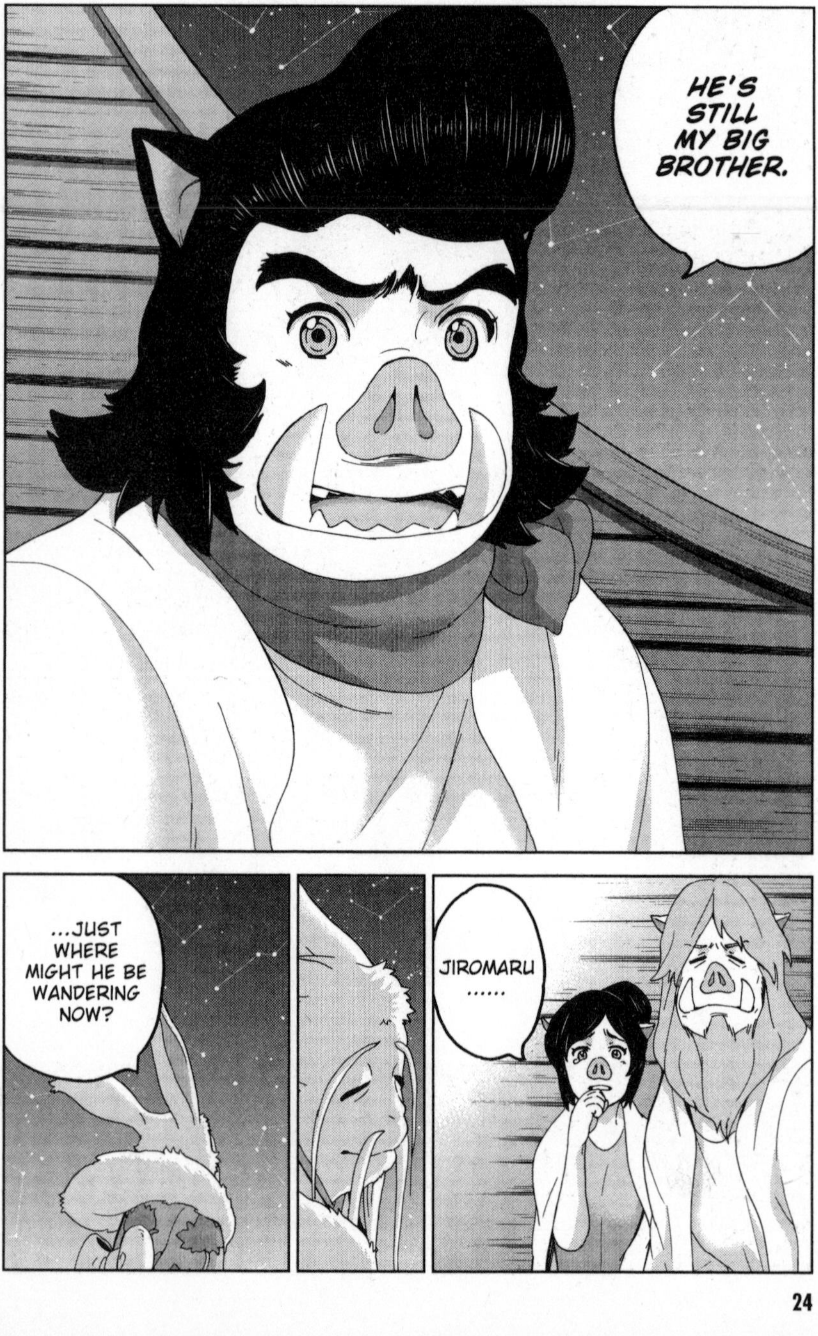
HE'S STILL MY BIG BROTHER.
JIROMARU ......
...JUST WHERE MIGHT HE BE WANDERING NOW?

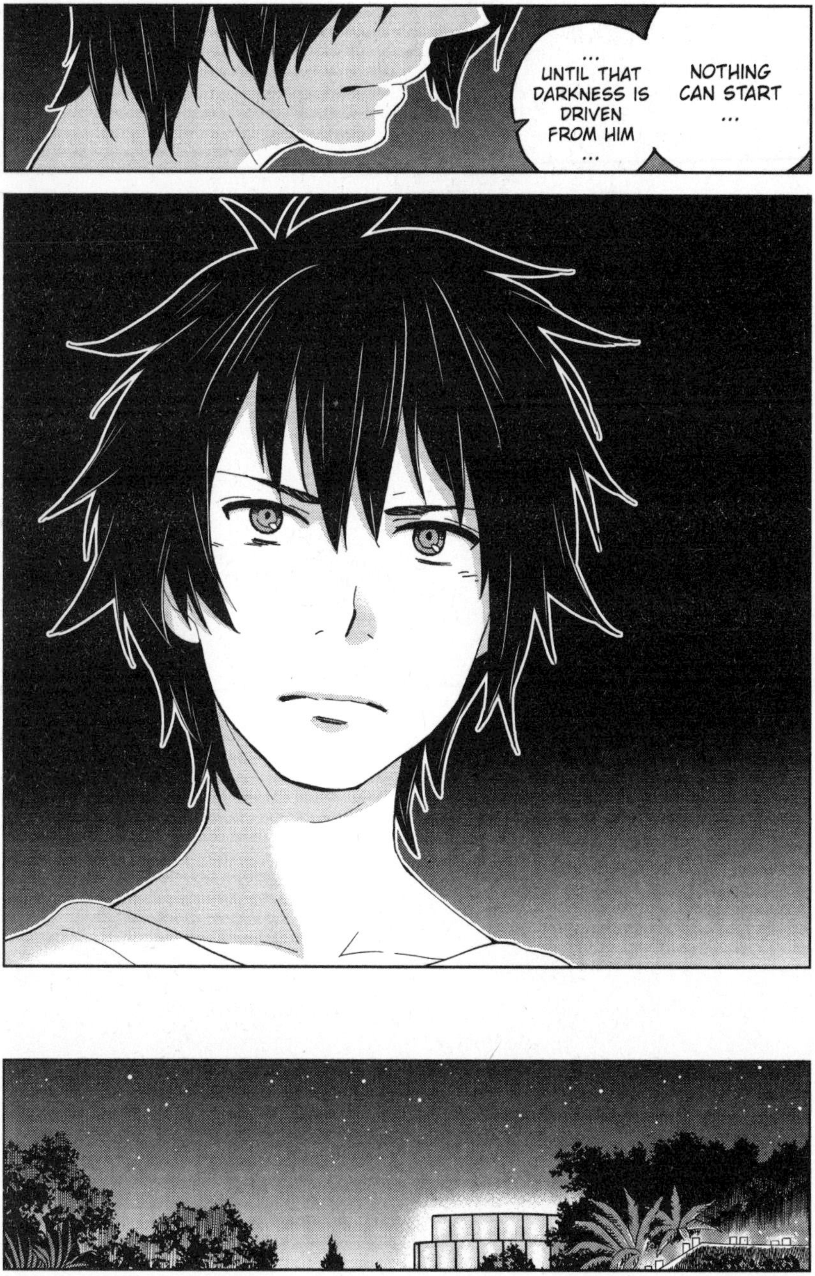
NOTHING CAN START ...
... UNTIL THAT DARKNESS IS DRIVEN FROM HIM ...

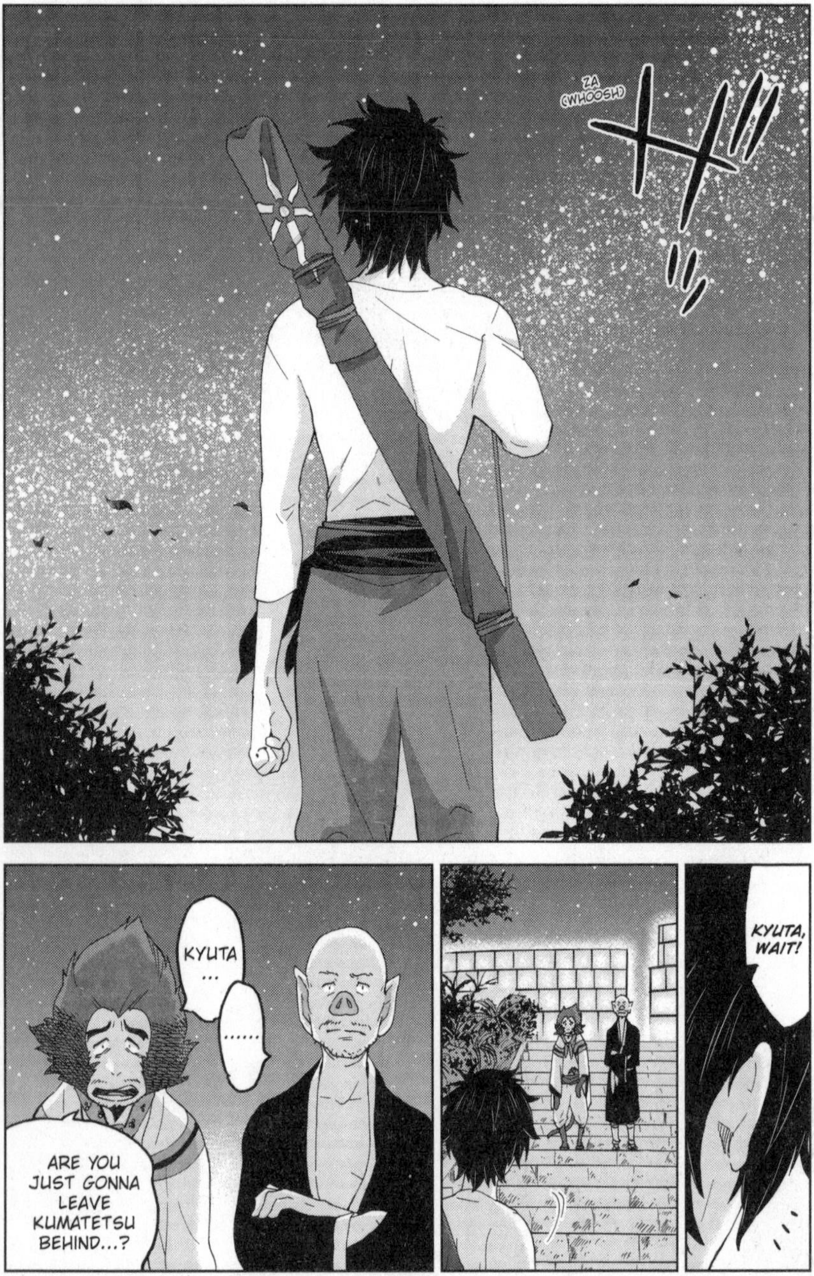
ZA (WHOOSH)
KYUTA, WAIT!
KYUTA ...
......
ARE YOU JUST GONNA LEAVE KUMATETSU BEHIND...?

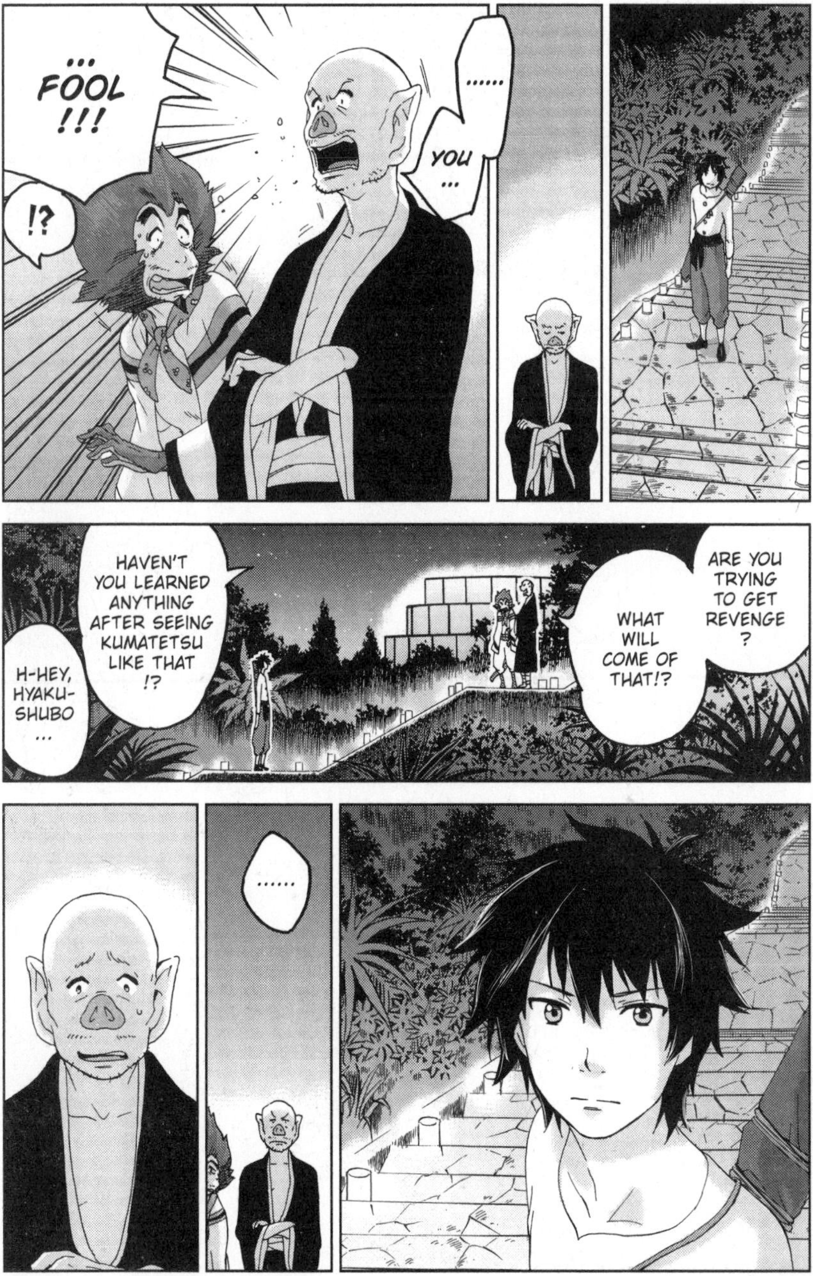
......
YOU ...
... FOOL !!!
!?
ARE YOU TRYING TO GET REVENGE ?
WHAT WILL COME OF THAT!?
HAVEN'T YOU LEARNED ANYTHING AFTER SEEING KUMATETSU LIKE THAT !?
H-HEY, HYAKU-SHUBO ...
......

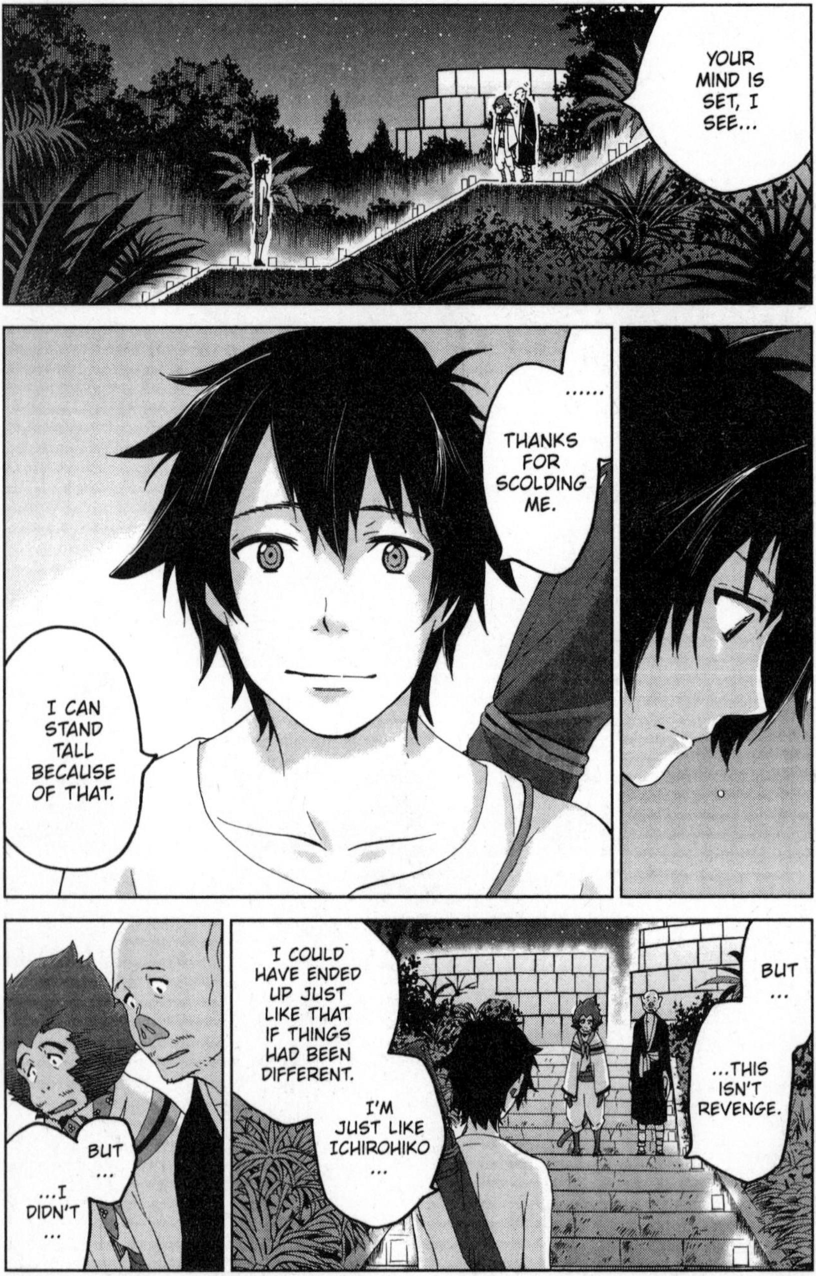
YOUR MIND IS SET, I SEE...
......
THANKS FOR SCOLDING ME.
I CAN STAND TALL BECAUSE OF THAT.
BUT ...
...THIS ISN'T REVENGE.
I COULD HAVE ENDED UP JUST LIKE THAT IF THINGS HAD BEEN DIFFERENT.
I'M JUST LIKE ICHIROHIKO ...
BUT ...
...I DIDN'T ...

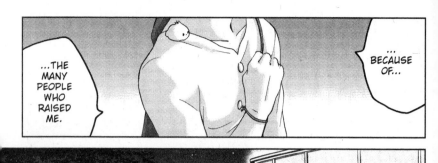

...THE MANY PEOPLE WHO RAISED ME.

...BECAUSE OF...

LIKE YOU, TATA-SAN...

...AND YOU, HYAKU-SAN...

...AND EVERYONE ELSE...

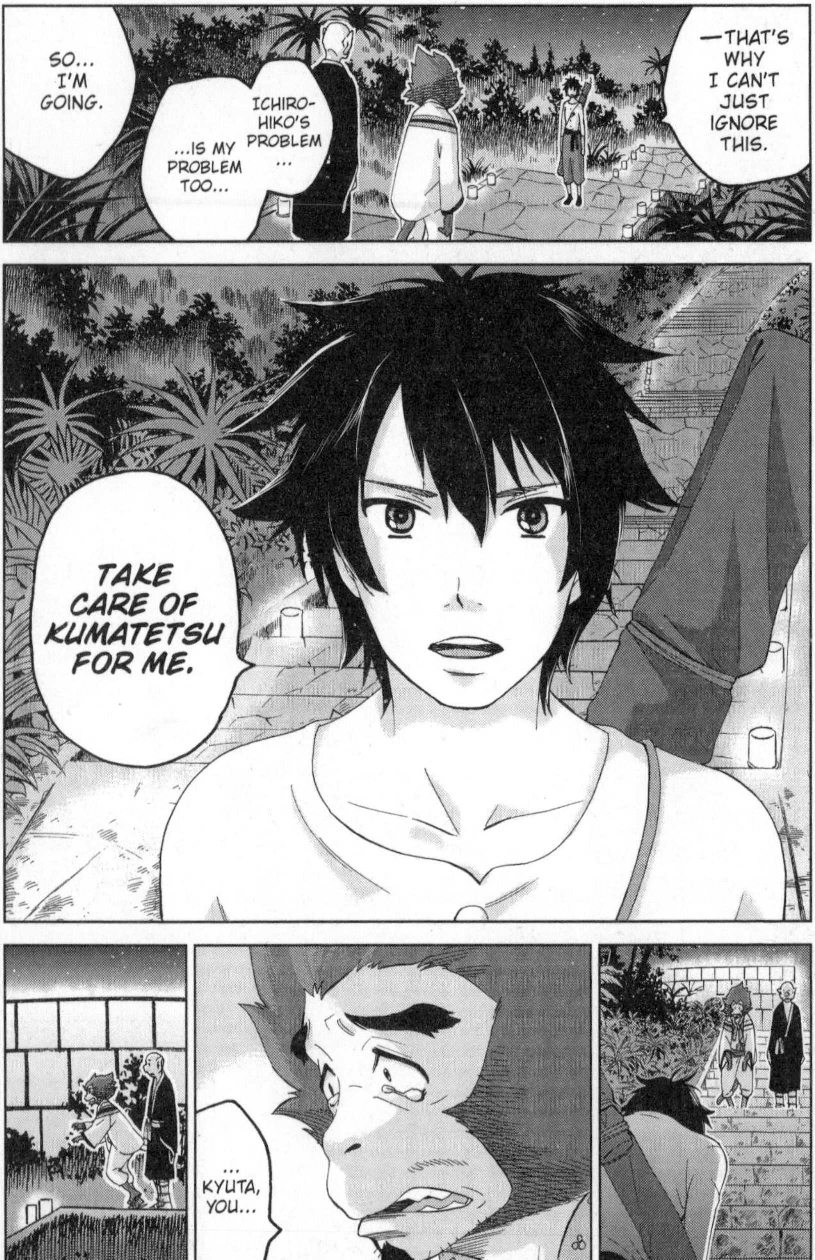
—THAT'S WHY I CAN'T JUST IGNORE THIS.
ICHIRO-HIKO'S PROBLEM...
...IS MY PROBLEM TOO...
SO... I'M GOING.
TAKE CARE OF KUMATETSU FOR ME.
...KYUTA, YOU...

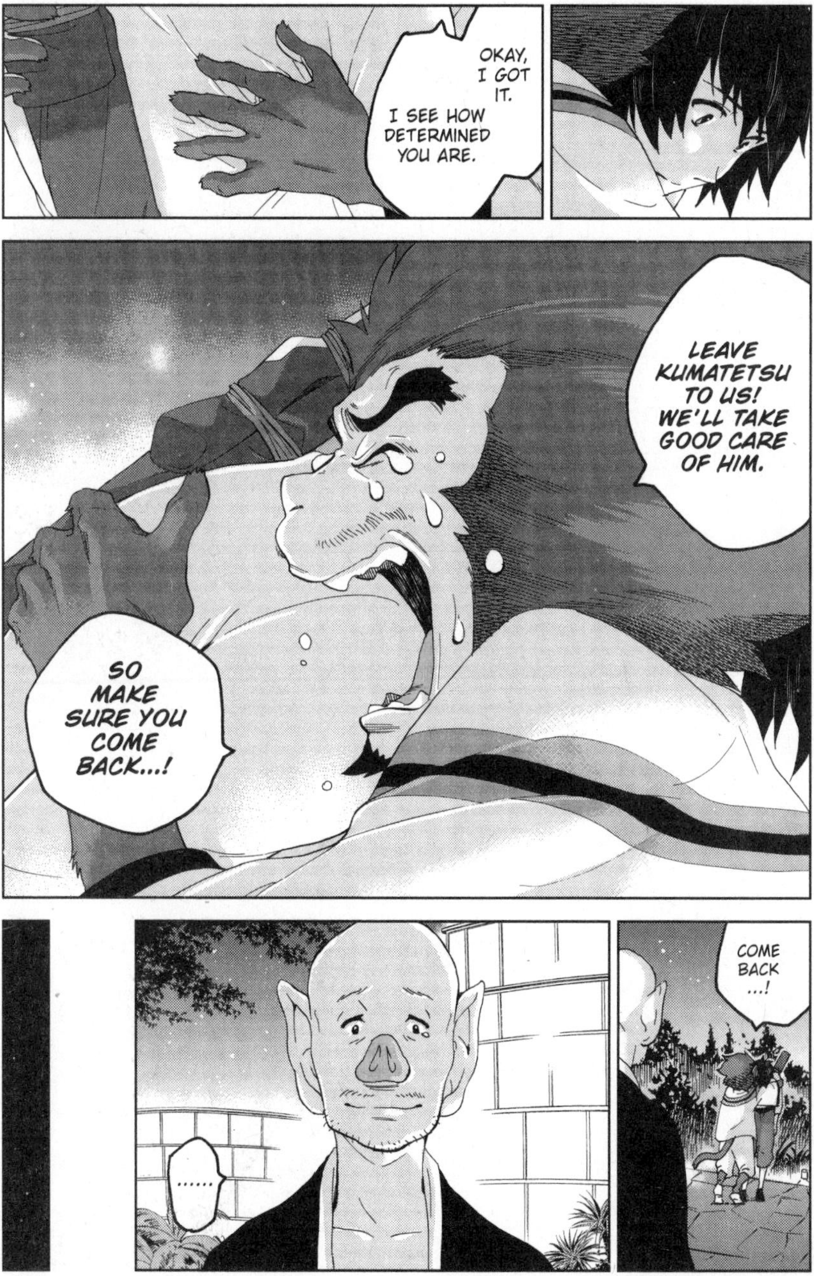
OKAY, I GOT IT.
I SEE HOW DETERMINED YOU ARE.
LEAVE KUMATETSU TO US! WE'LL TAKE GOOD CARE OF HIM.
SO MAKE SURE YOU COME BACK...!
COME BACK ...!
....

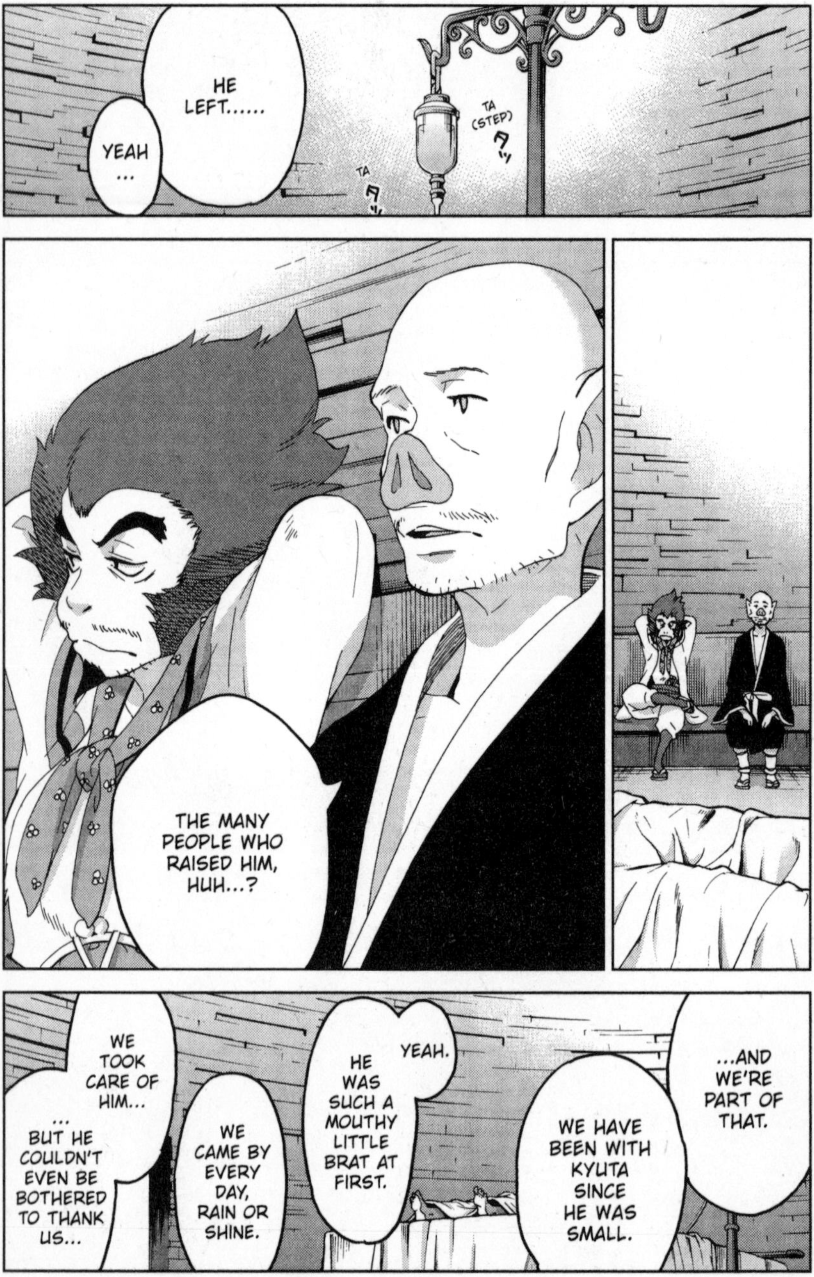
TA (STEP)
HE LEFT......
YEAH ...
TA
THE MANY PEOPLE WHO RAISED HIM, HUH...?
...AND WE'RE PART OF THAT.
WE HAVE BEEN WITH KYUTA SINCE HE WAS SMALL.
YEAH.
HE WAS SUCH A MOUTHY LITTLE BRAT AT FIRST.
WE CAME BY EVERY DAY, RAIN OR SHINE.
WE TOOK CARE OF HIM...
... BUT HE COULDN'T EVEN BE BOTHERED TO THANK US...

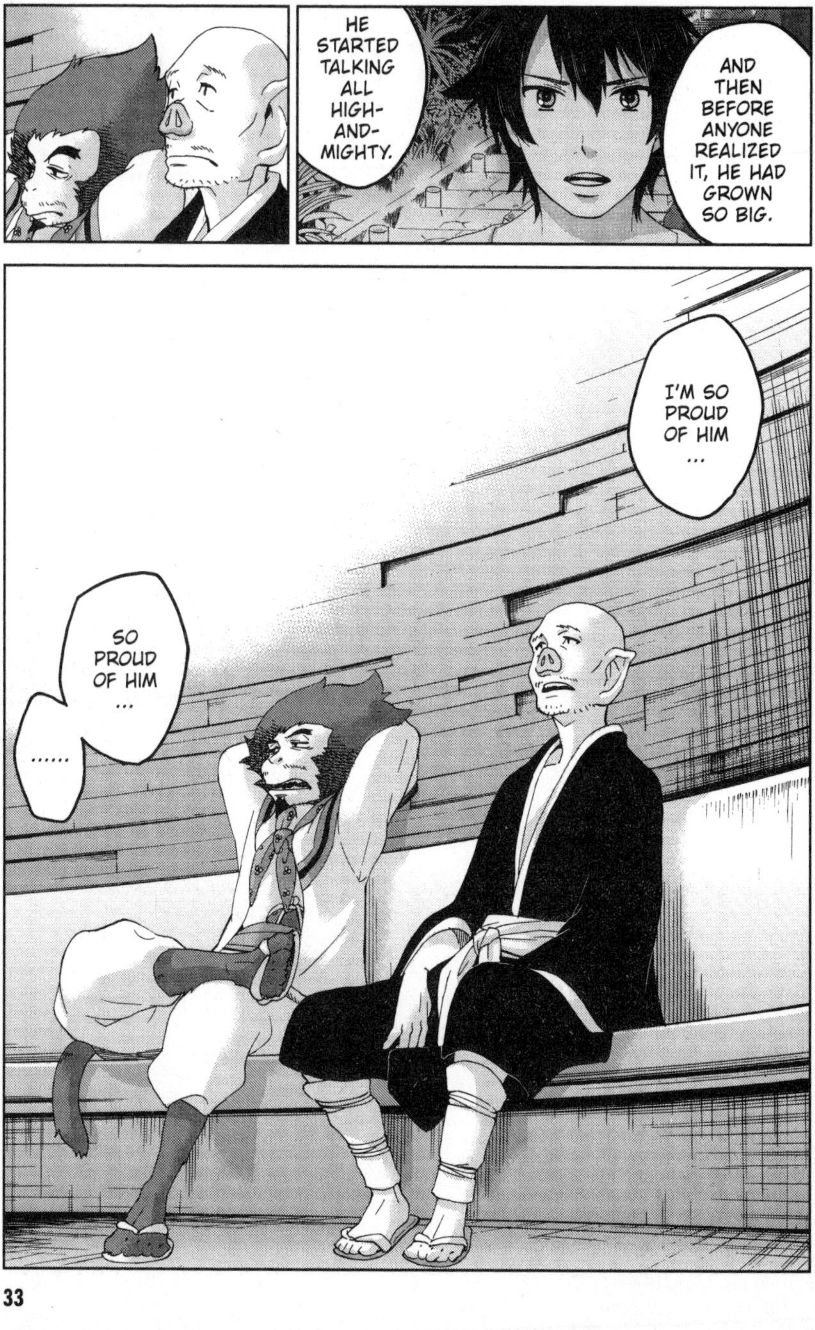
HE STARTED TALKING ALL HIGH-AND-MIGHTY.
AND THEN BEFORE ANYONE REALIZED IT, HE HAD GROWN SO BIG.
I'M SO PROUD OF HIM ...
SO PROUD OF HIM ...
......

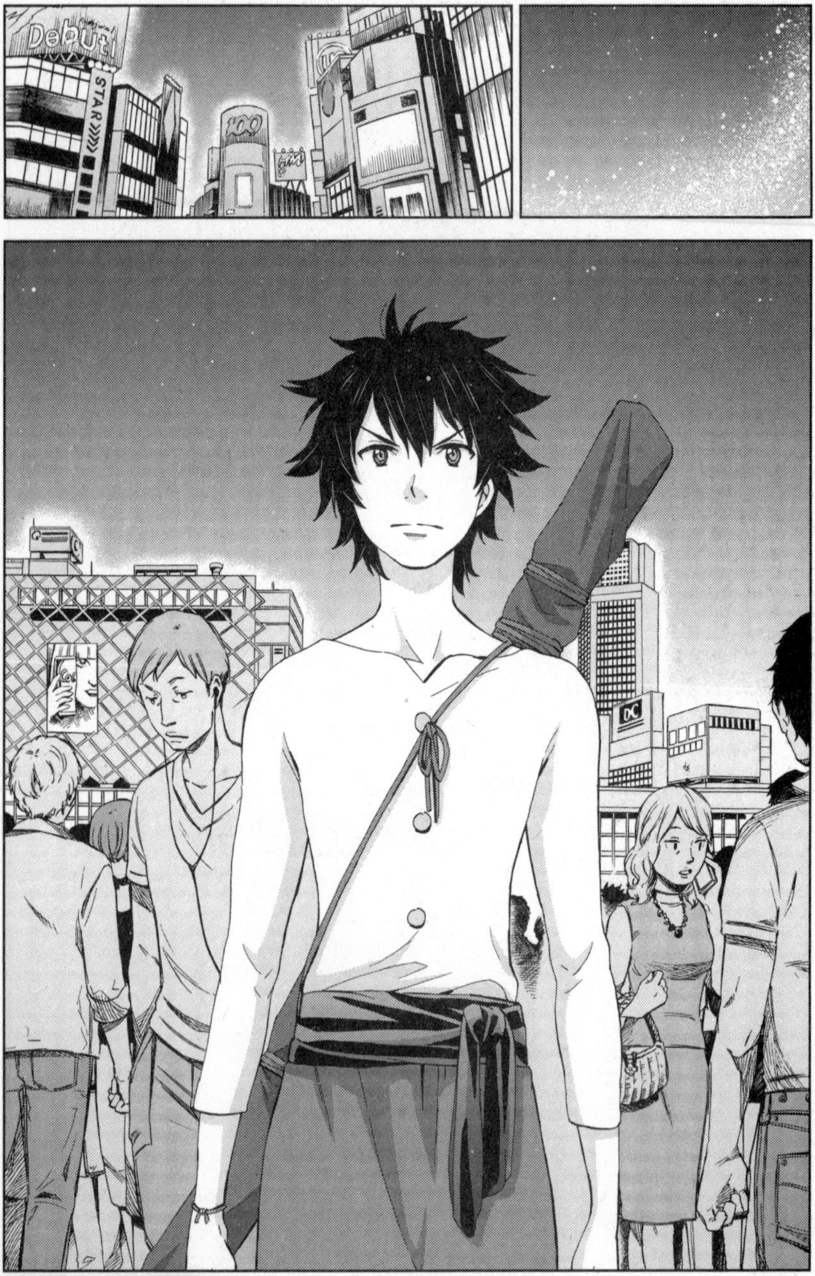
STAR
109
DC

CHAPTER 15 END

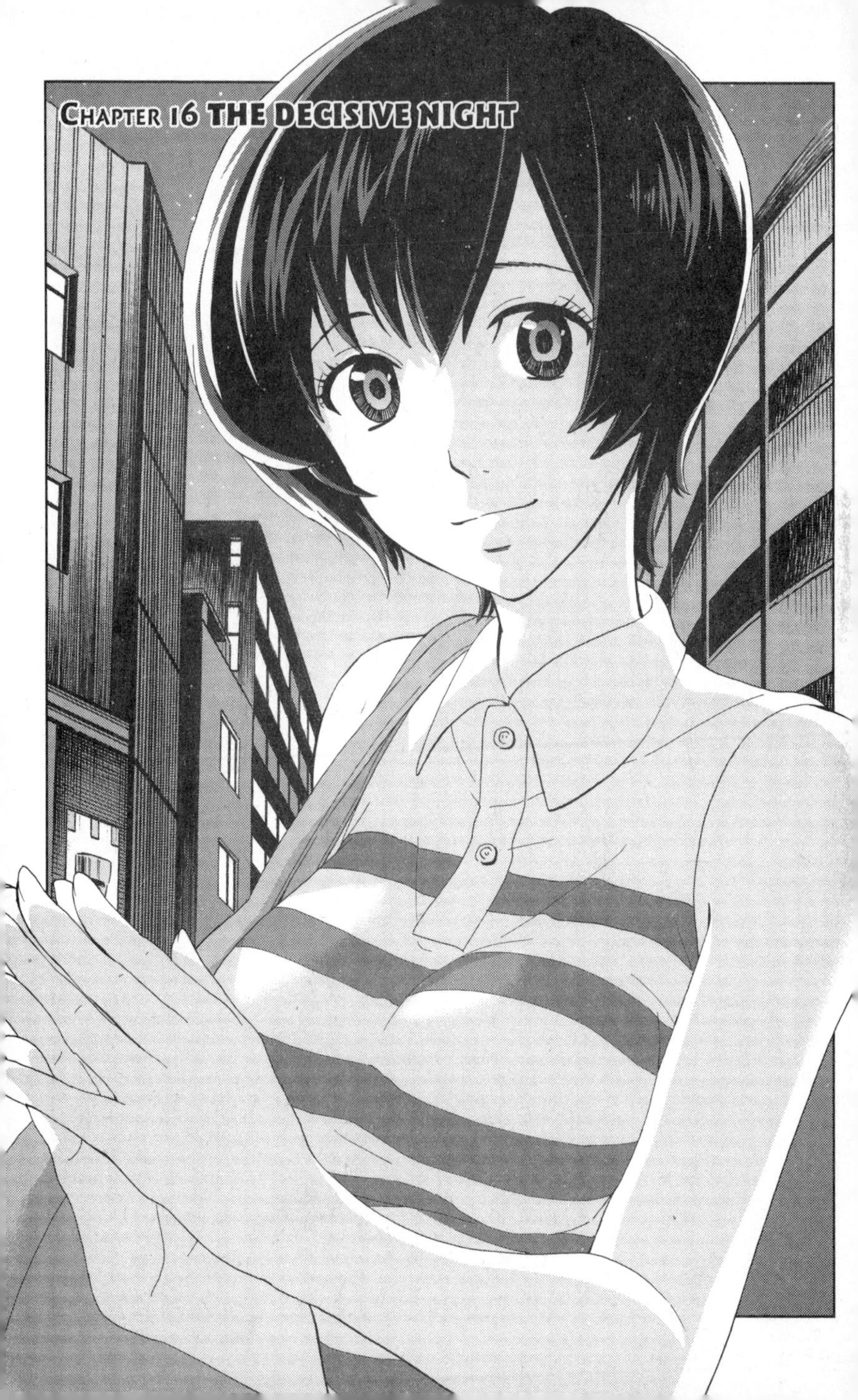
CHAPTER 16 THE DECISIVE NIGHT

SIGNS: ...THEY WERE TOLD... / SALONPAS

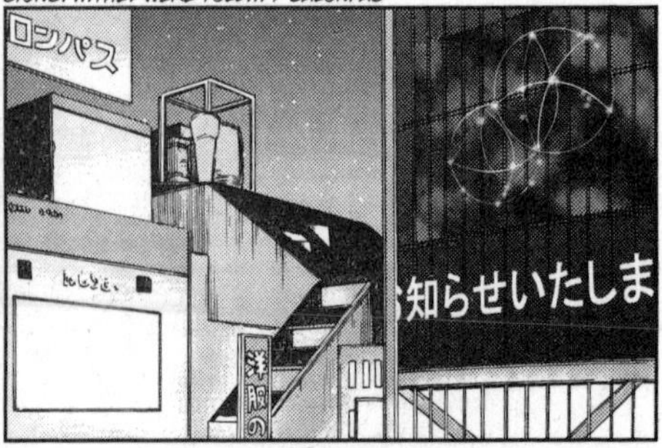
ロンパス
知らせいたしま
洋服の

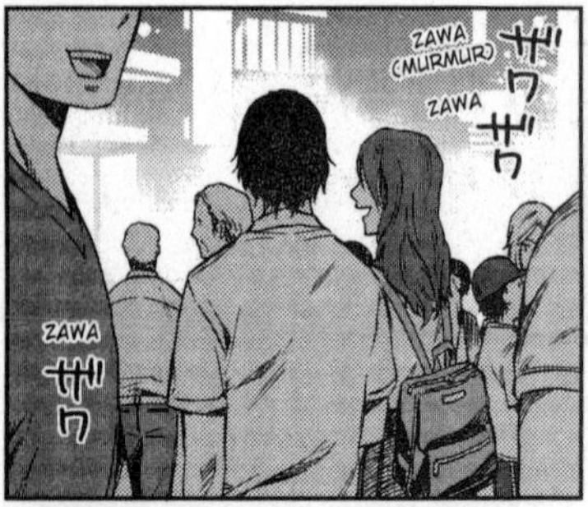
ZAWA (MURMUR) ザワ
ZAWA ザワ
ZAWA ザワ

SIGNS: SHIBUYA CENTER STREET / BUILDING

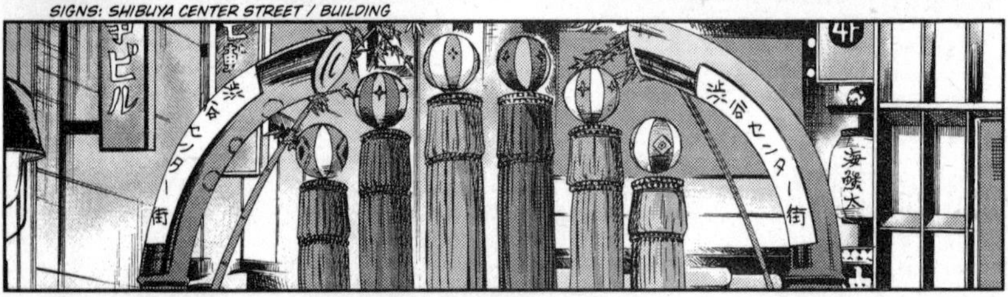
渋谷センター街
ビル
渋谷センター街
4F

SIGNS: KARAOKE SONG PLAZA / KARAOKE HALL

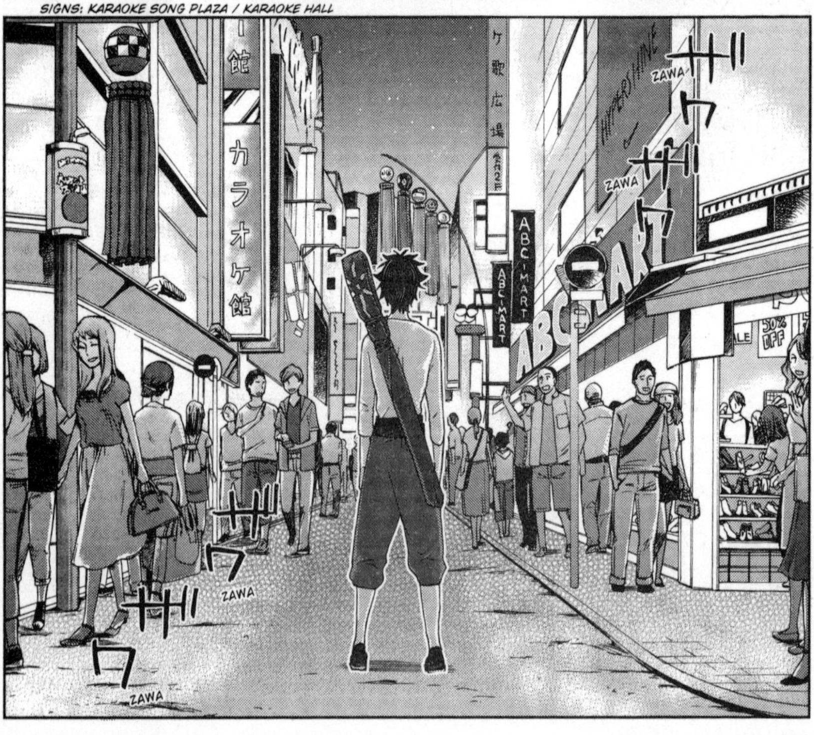
ZAWA ザワ
ZAWA ザワ
ケ歌広場
ー館
カラオケ館
ABC-MART
ABC-MART
ABC-MART
50% OFF
ZAWA ザワ
ZAWA ザワ

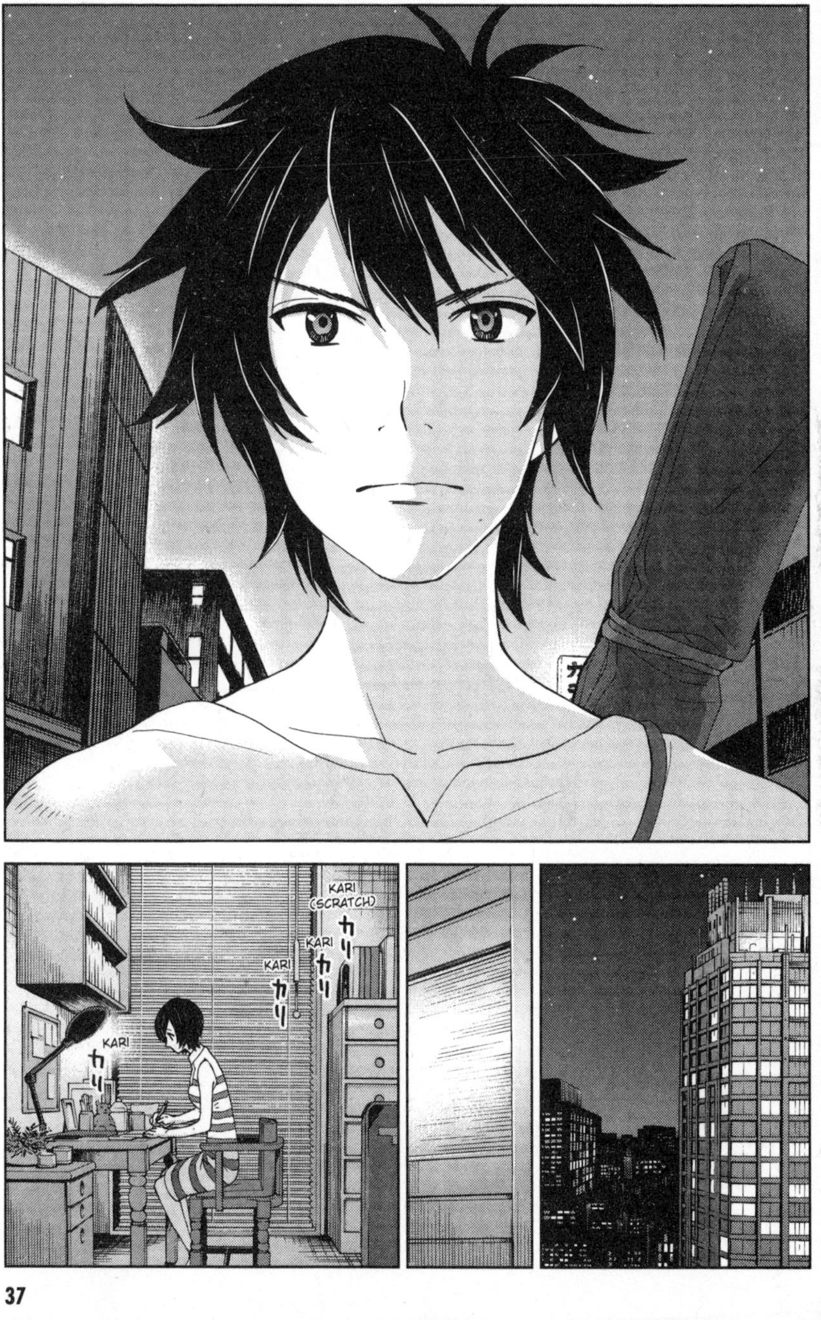
KARI (SCRATCH)
カリ
KARI
カリ
KARI
カリ
KARI
カリ

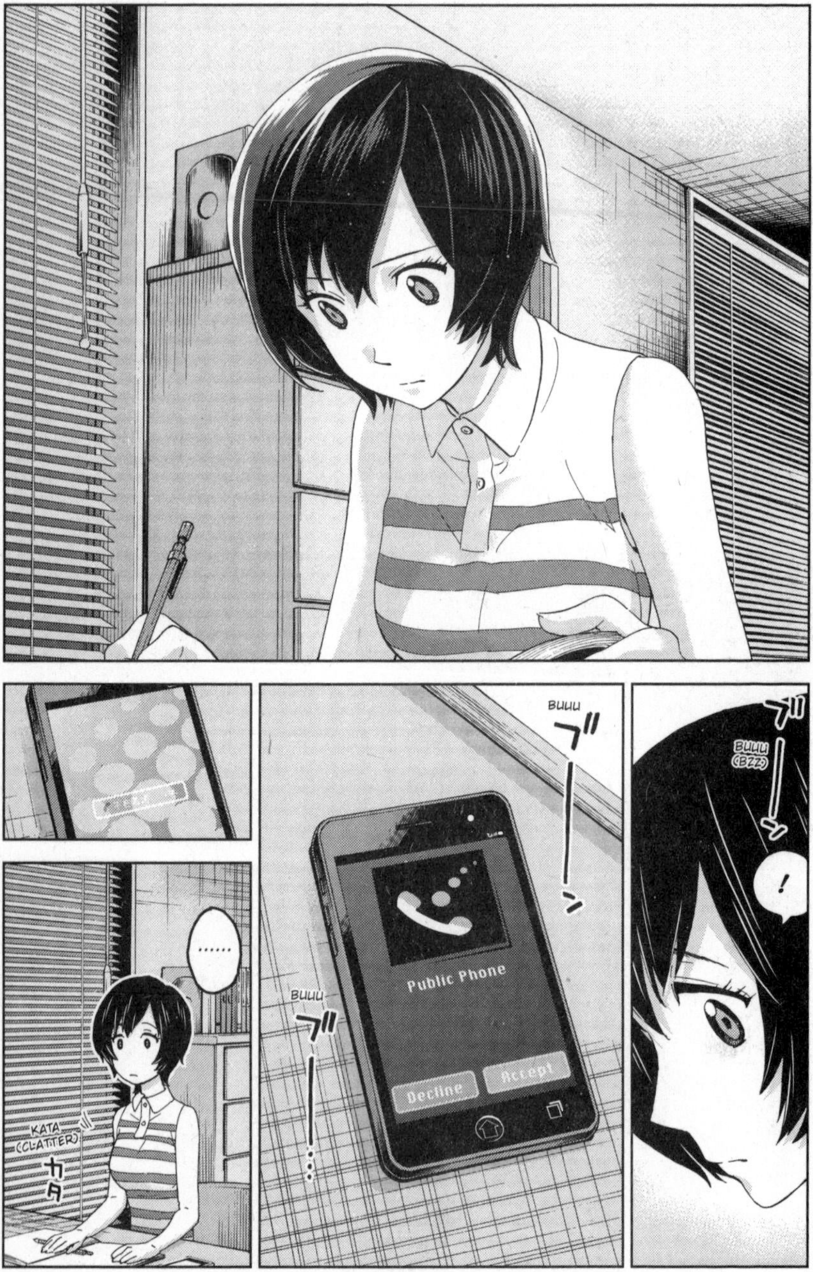
BUUU (BZZ)
!
BUUU
Public Phone
Decline
Accept
BUUU
......
KATA (CLATTER)

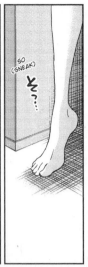

SO
(SNEAK)

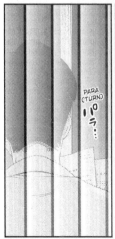

KACHA
(CLICK)

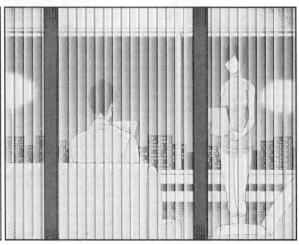

PARA
(TURN)

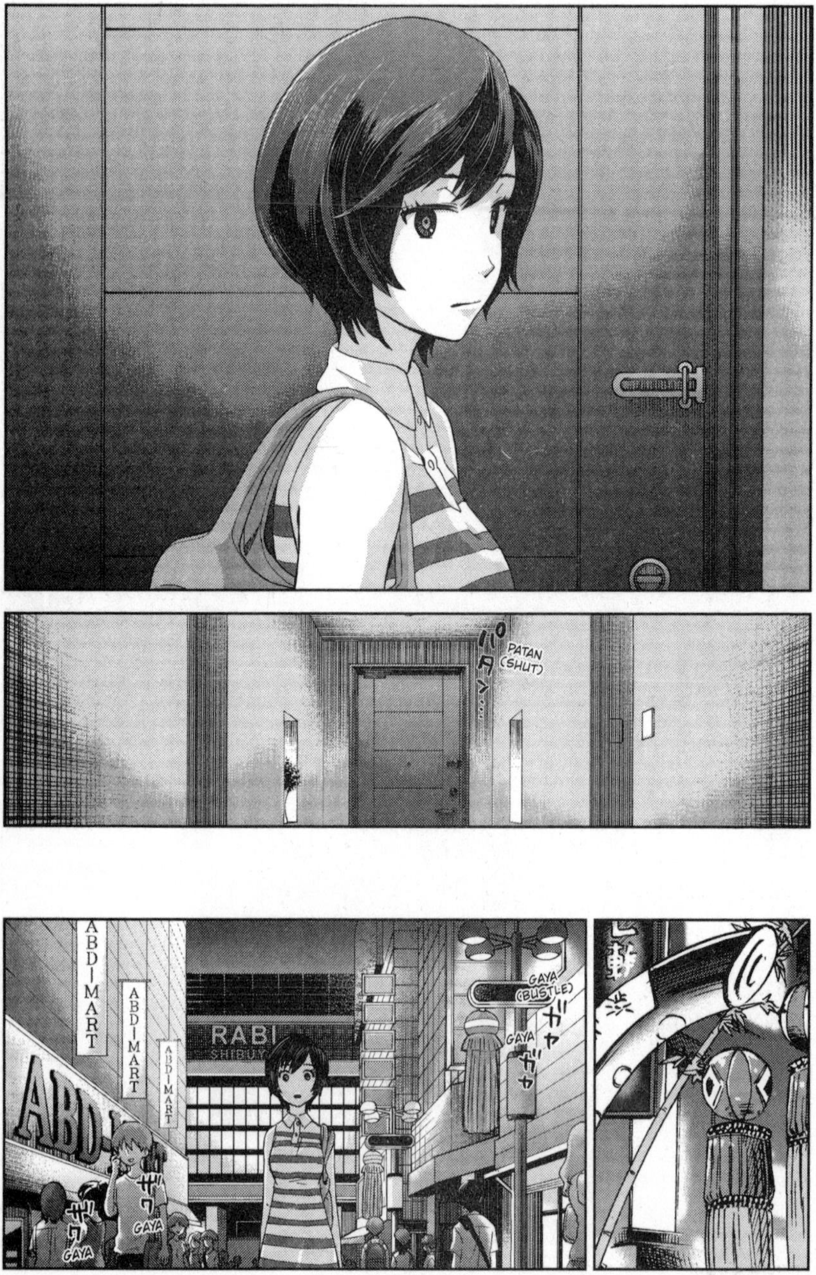
パタン…
PATAN (SHUT)
GAYA (BUSTLE)
ガヤ
GAYA
ガヤ
ABDIMART
ABDIMART
ABDIMART
RABI
ザワ
GAYA
ザワ
GAYA

SIGN: KARAOKE & PARTY HALL

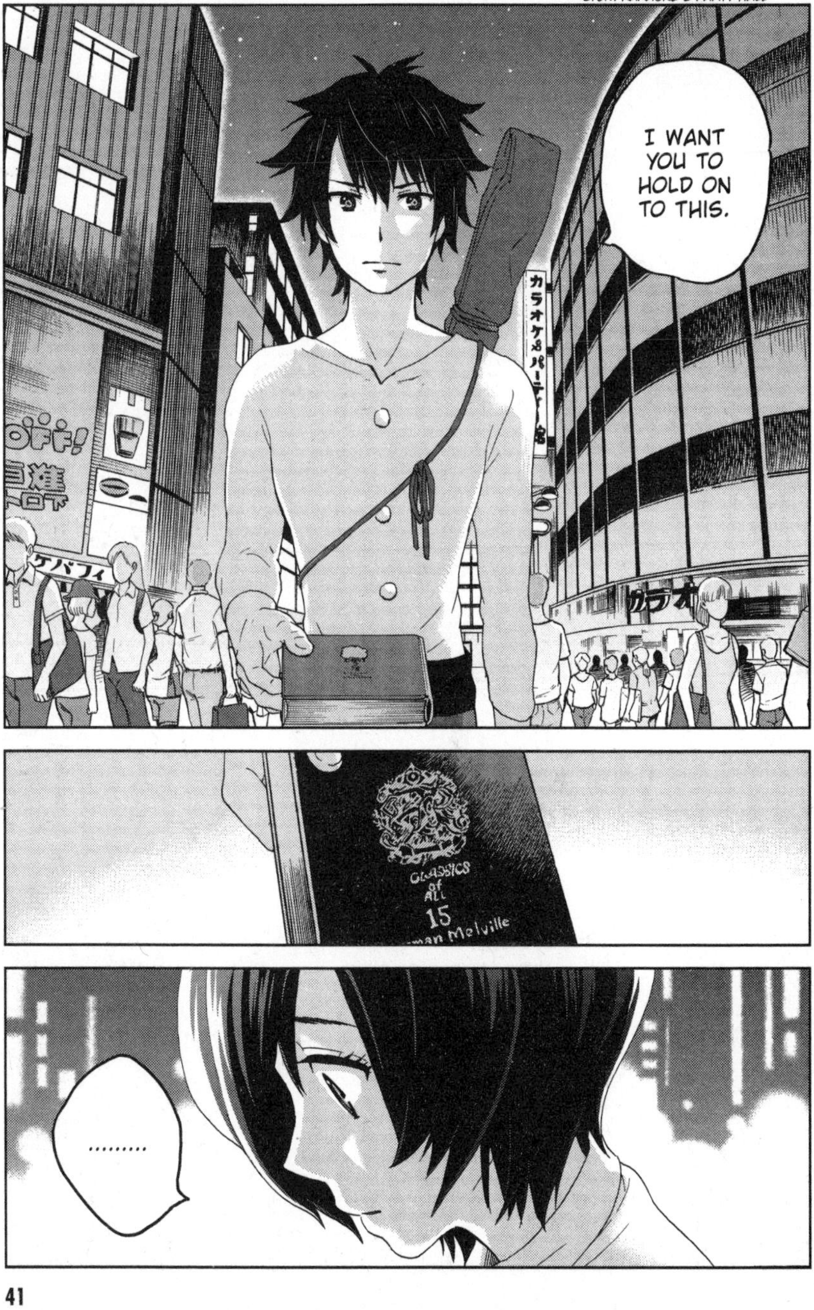
I WANT YOU TO HOLD ON TO THIS.
CLASSICS of ALL
15
....

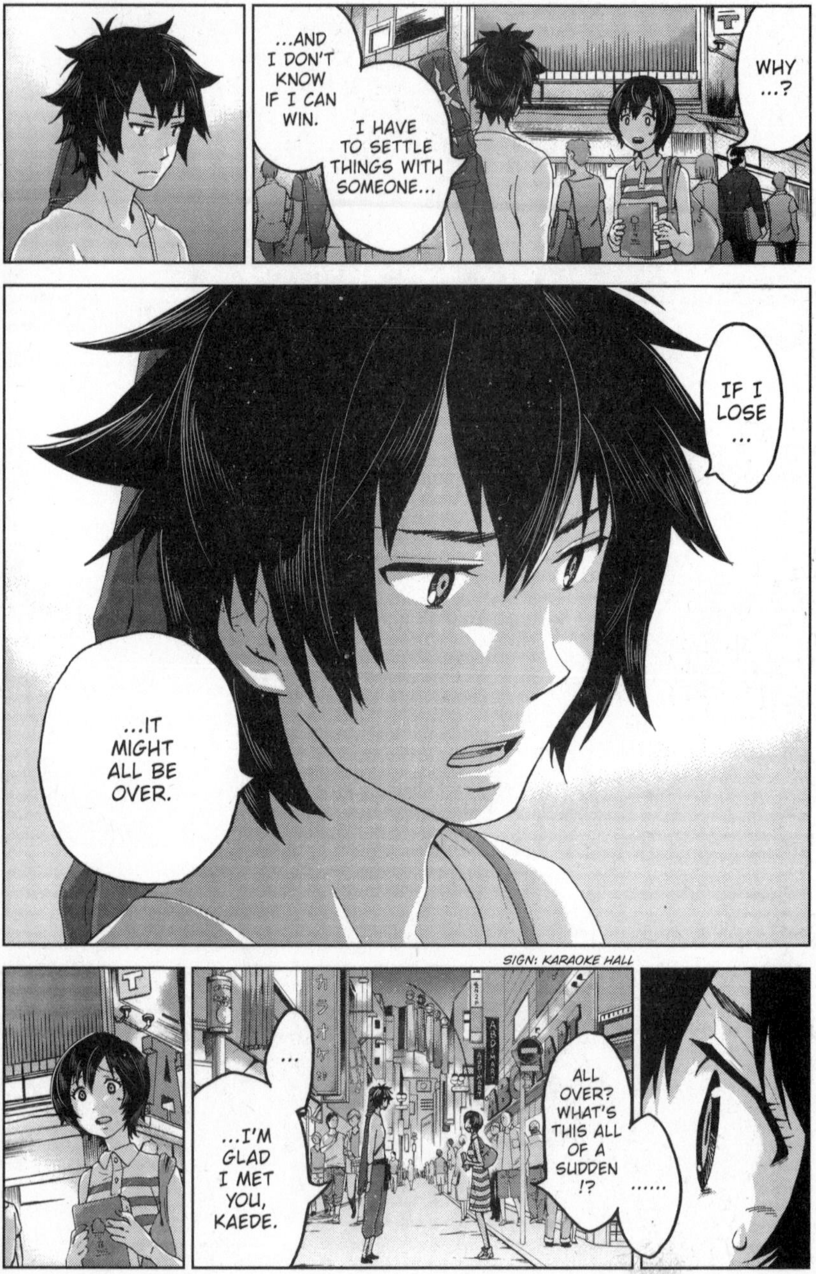
WHY ...?
I HAVE TO SETTLE THINGS WITH SOMEONE...
...AND I DON'T KNOW IF I CAN WIN.
IF I LOSE ...
...IT MIGHT ALL BE OVER.
SIGN: KARAOKE HALL
......
ALL OVER? WHAT'S THIS ALL OF A SUDDEN !?
...
...I'M GLAD I MET YOU, KAEDE.

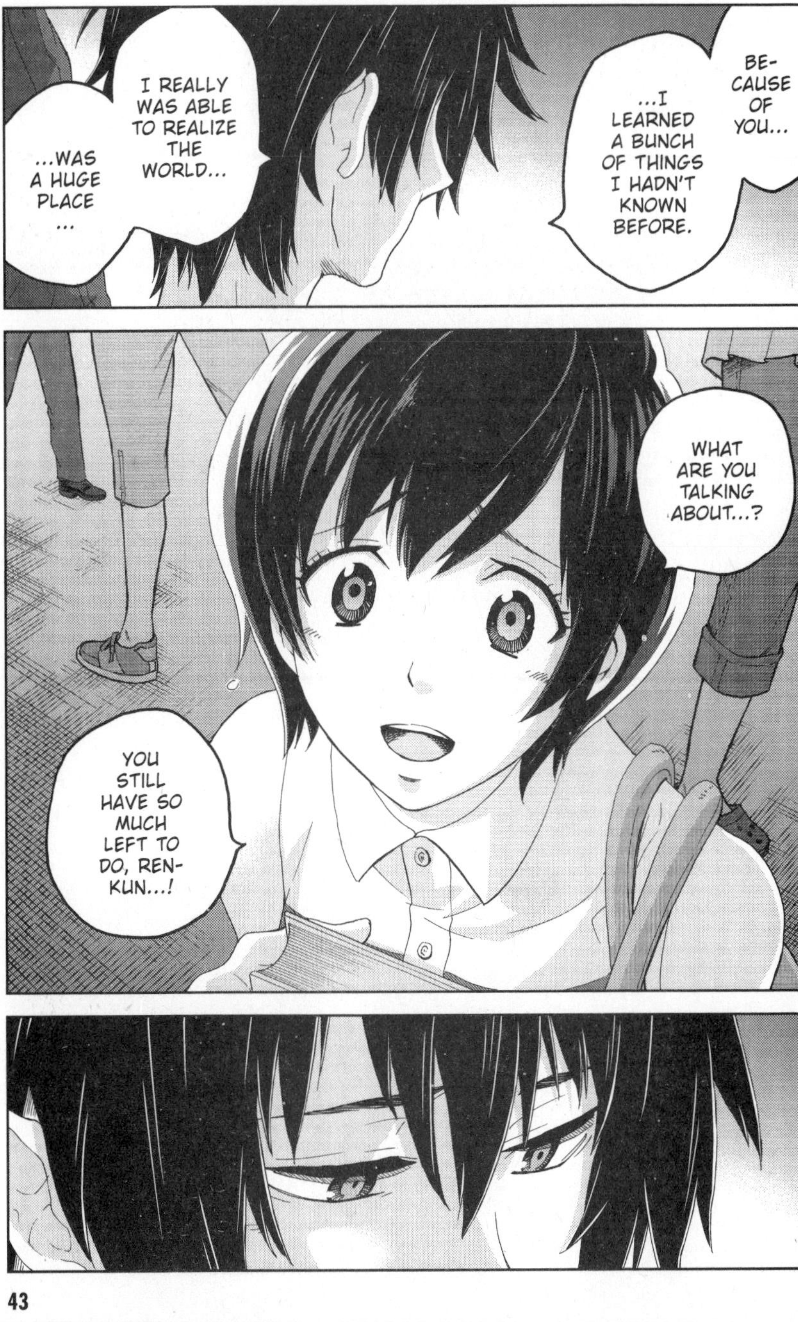
BE-CAUSE OF YOU...
...I LEARNED A BUNCH OF THINGS I HADN'T KNOWN BEFORE.
I REALLY WAS ABLE TO REALIZE THE WORLD...
...WAS A HUGE PLACE...
WHAT ARE YOU TALKING ABOUT...?
YOU STILL HAVE SO MUCH LEFT TO DO, REN-KUN...!

SIGN: KARAOKE & PARTY

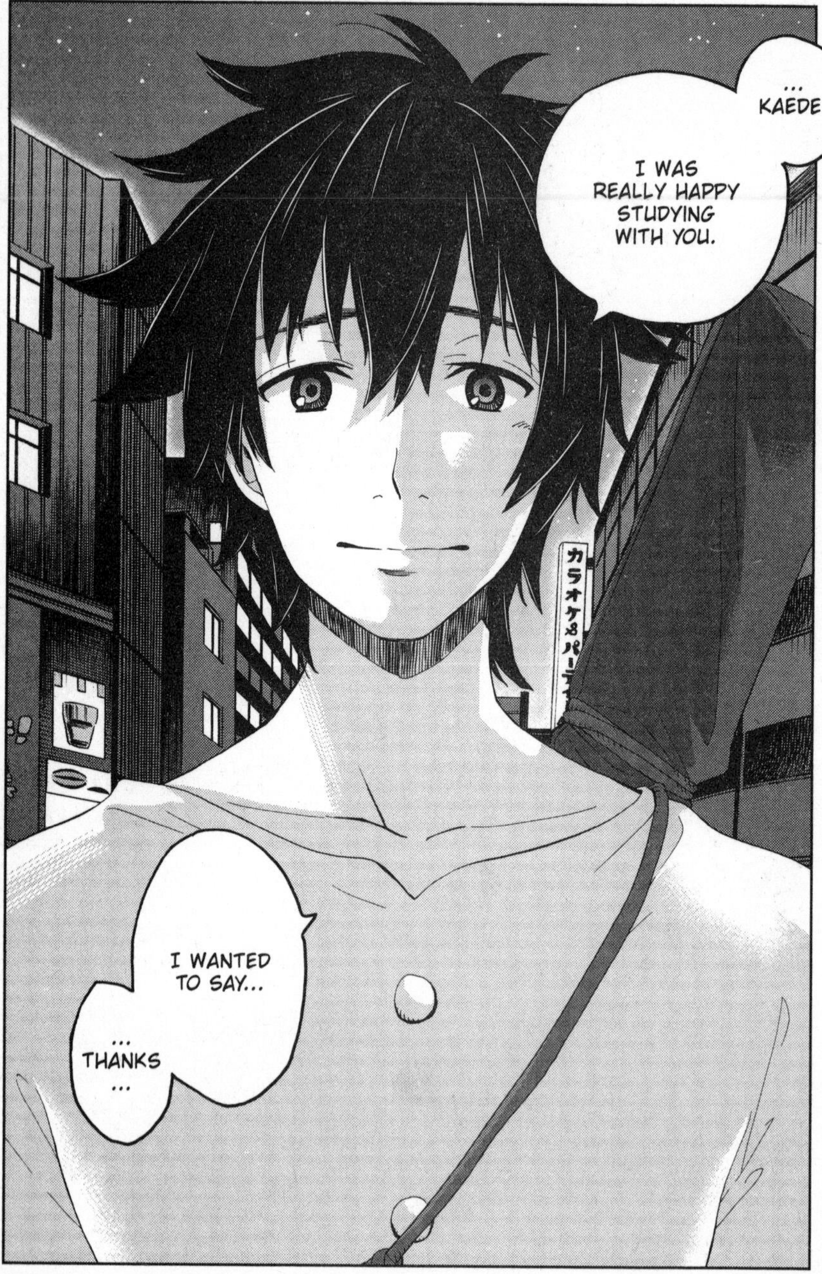
... KAEDE.
I WAS REALLY HAPPY STUDYING WITH YOU.
I WANTED TO SAY...
... THANKS ...

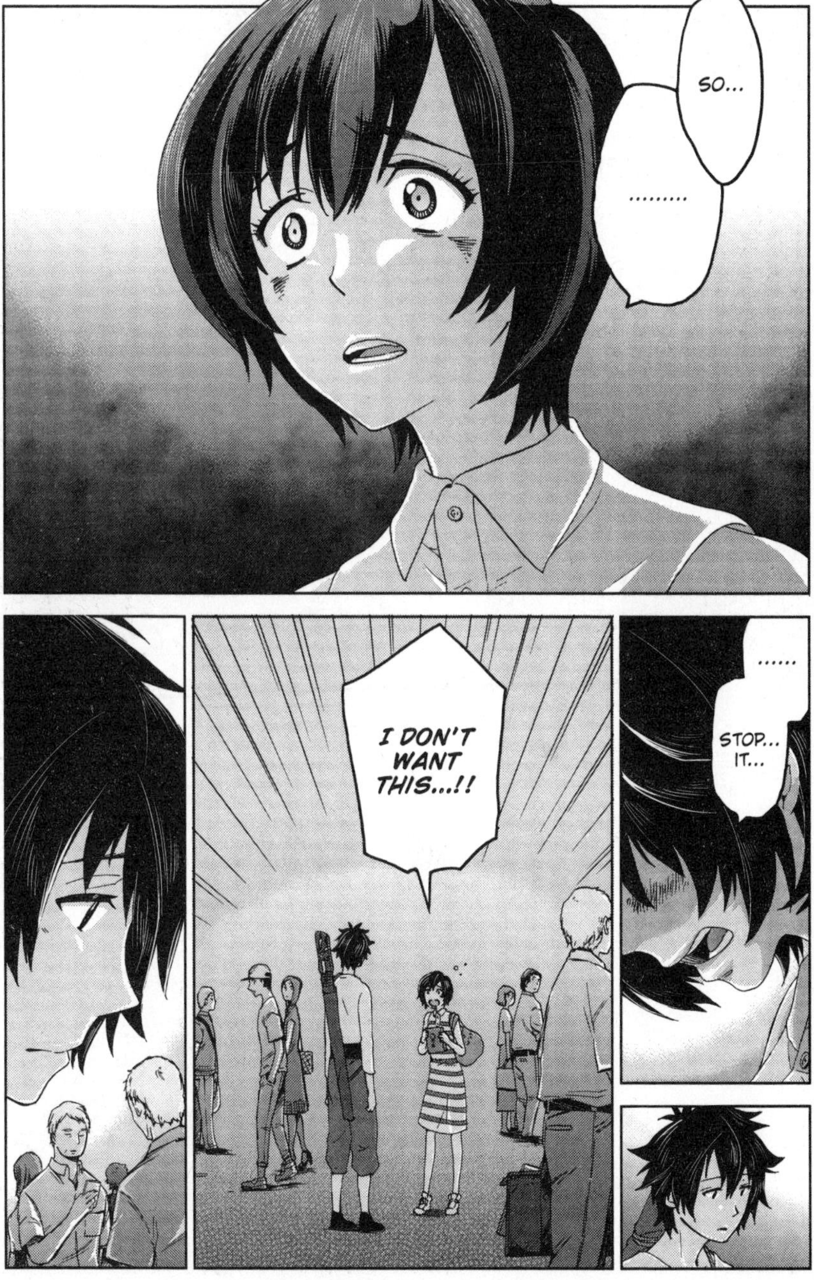
SO...
....
......
STOP... IT...
I DON'T WANT THIS...!!

SIGN: HALL

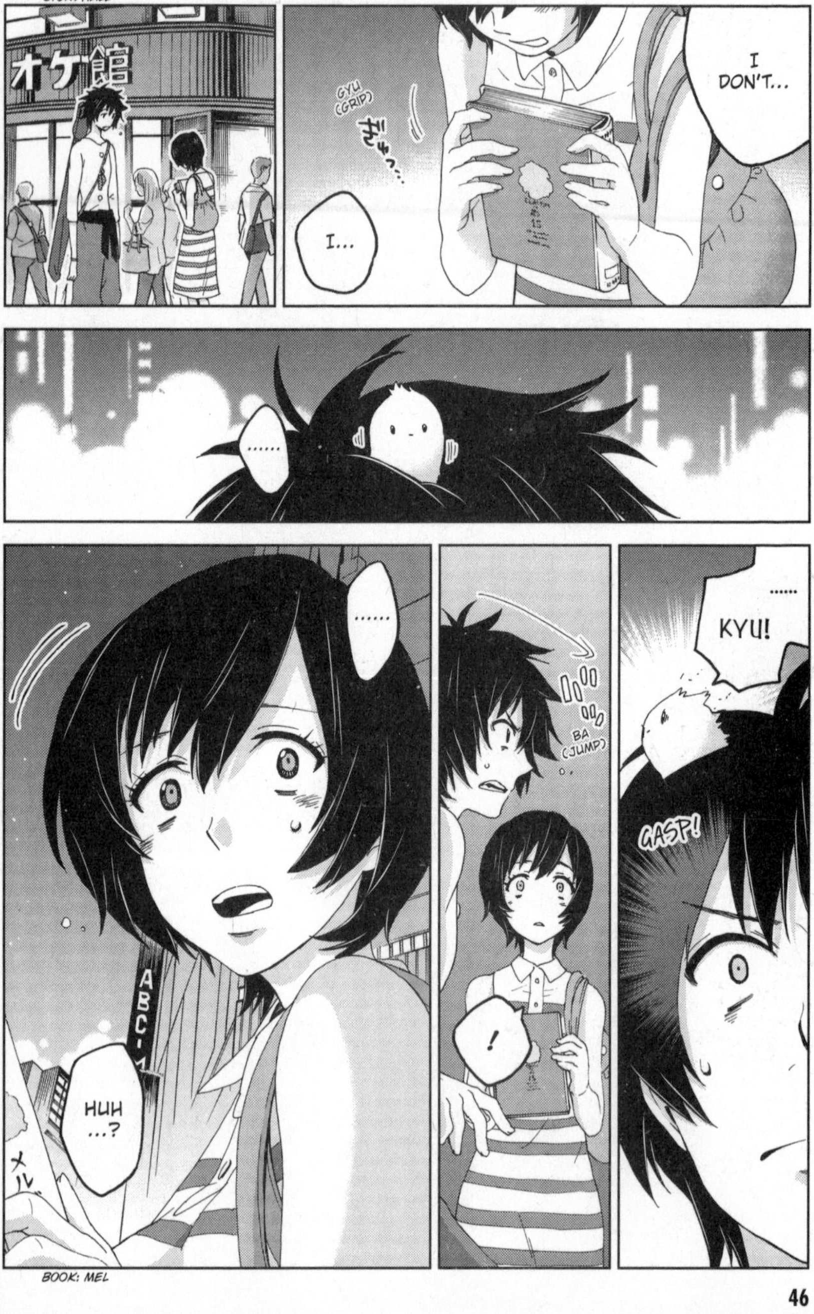

I DON'T...
GYU (GRIP)
ぎゅっ…
I...
オケ館
......
......
KYU!
GASP!
BA (JUMP)
!
......
HUH ...?
ABC

BOOK: MEL

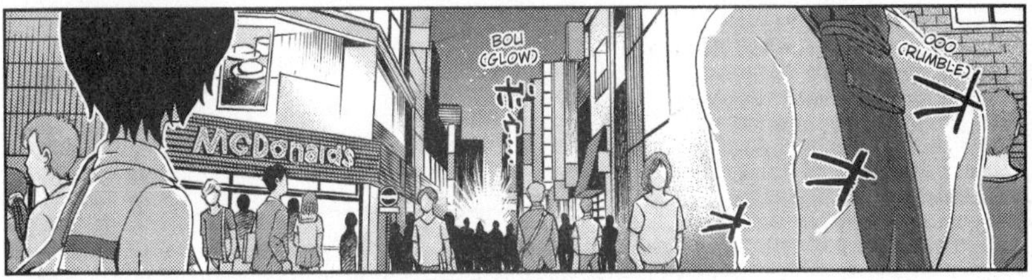
ooo
(RUMBLE)
BOU
(GLOW)
McDonald's

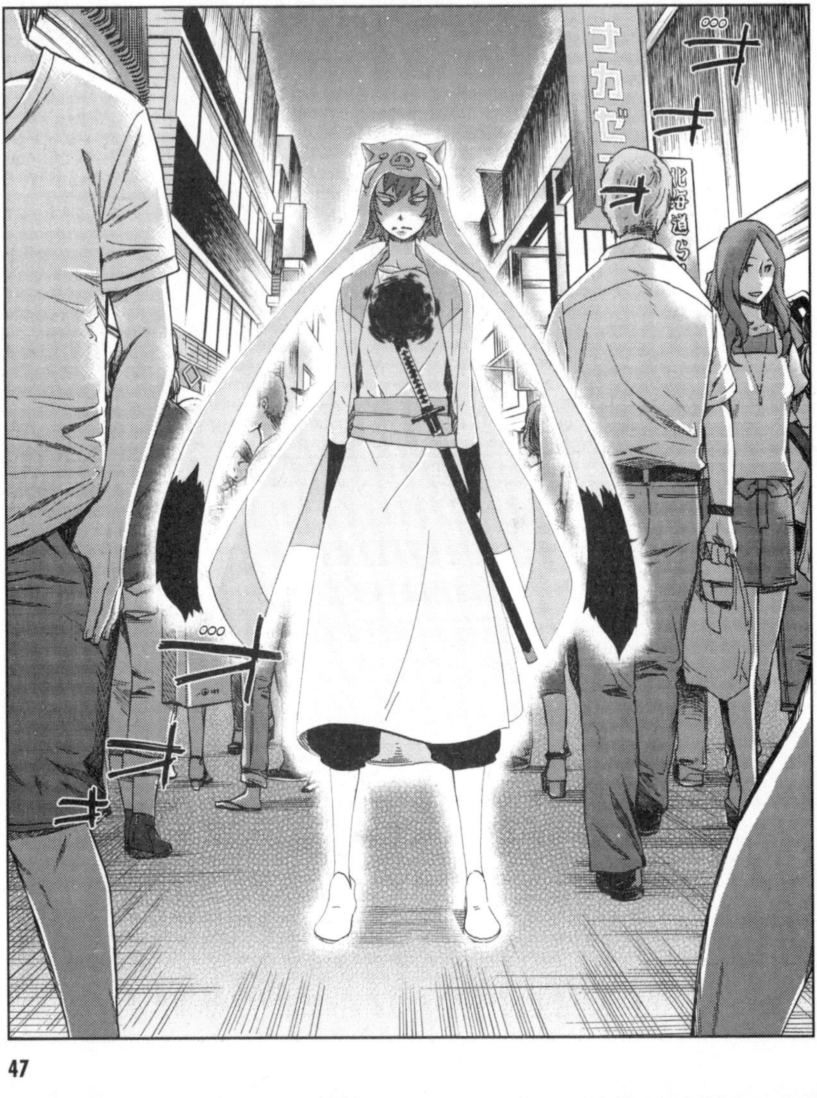
ooo
ooo

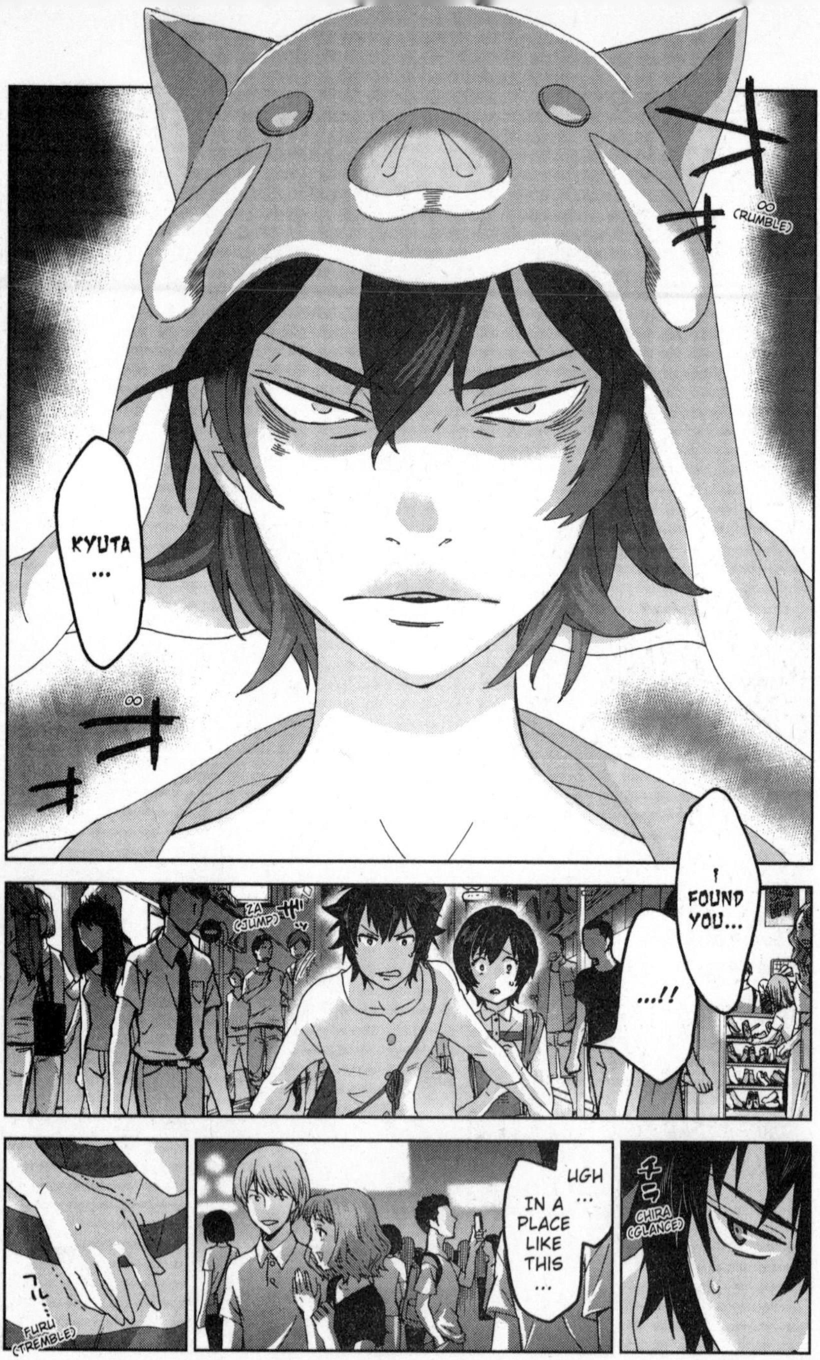
OO
(RUMBLE)
OO
KYUTA ...
I FOUND YOU...
...!!
ZA
(JUMP)
ザッ
チラ
CHIRA
(GLANCE)
UGH ...
IN A PLACE LIKE THIS ...
フル…
FURU
(TREMBLE)

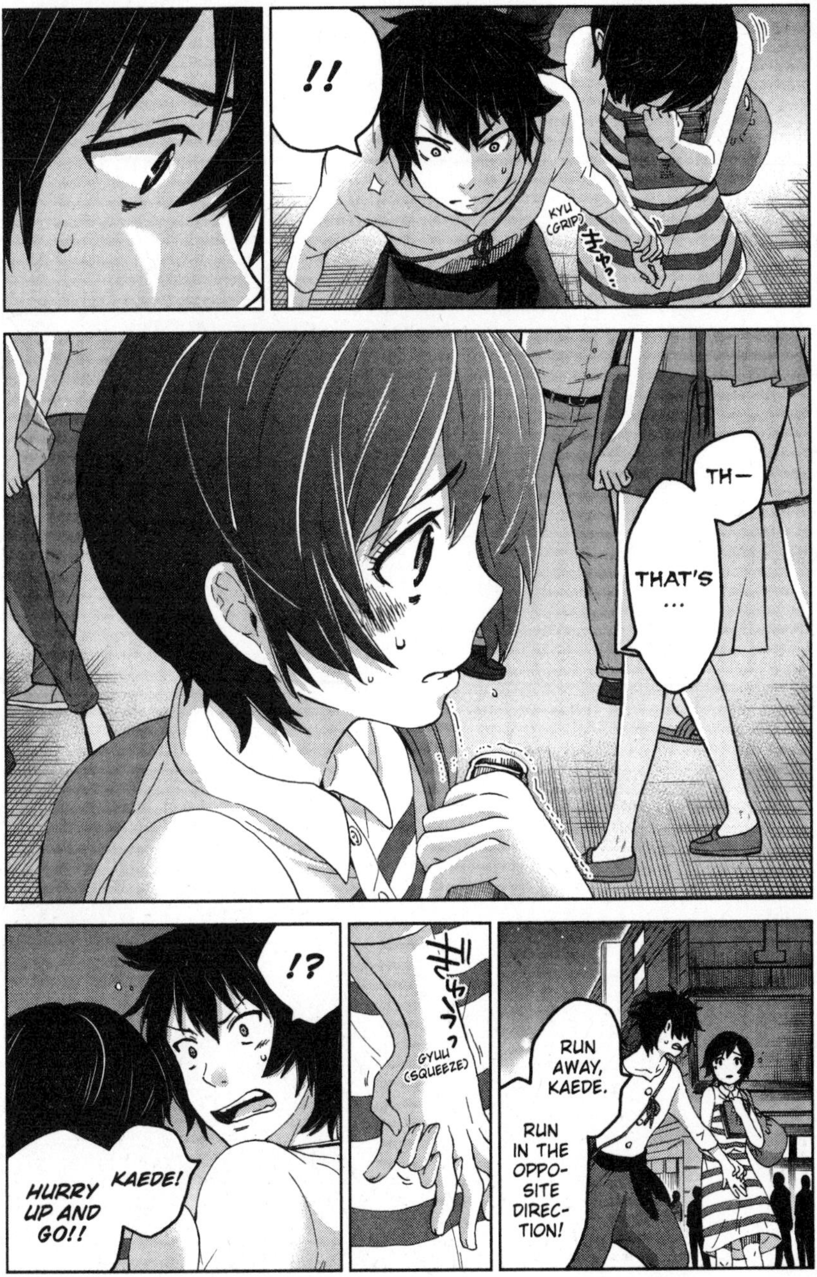
!!
KYU (GRIP)
TH—
THAT'S ...
RUN AWAY, KAEDE.
RUN IN THE OPPOSITE DIRECTION!
GYUU (SQUEEZE)
!?
KAEDE!
HURRY UP AND GO!!

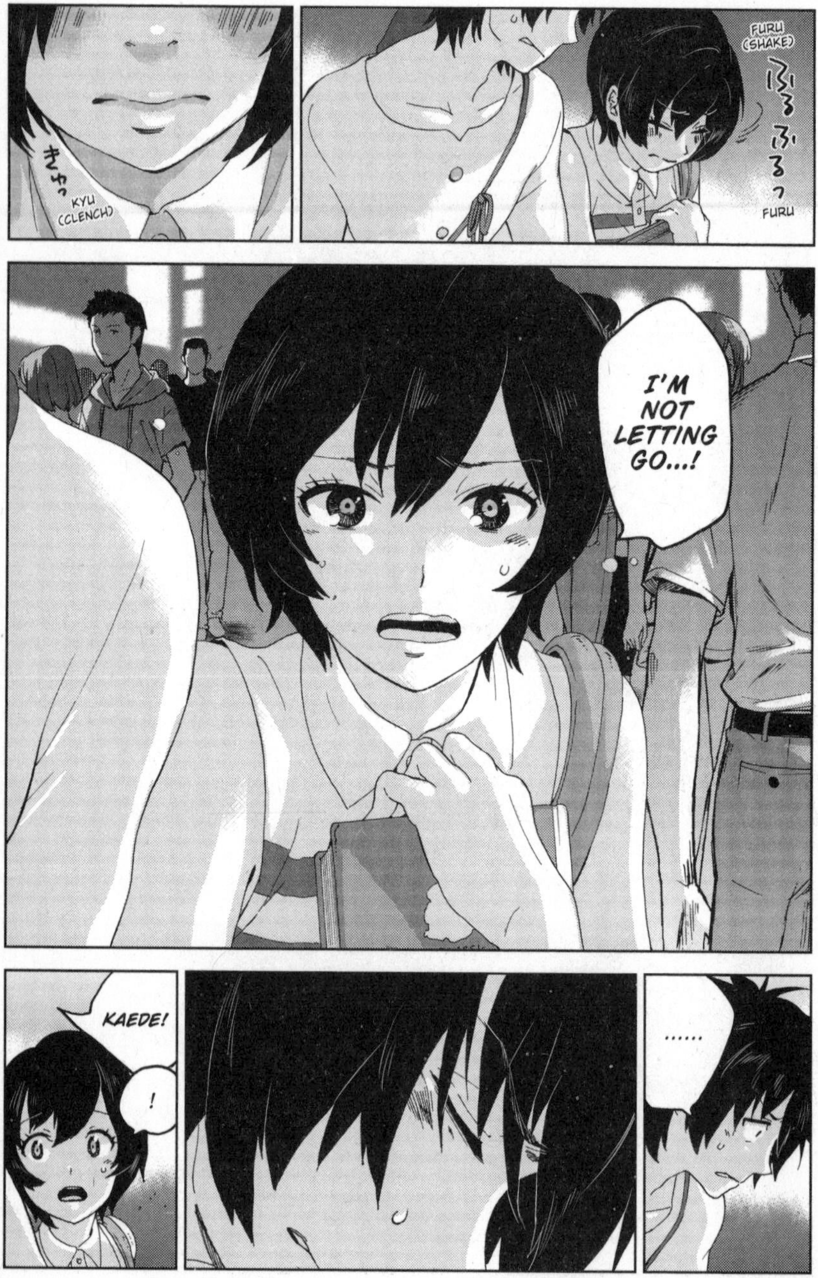
FURU (SHAKE)
ふるふるっ
FURU
きゅっ
KYU (CLENCH)
I'M NOT LETTING GO...!
......
KAEDE!
!

SIGN: SHIBUYA CENTER

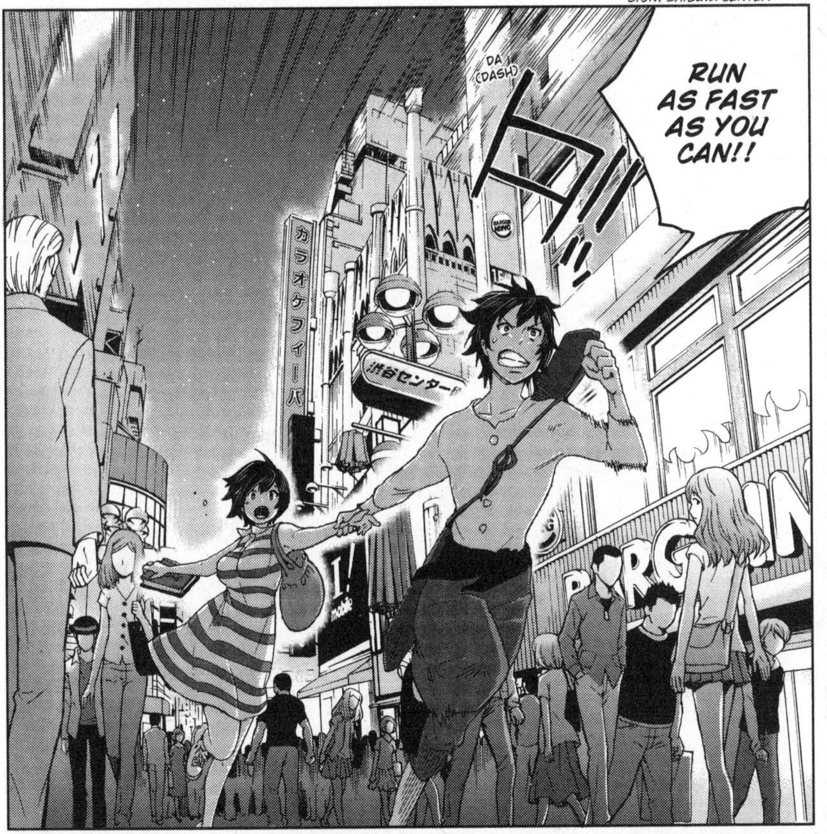
DA (DASH)
RUN AS FAST AS YOU CAN!!

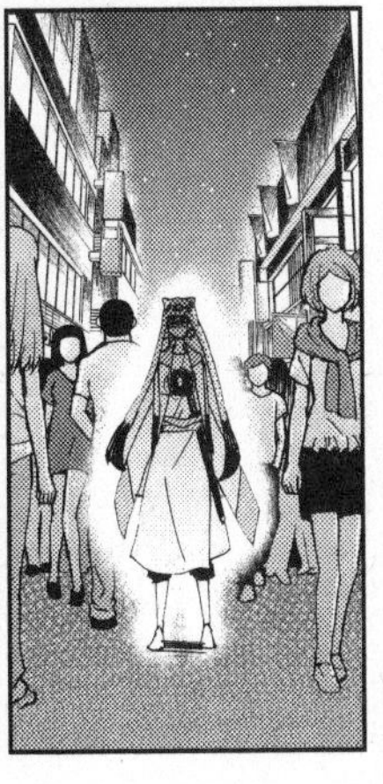

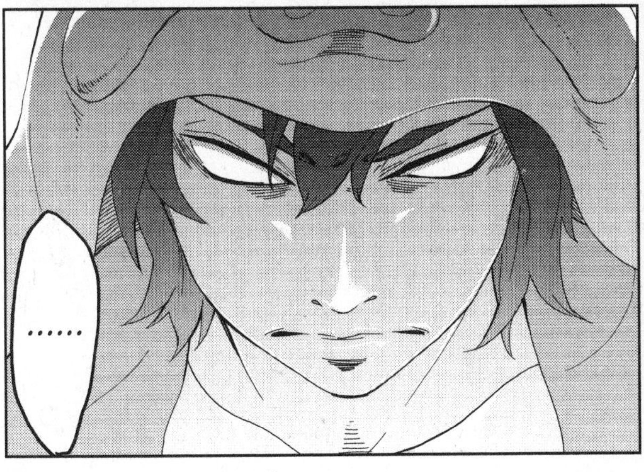
......

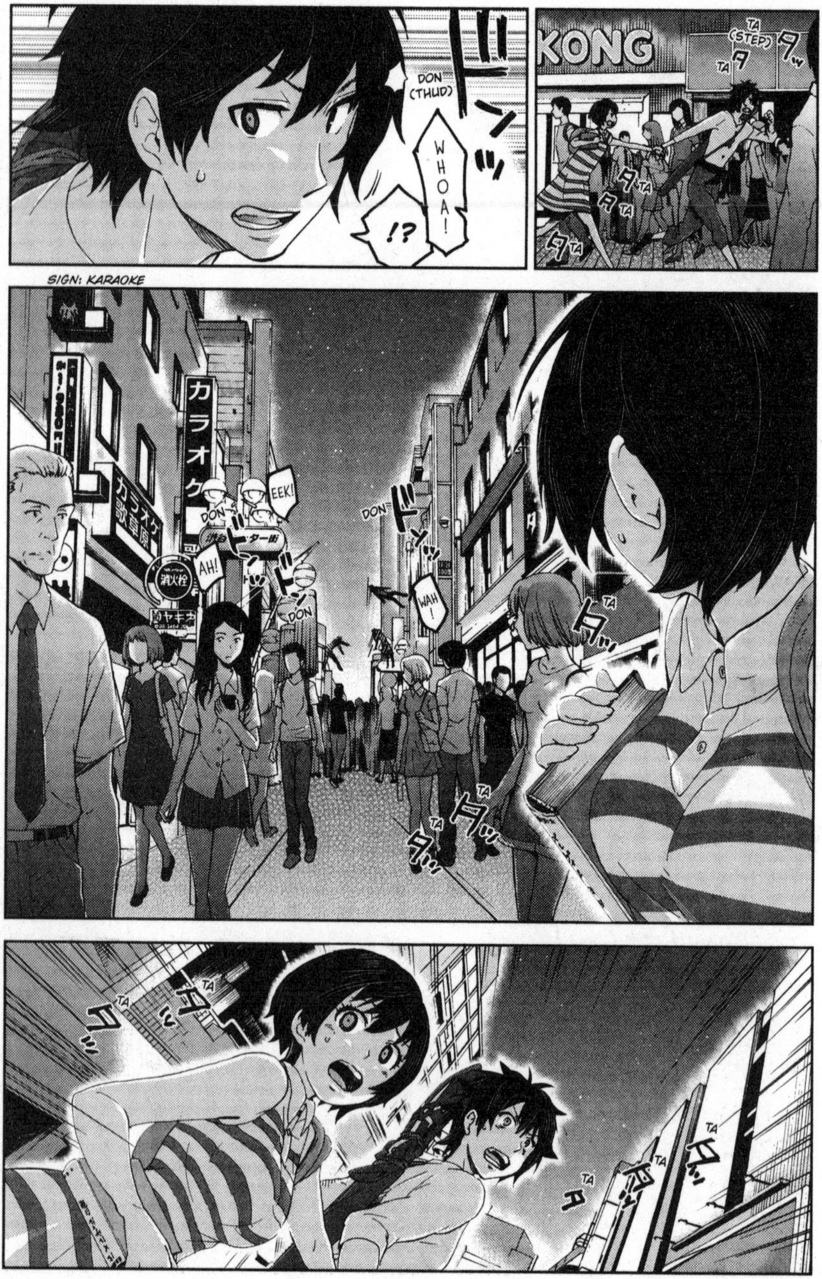
KONG
TA (STEP)
TA
TA
TA
TA
TA
DON (THUD)
WHOA!
!?
SIGN: KARAOKE
TA
TA
TA
DON
WAH!
DON
EEK!
DON
AH!
TA
TA
TA
TA
TA
TA

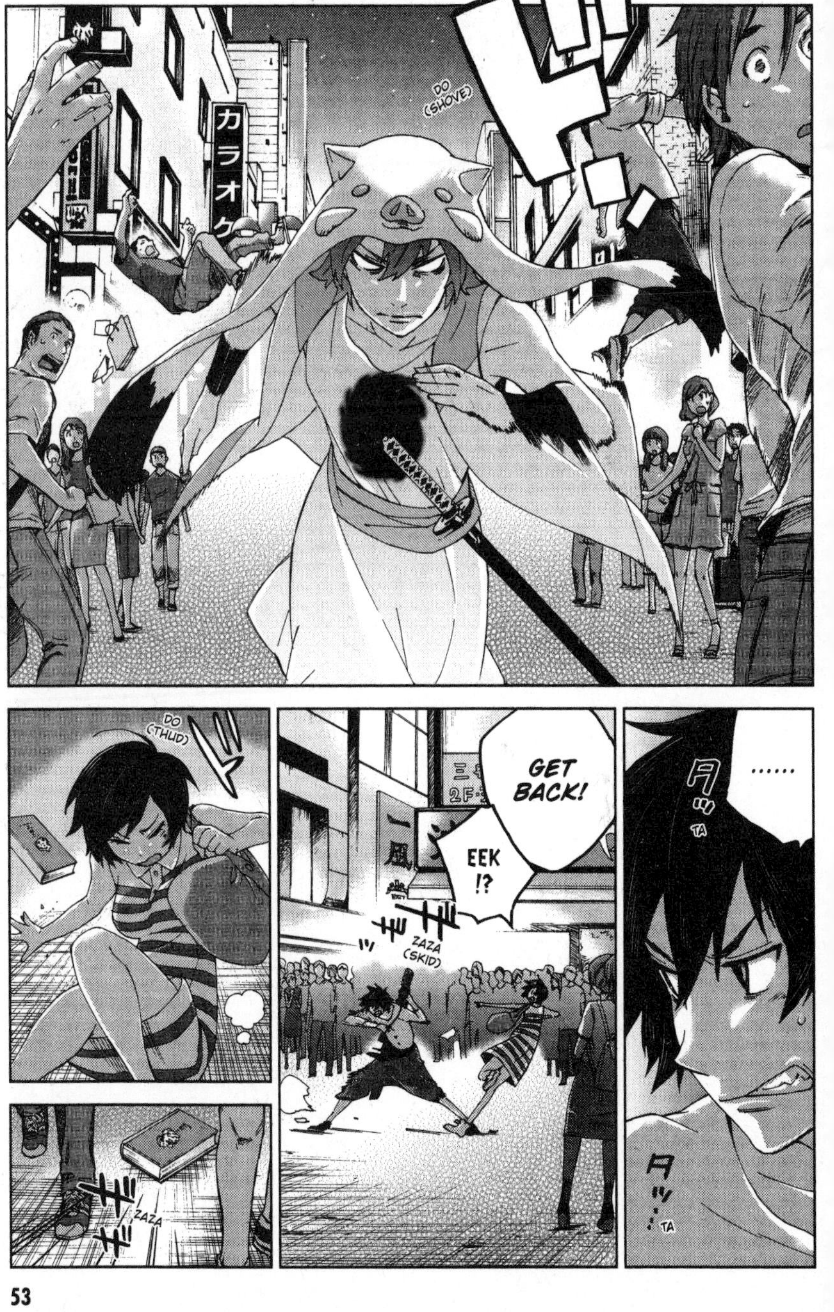

DO (SHOVE)
カラオケ
....
TA
TA
GET BACK!
EEK !?
ZAZA (SKID)
DO (THUD)
ZAZA

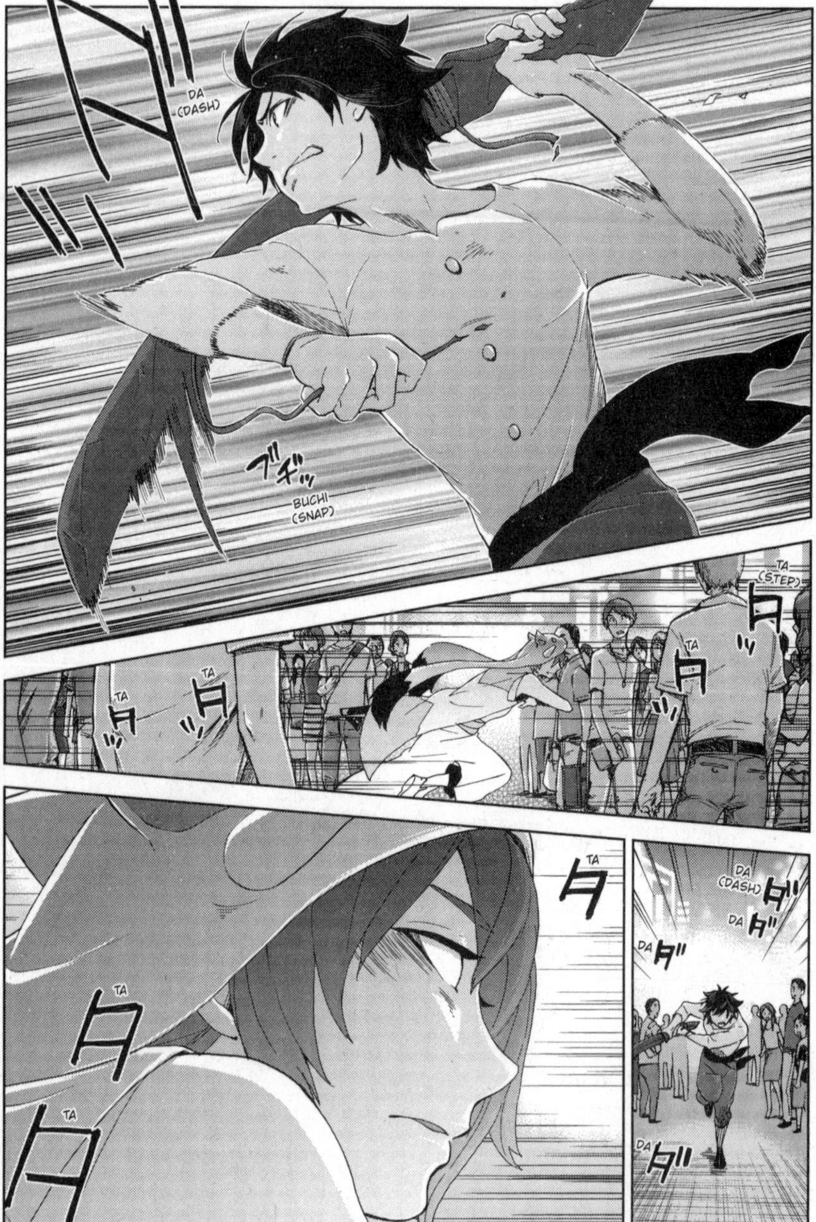

DA
(DASH)
BUCHI
(SNAP)
TA
(STEP)
タッ
TA
タッ
TA
タッ
TA
タッ
DA
(DASH)
ダ
DA
ダ
DA
ダ
DA
ダ
TA
タ
TA
タ
TA
タ

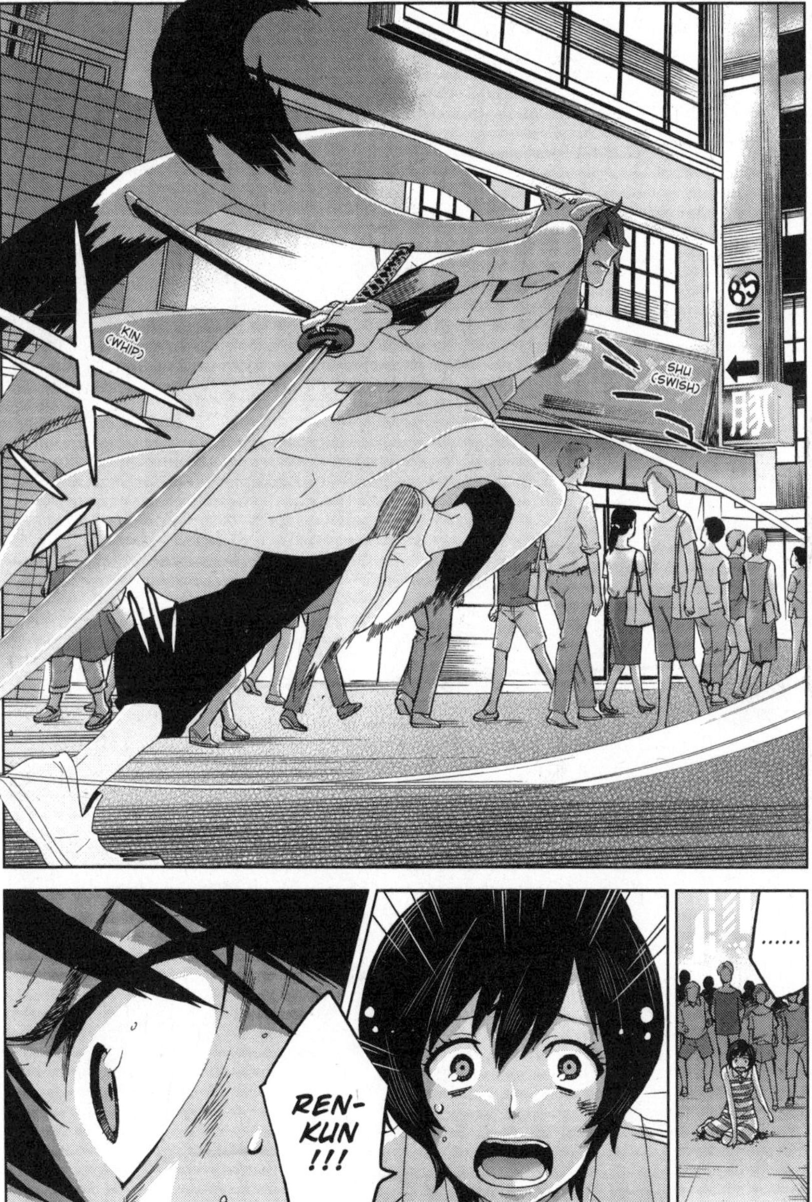
SHU (SWISH)
KIN (WHIP)
豚
......
REN-KUN!!!

SIGNS: YAMUBAL SOBA / KARAOKE

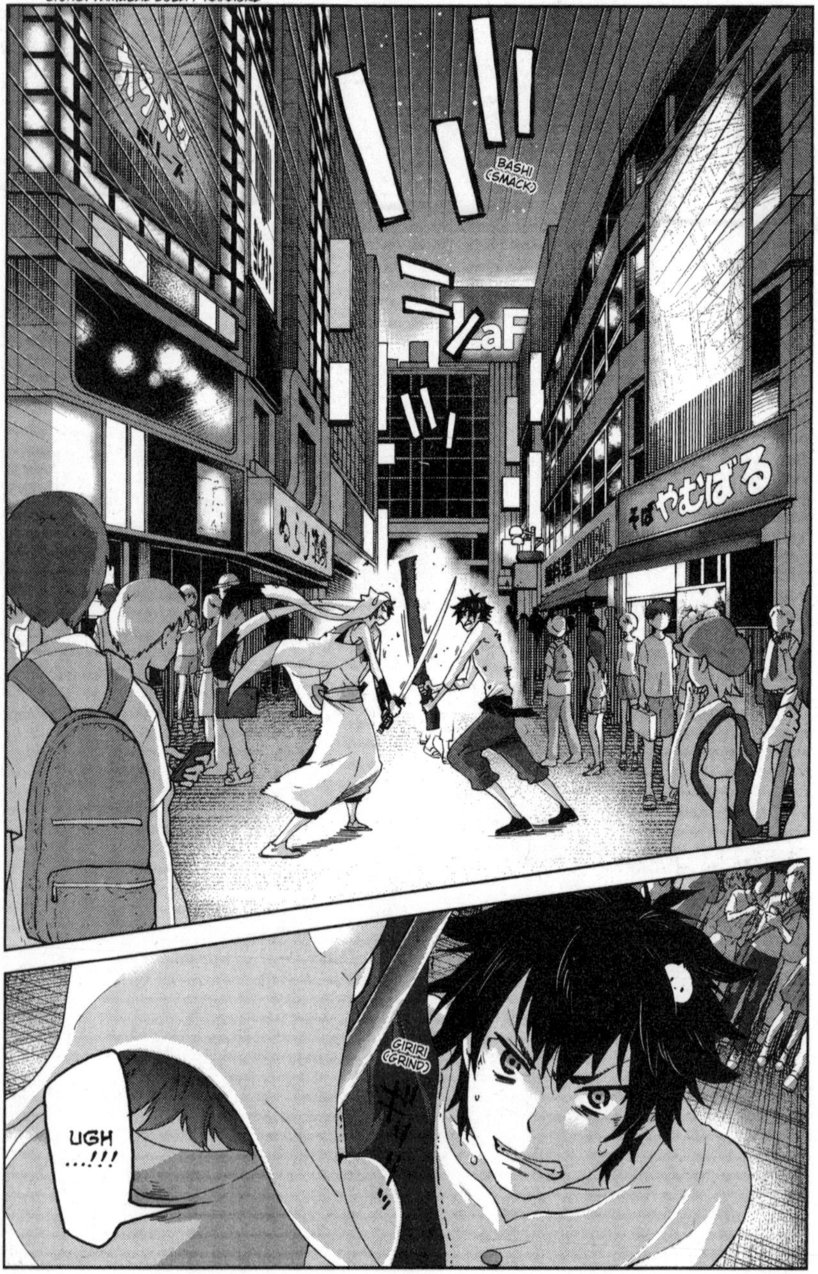
BASHI (SMACK)
そば やむばる
GIRIRI (GRIND)
UGH ...!!!

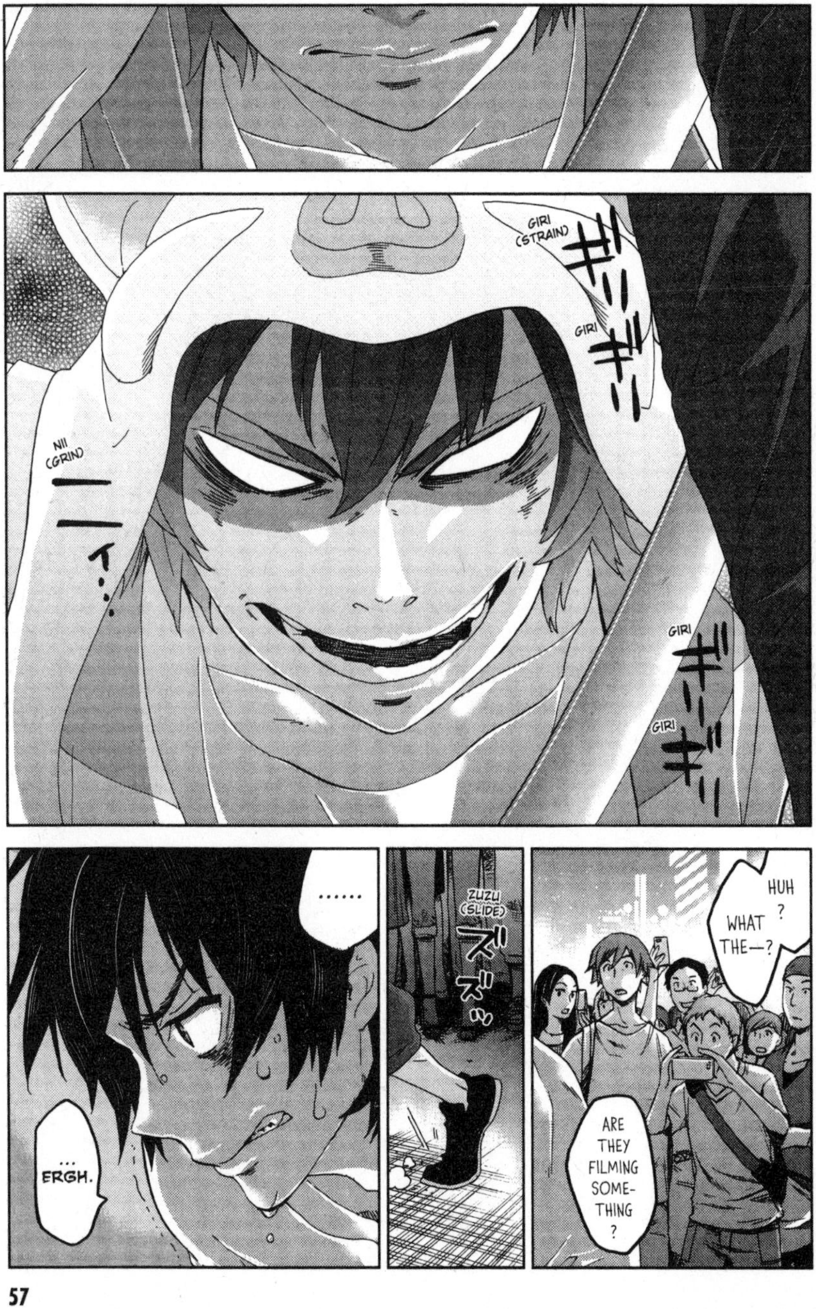
GIRI (STRAIN)
GIRI
NII (GRIN)
GIRI
GIRI
HUH?
WHAT THE—?
ARE THEY FILMING SOMETHING?
ZUZU (SLIDE)
......
...ERGH.

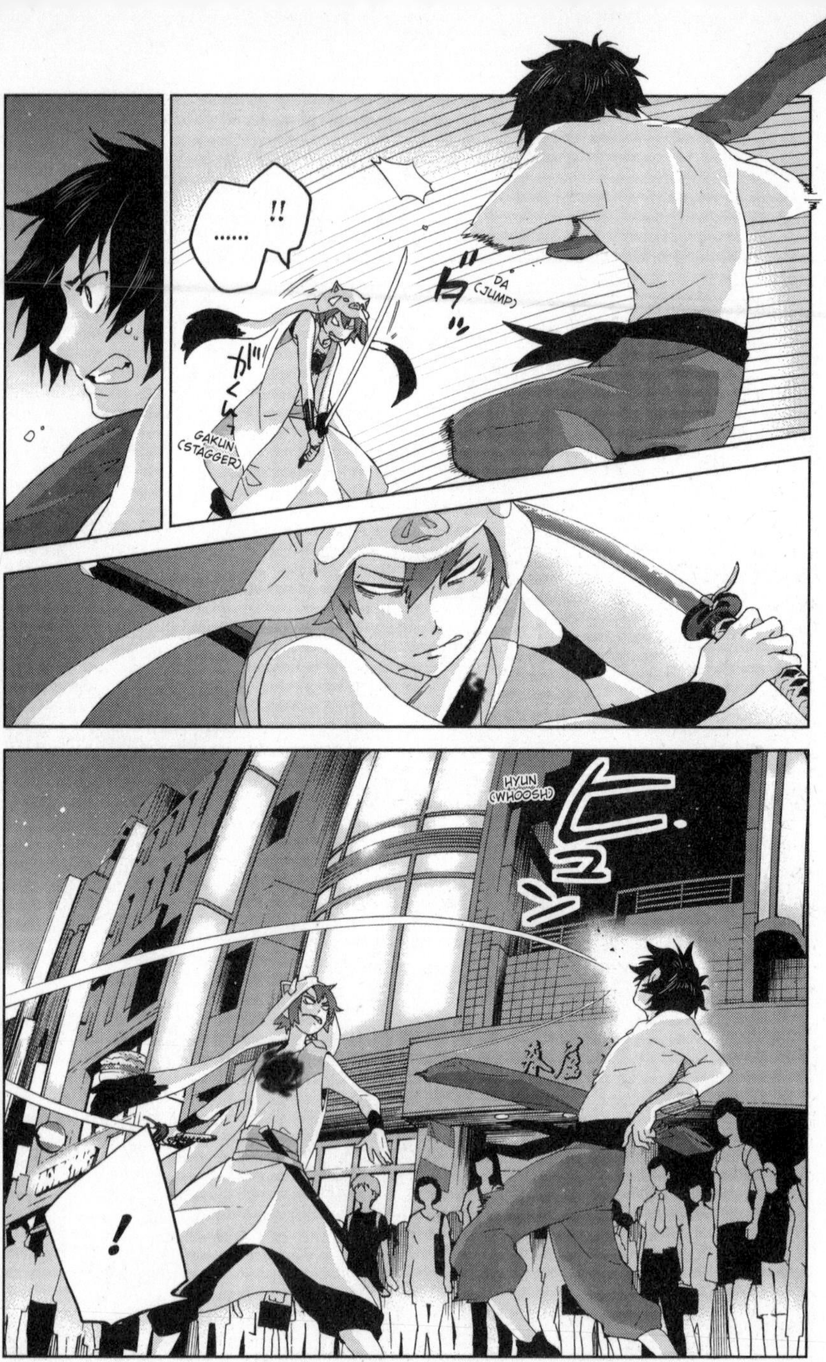
!!
......
DA (JUMP)
GAKUN (STAGGER)
HYUN (WHOOSH)
!

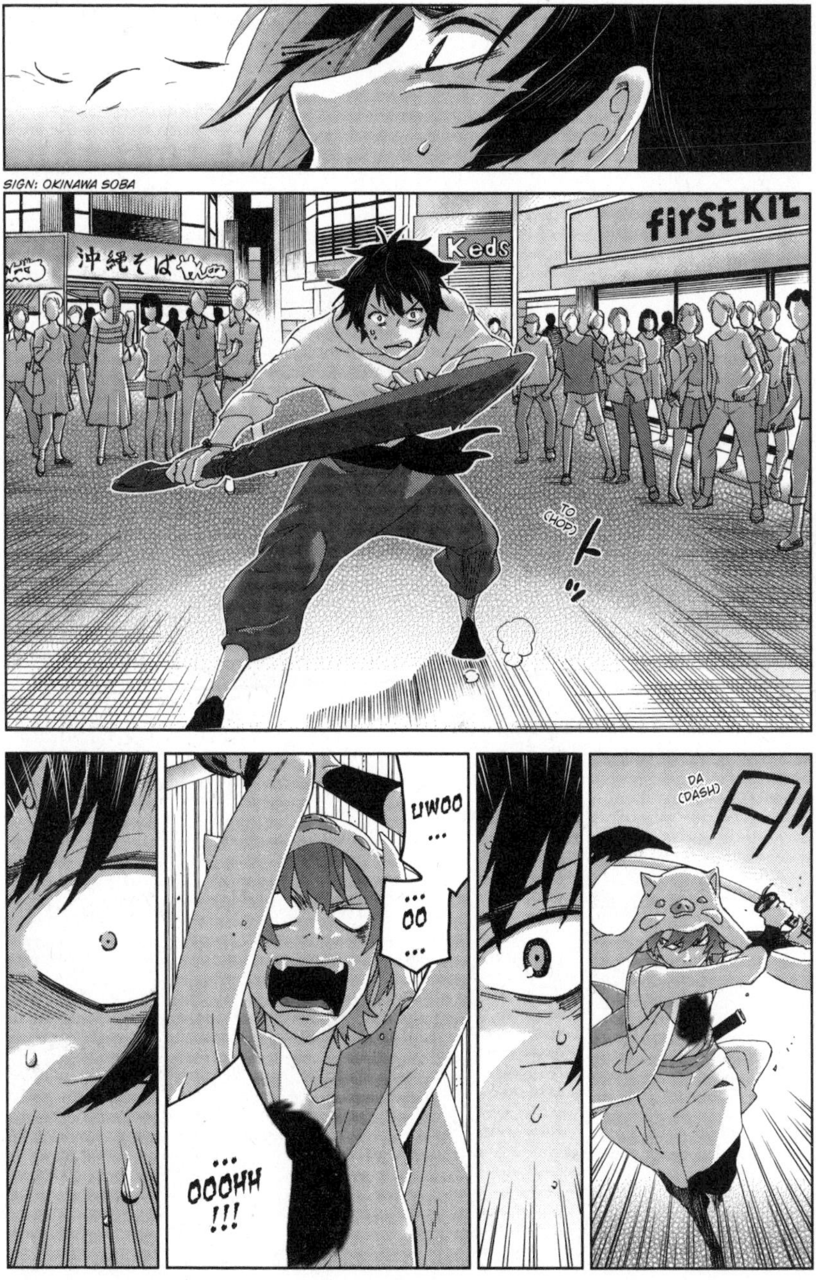
SIGN: OKINAWA SOBA
沖縄そば
first Kit
Keds
TO (HOP)
トッ
DA (DASH)
UWOO ...
... OO ...
... OOOHH !!!

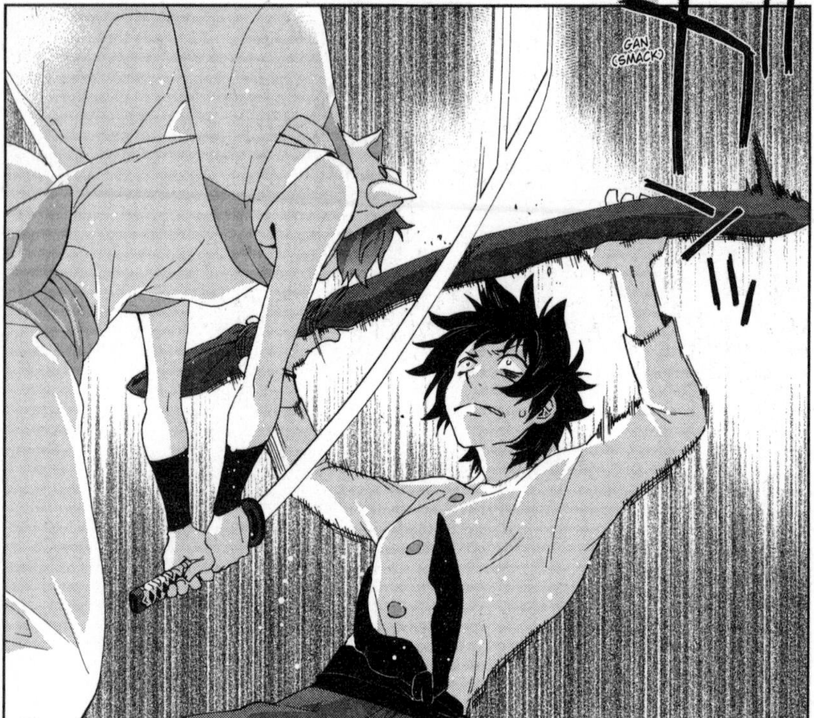
GAN
(SMACK)
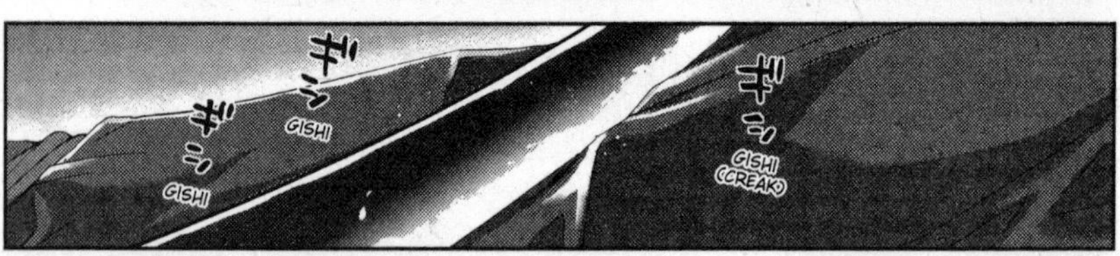
GISHI
(CREAK)
GISHI
GISHI
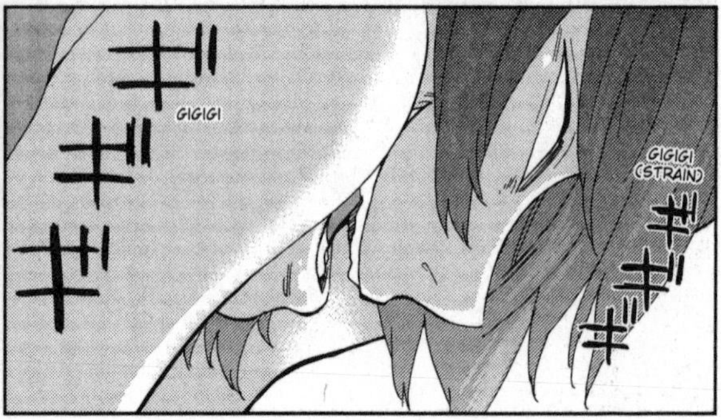
GIGIGI
(STRAIN)
GIGIGI
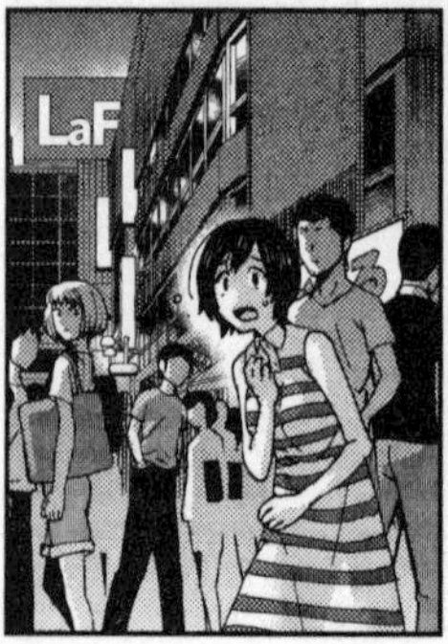

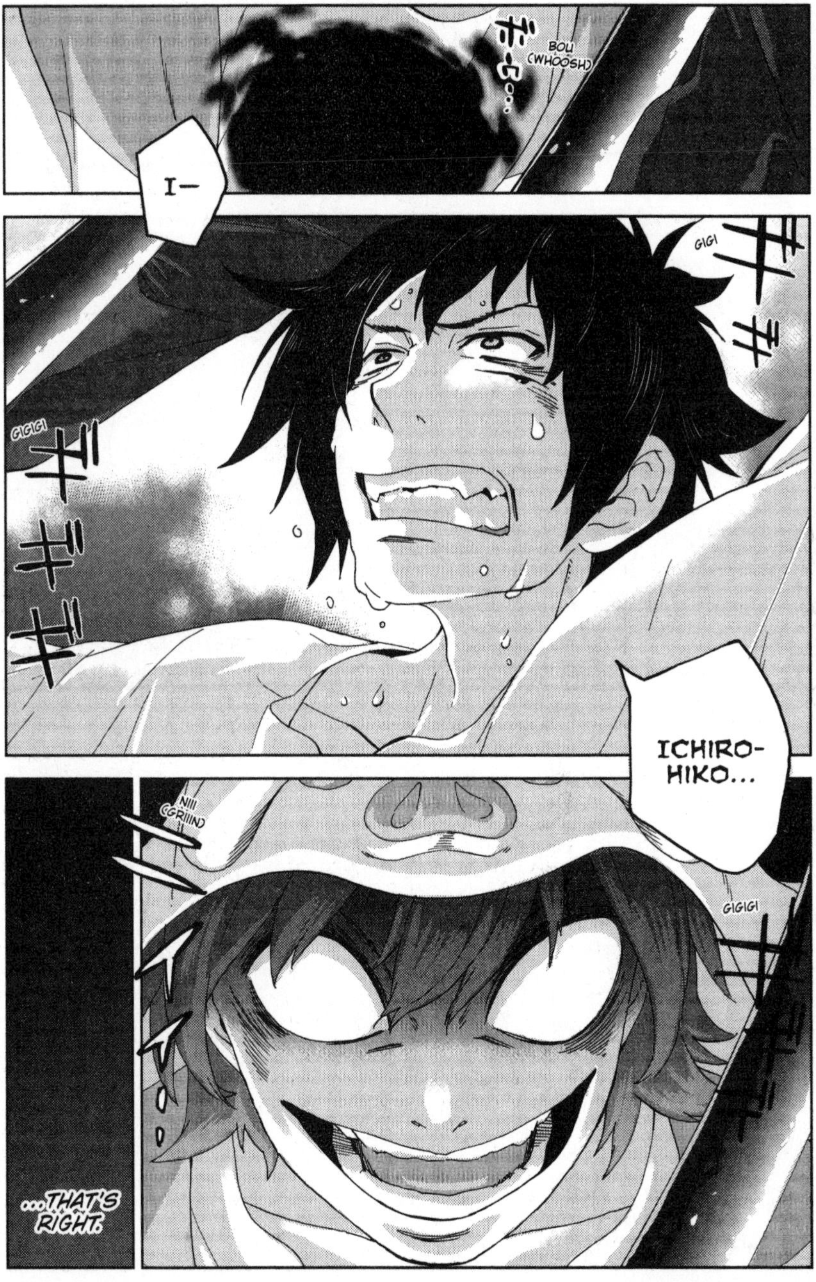
BOU (WHOOSH)
I—
GIGI
GIGIGI
ICHIRO-HIKO...
NIII (GRIIIN)
GIGIGI
...THAT'S RIGHT.

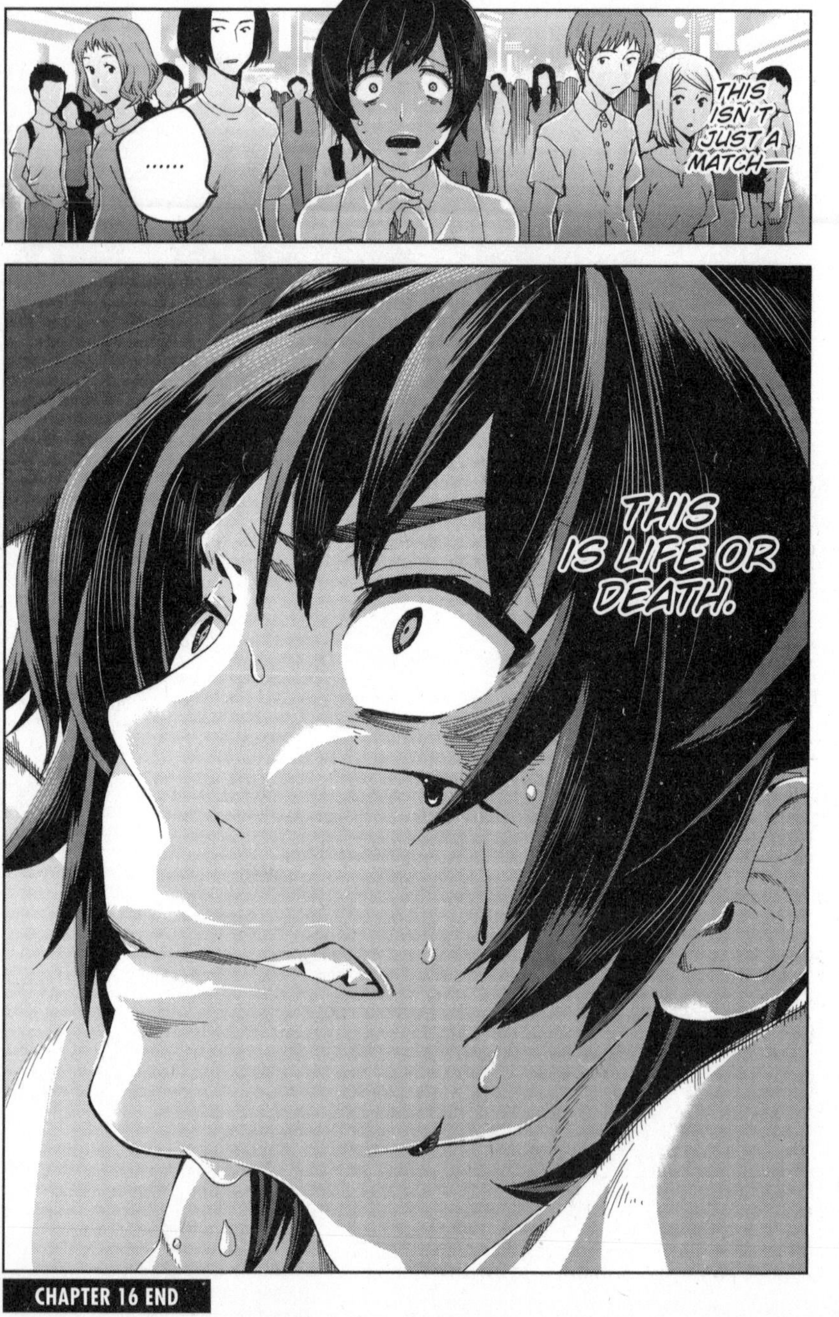
THIS ISN'T JUST A MATCH—
......
THIS IS LIFE OR DEATH.

CHAPTER 16 END

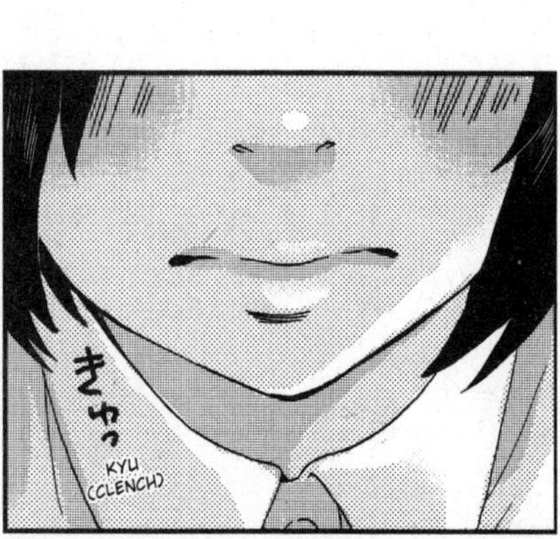
きゅっ
KYU
(CLENCH)

THE BOY & THE BEAST

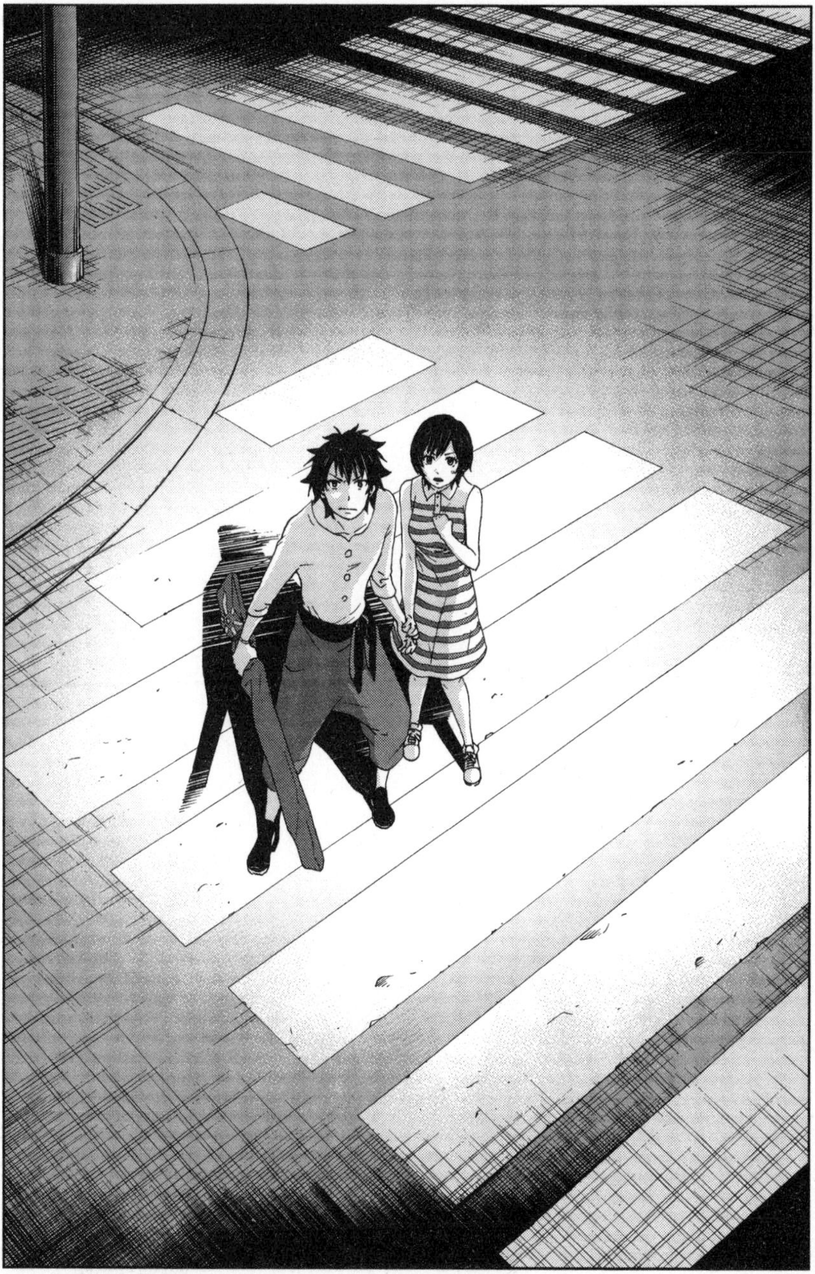

Chapter 17 THE COURAGE TO FIGHT

SIGNS: SHIBUYA STORE #2 / LOW LOW PRICES / SHOES

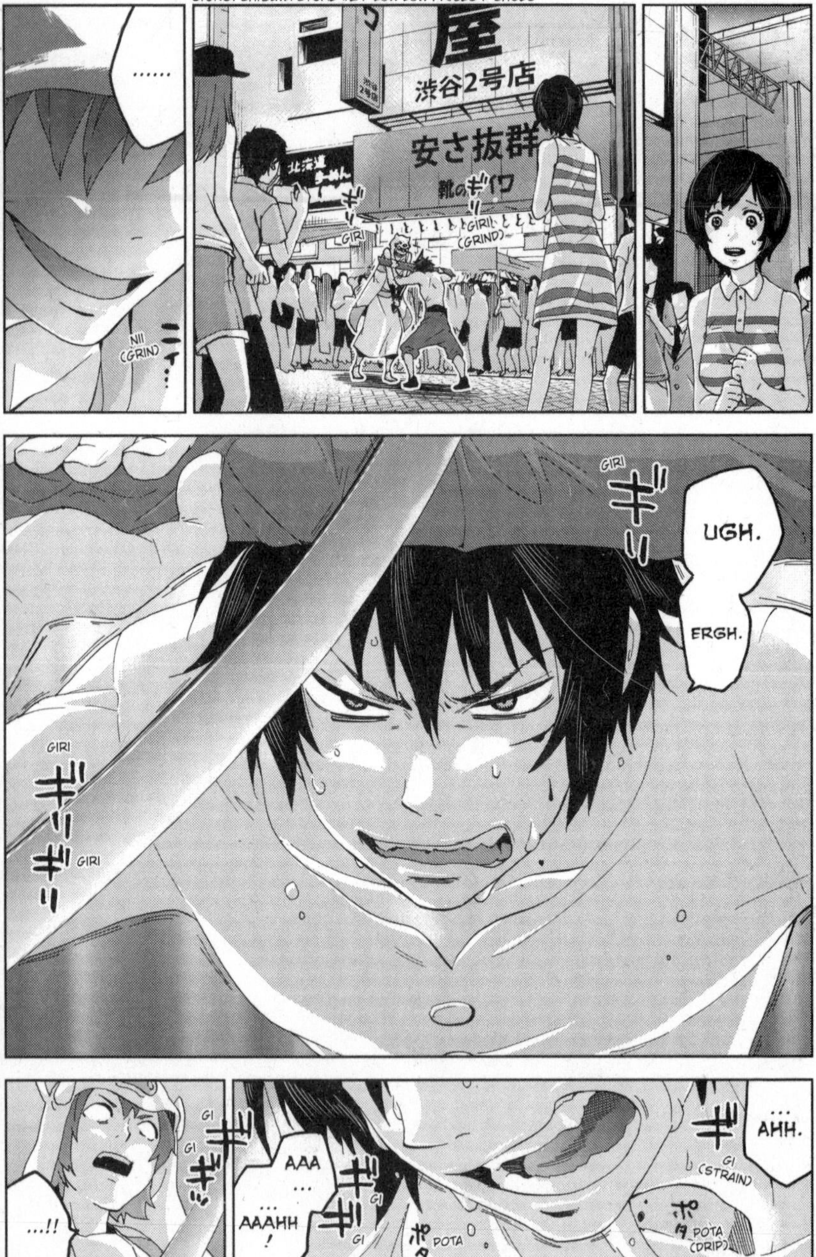

屋
渋谷2号店
安さ抜群
GIRI
GIRI (GRIND)
......
NII (GRIN)
GIRI
UGH.
ERGH.
GIRI
GIRI
...AHH.
GI (STRAIN)
POTA (DRIP)
POTA
AAA...
...AAAHH!
GI
GI
GI
GI
...!!

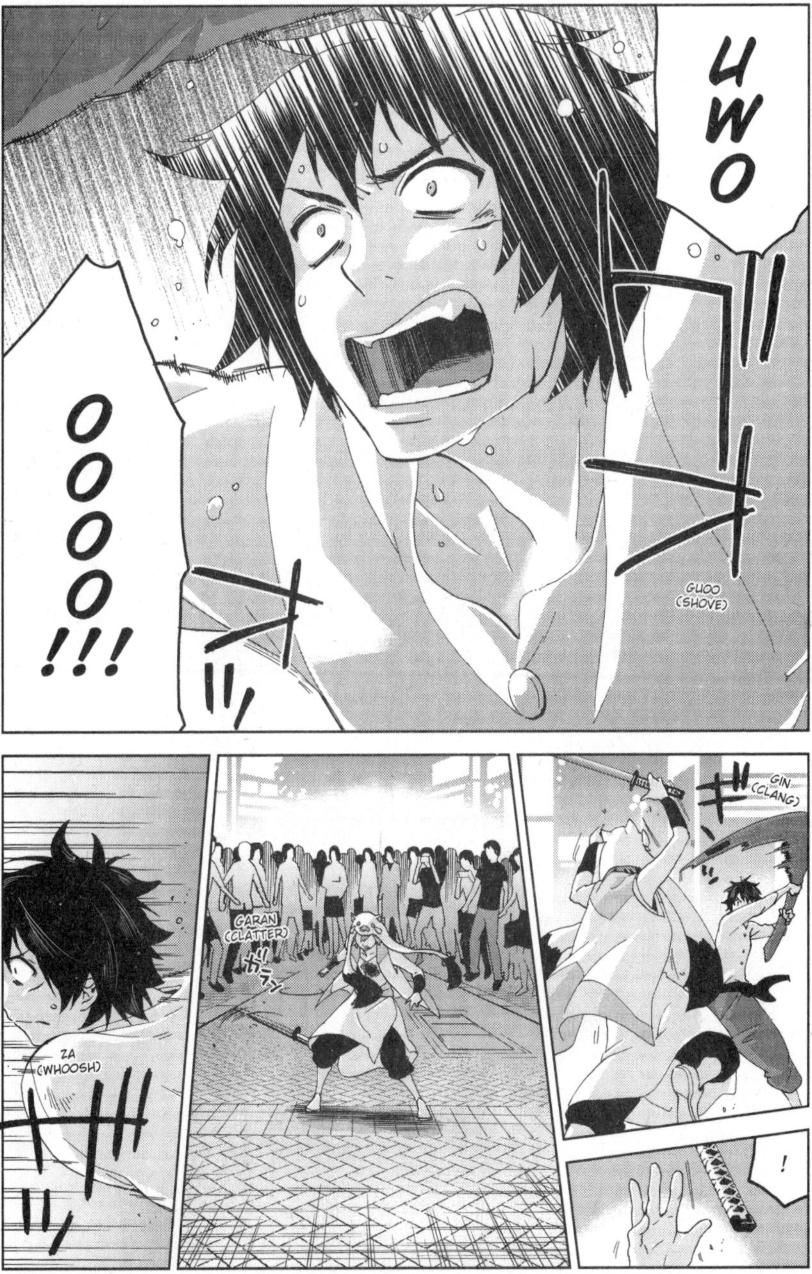
UWO
OOOOO!!!
GUOO (SHOVE)
GIN (CLANG)
!
GARAN (CLATTER)
ZA (WHOOSH)

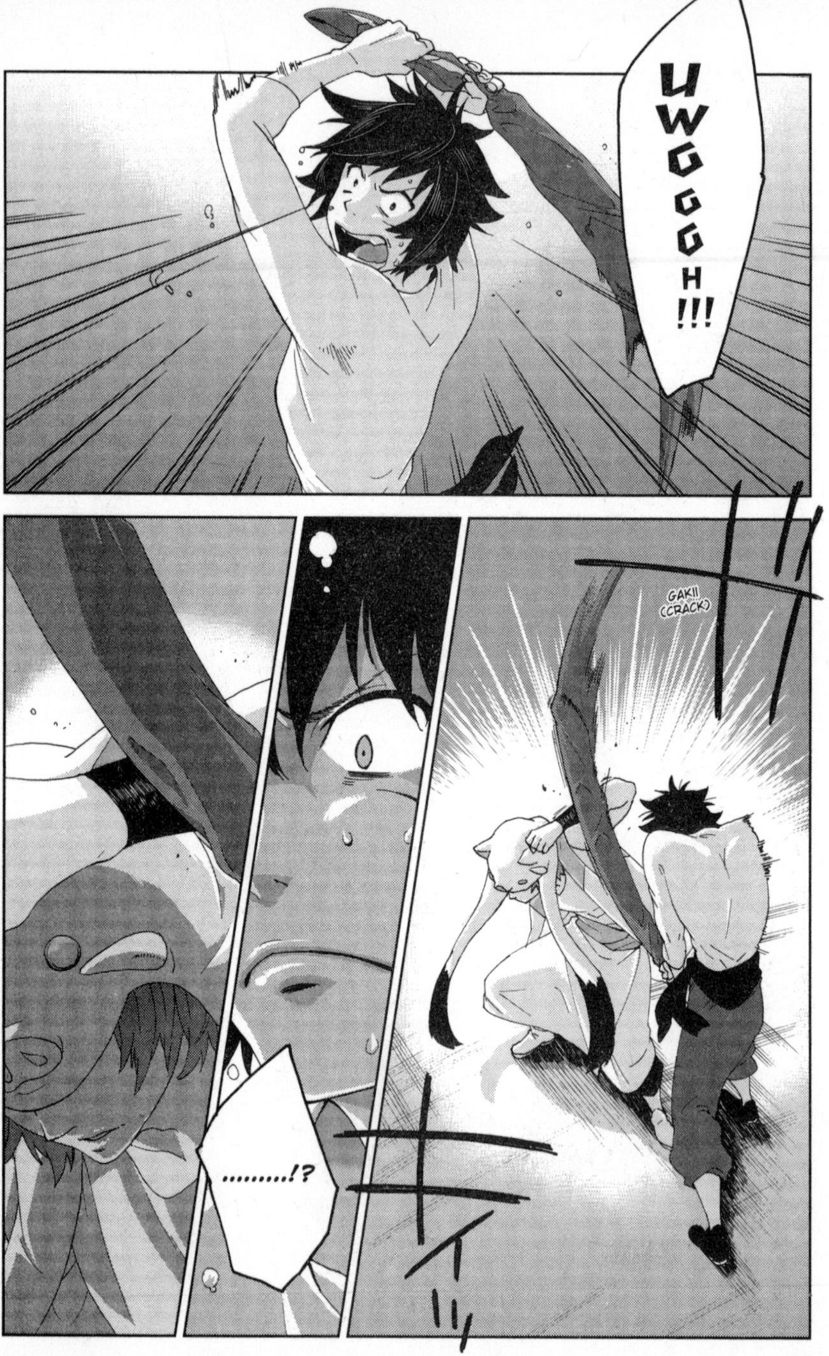
UWGGGH!!!
GAKII (CRACK)
.........!?

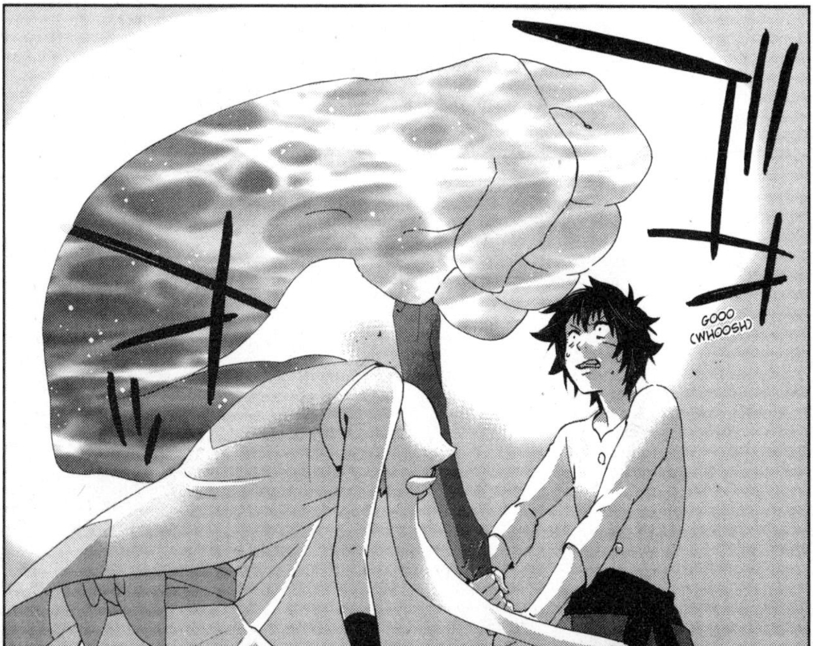
GOOO
(WHOOSH)

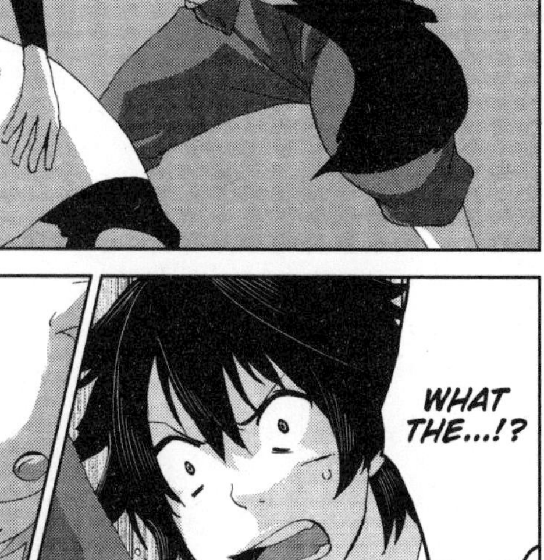
WHAT THE...!?

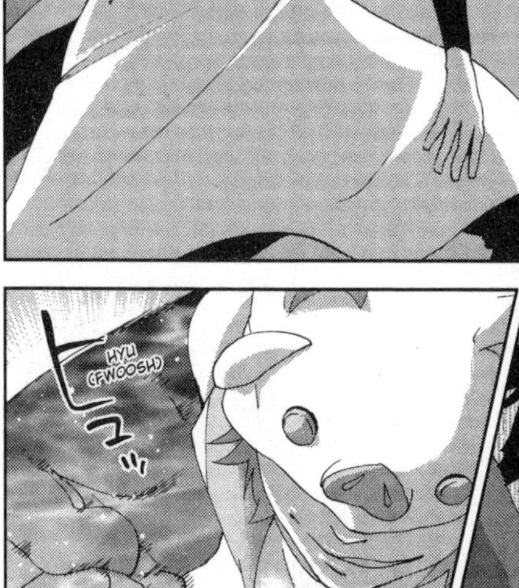
HYU
(FWOOSH)

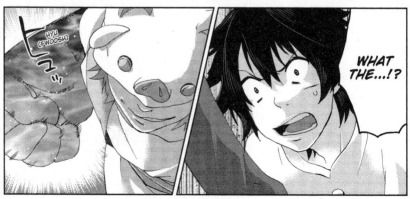

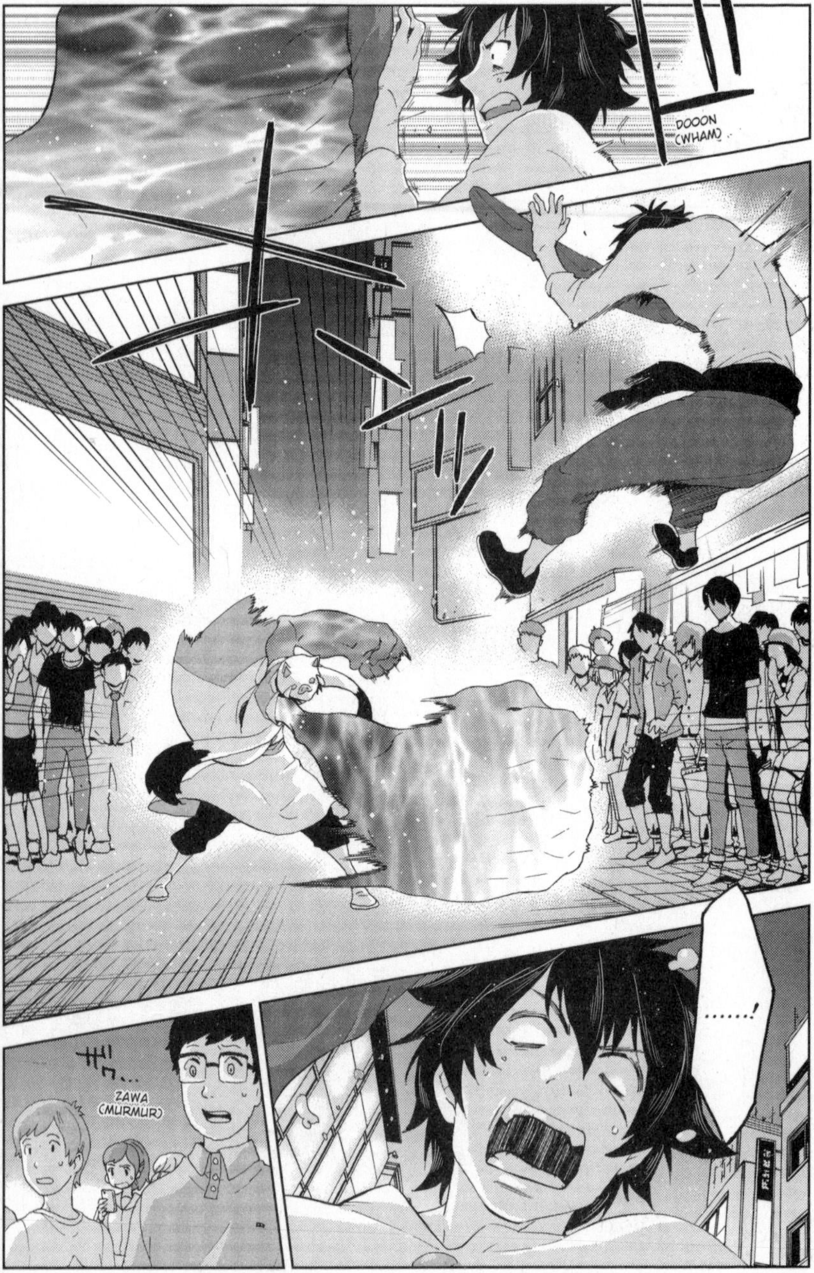
DOOON
(WHAM)
......!
ZAWA
(MURMUR)

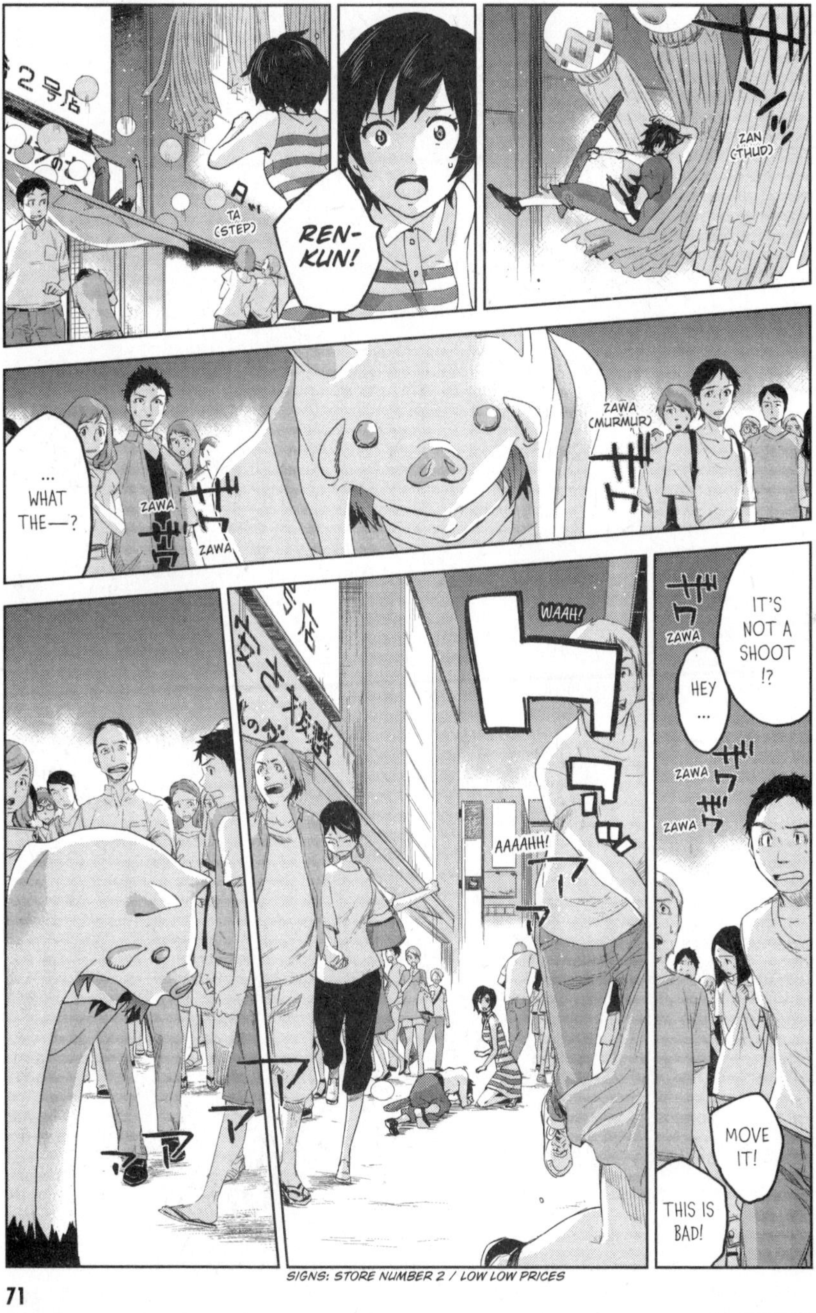
ZAN (THUD)
REN-KUN!
TA (STEP)
ZAWA (MURMUR)
... WHAT THE—?
ZAWA
ZAWA
IT'S NOT A SHOOT !?
ZAWA
HEY ...
ZAWA
ZAWA
MOVE IT!
THIS IS BAD!
WAAH!
AAAAHH!

SIGNS: STORE NUMBER 2 / LOW LOW PRICES

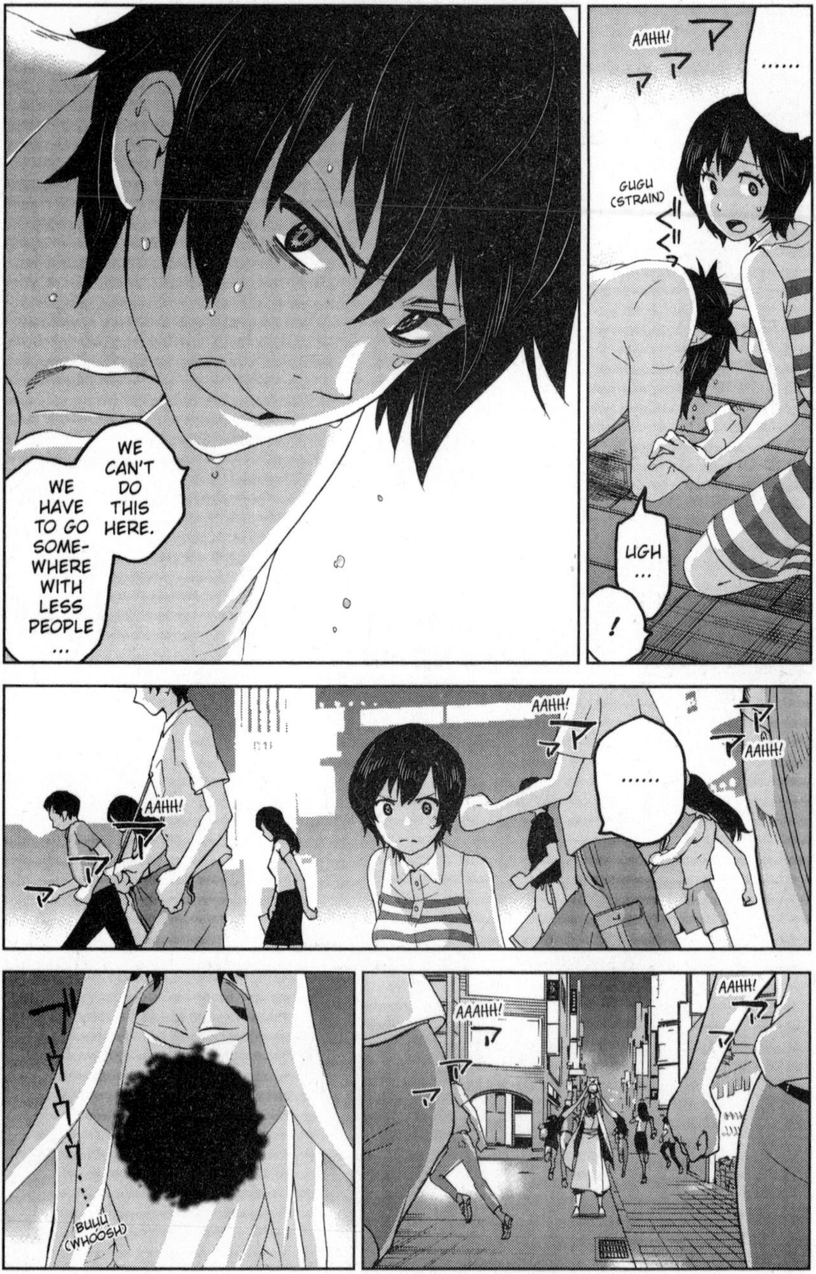
AAHH!
......
GUGU (STRAIN)
UGH ...
!
WE CAN'T DO THIS HERE.
WE HAVE TO GO SOME-WHERE WITH LESS PEOPLE ...
AAHH!
......
AAHH!
AAHH!
AAHH!
AAAHH!
BUUU (WHOOSH)

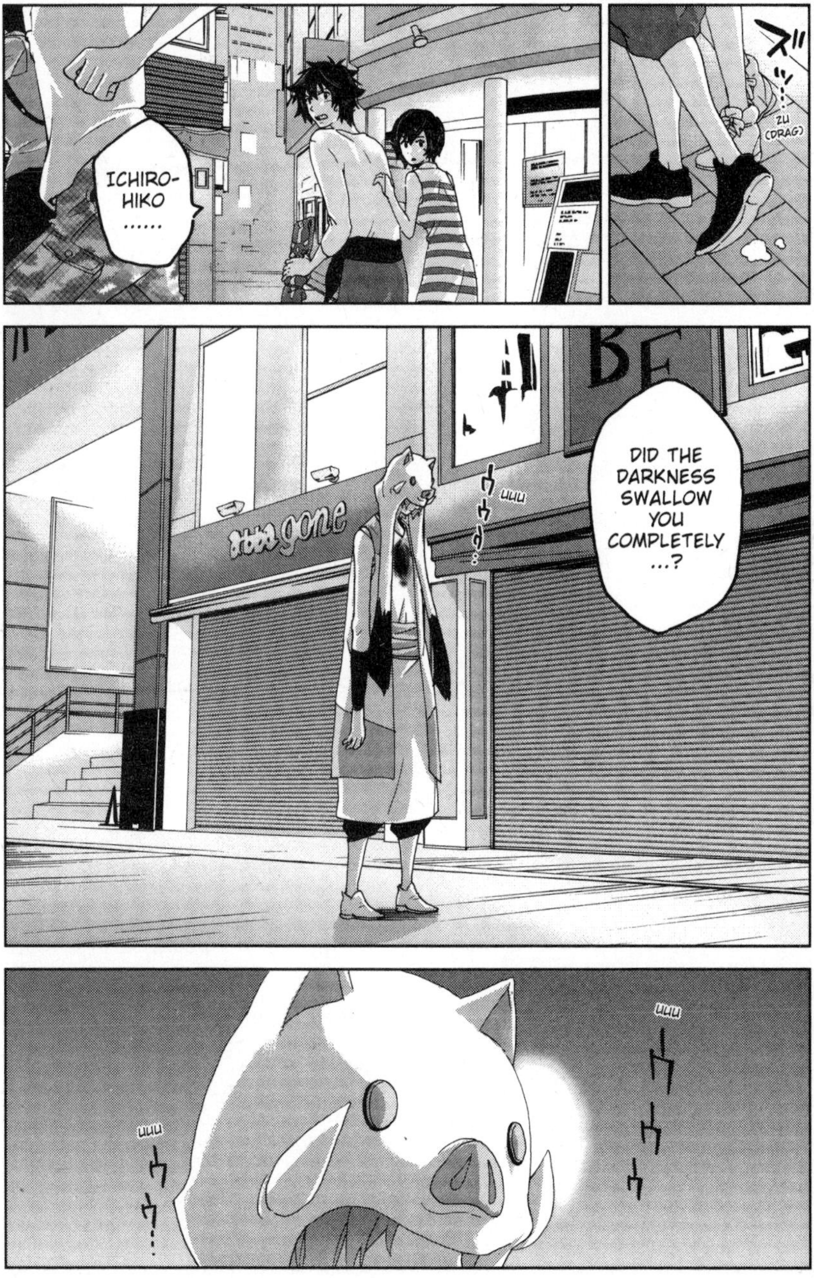
ズッ…
ZU (DRAG)
ICHIRO-HIKO ......
DID THE DARKNESS SWALLOW YOU COMPLETELY ...?
ウゥゥ…
UUU
UUU
ウゥゥ
UUU
ウゥ…

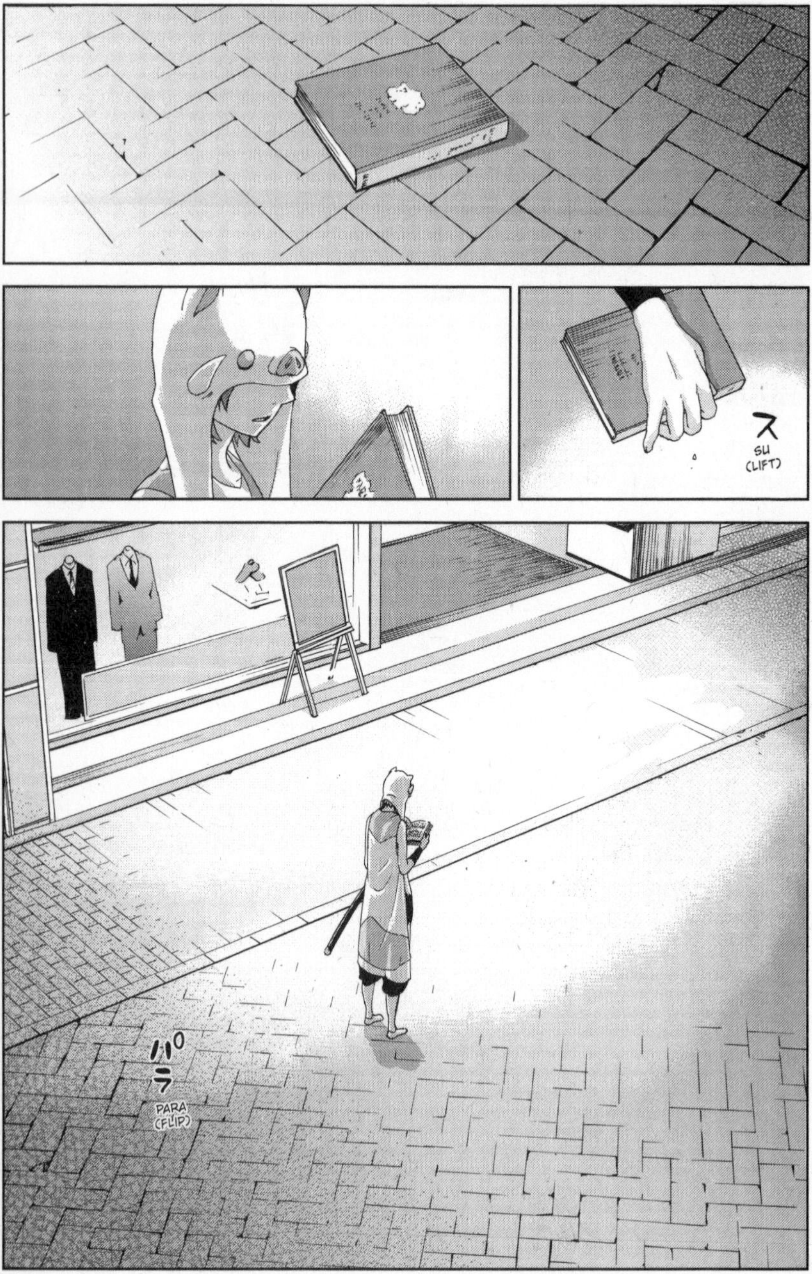
ス
SU
(LIFT)
パラ
PARA
(FLIP)

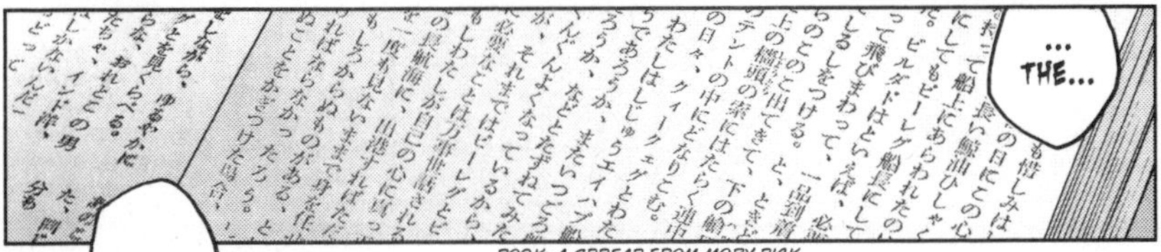
...THE...

BOOK: A SPREAD FROM MOBY DICK.

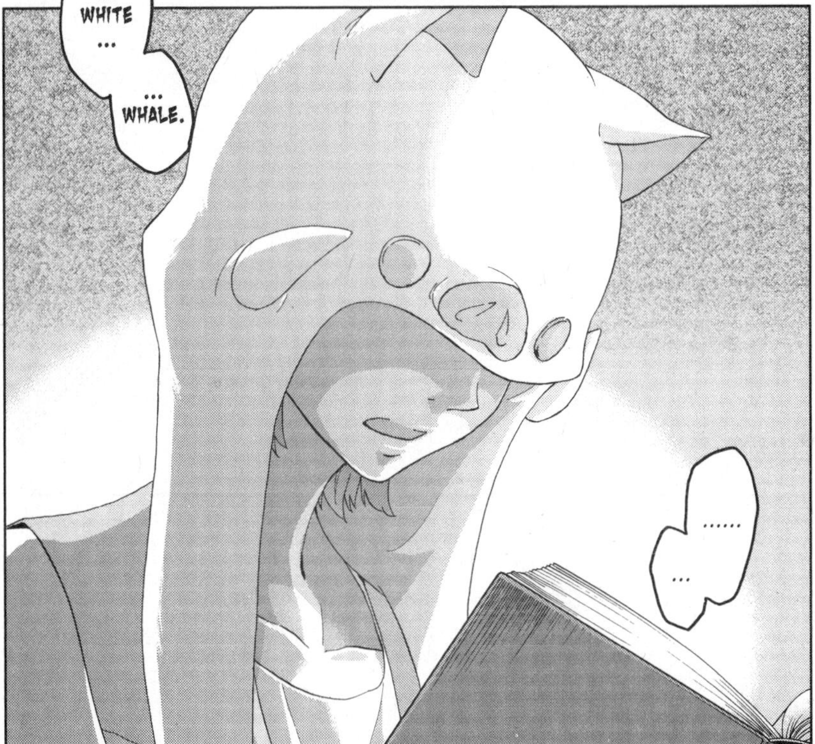
...WHITE... ...WHALE.
......
...

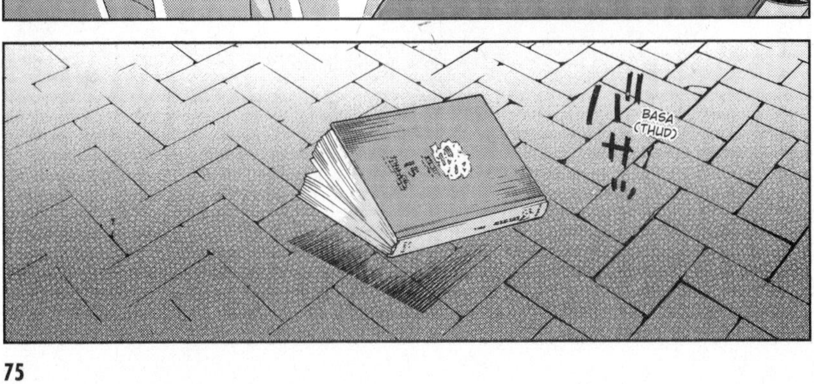
BASA (THUD)

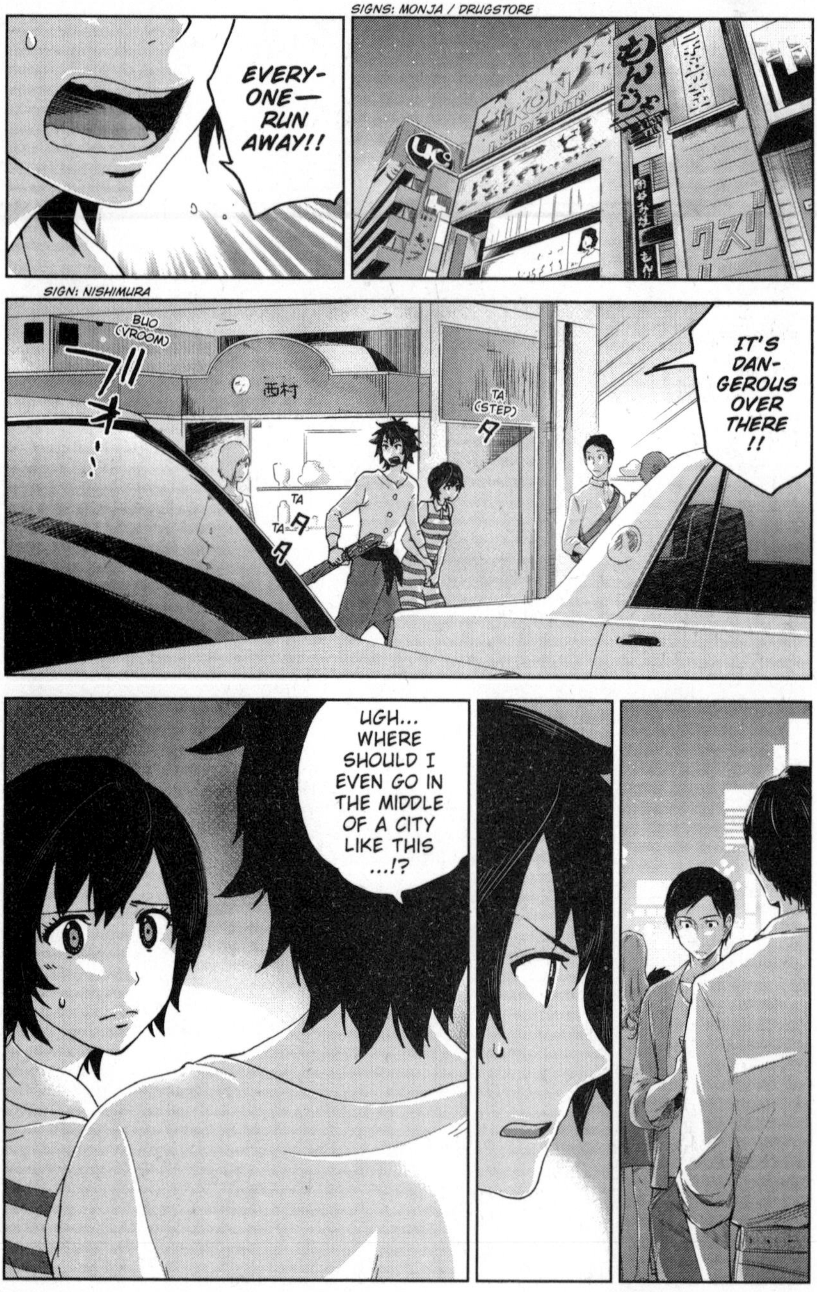
SIGNS: MONJA / DRUGSTORE
EVERY-ONE—RUN AWAY!!
SIGN: NISHIMURA
IT'S DAN-GEROUS OVER THERE!!
TA (STEP)
BUO (VROOM)
TA TA
UGH... WHERE SHOULD I EVEN GO IN THE MIDDLE OF A CITY LIKE THIS ...!?

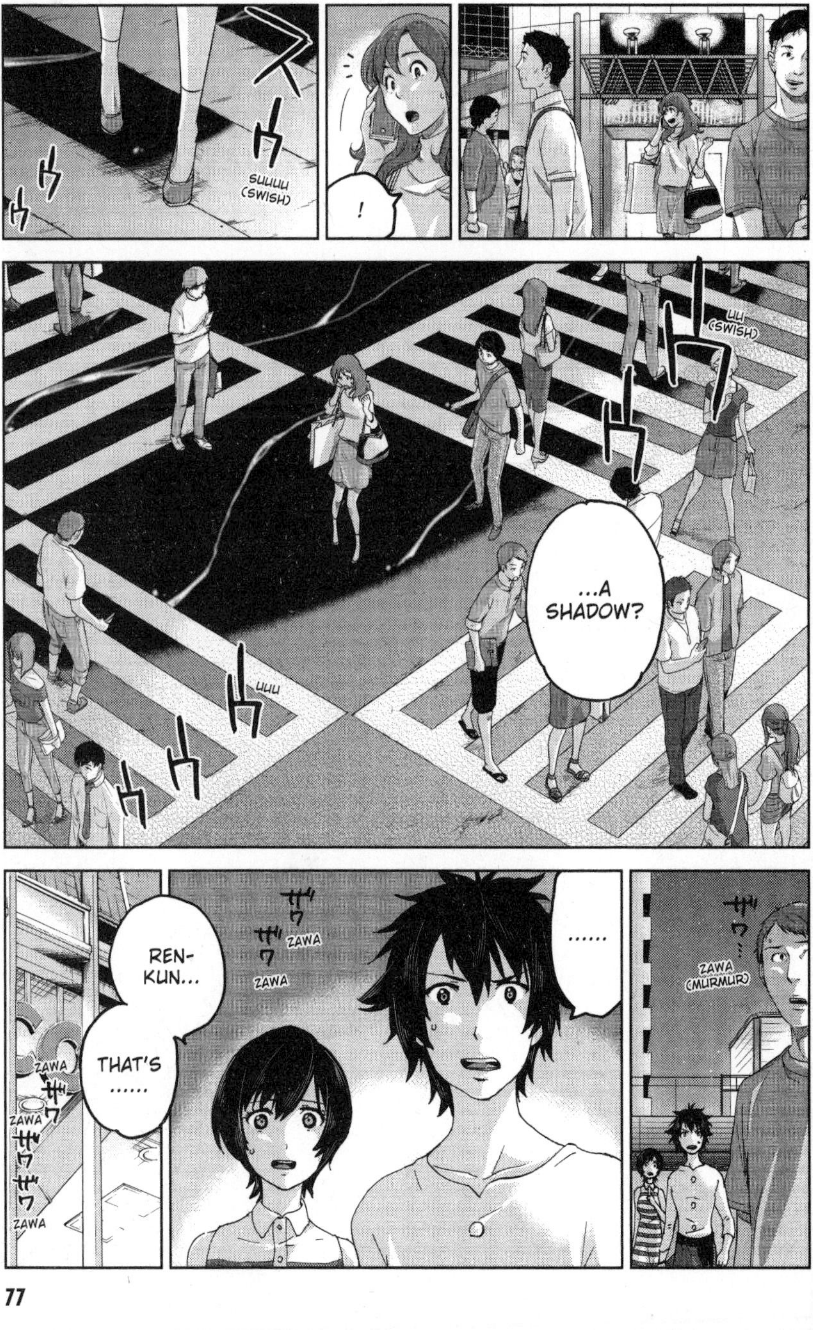
!
SUUUU (SWISH)
UU (SWISH)
...A SHADOW?
UUU
ZAWA (MURMUR)
......
ZAWA
ZAWA
REN-KUN...
THAT'S ......
ZAWA
ZAWA
ZAWA

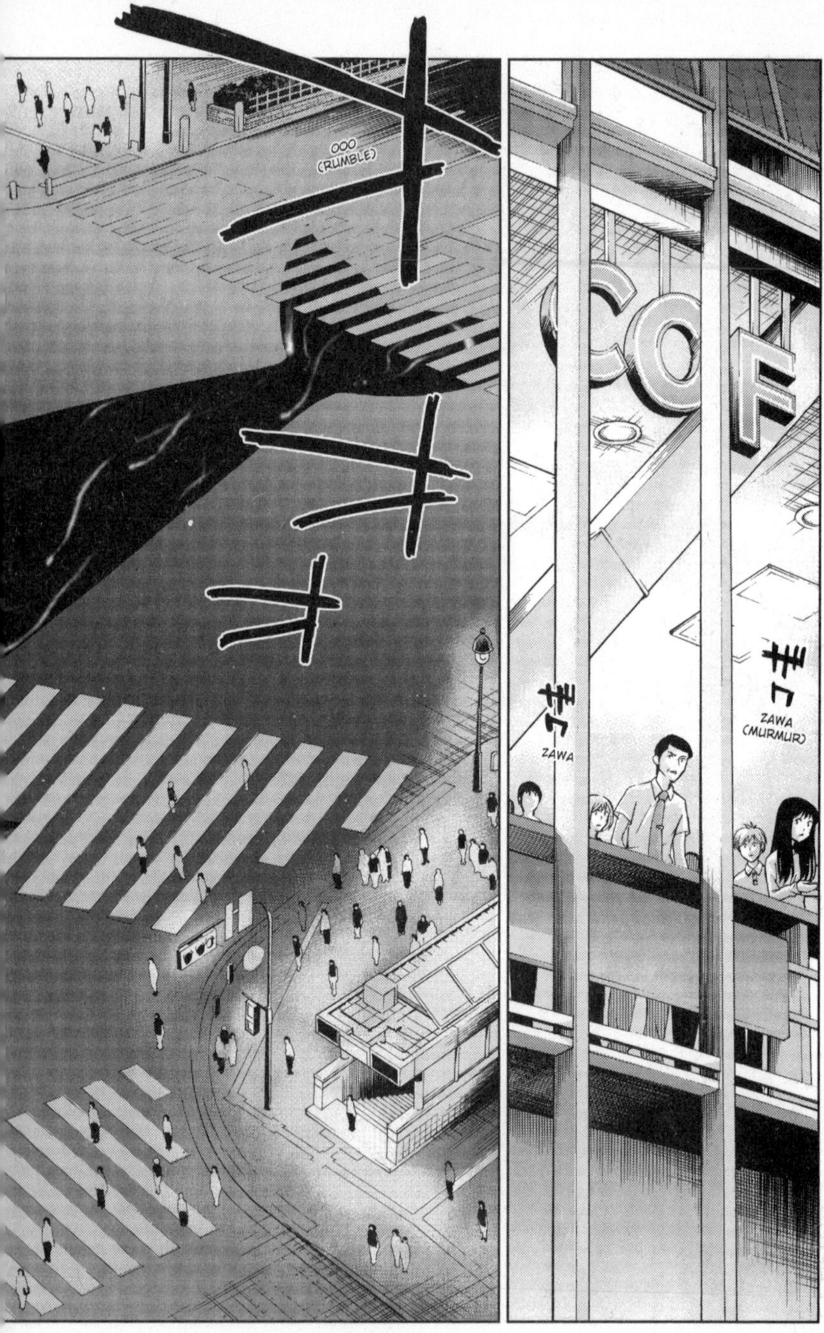
ZAWA (MURMUR)
ZAWA
OOO (RUMBLE)

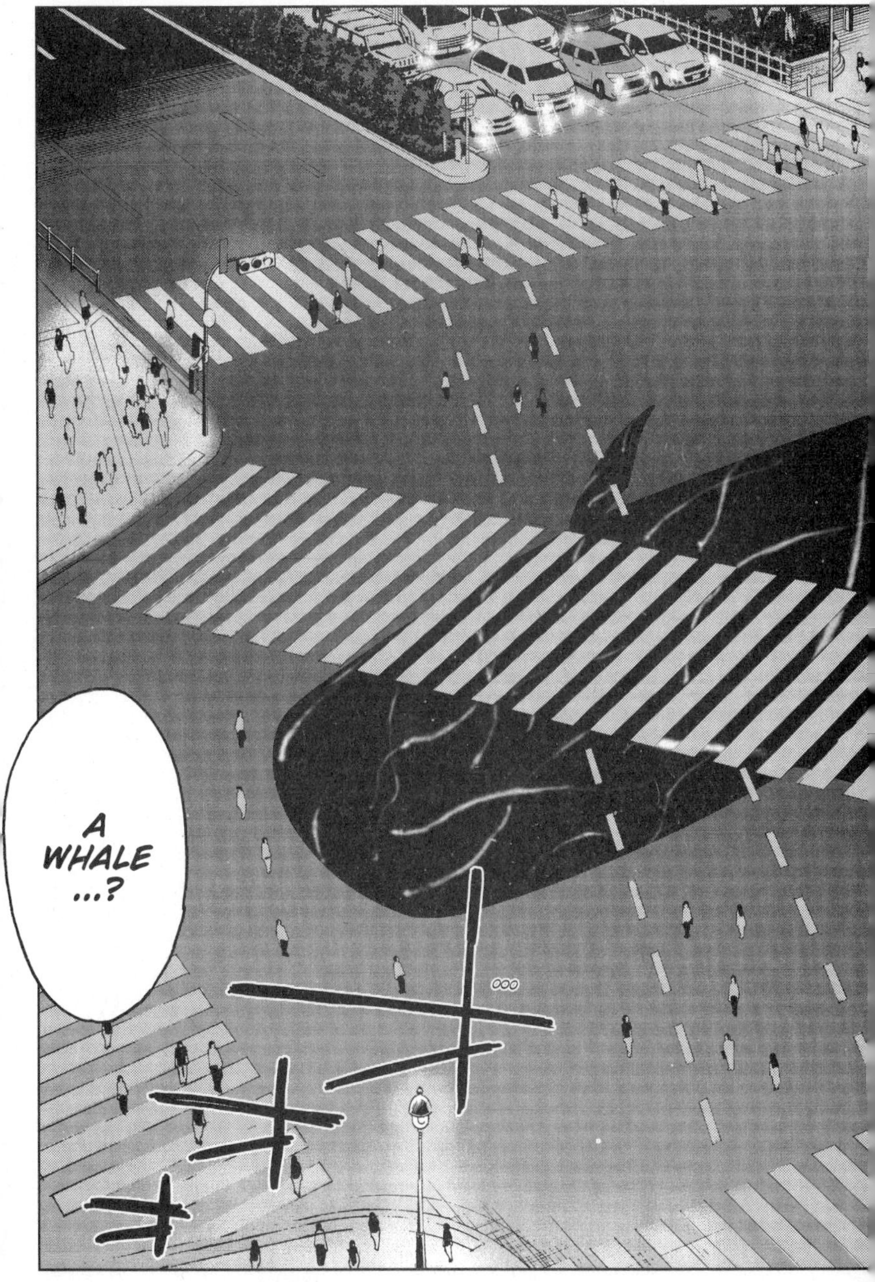
A WHALE ...?
ooo

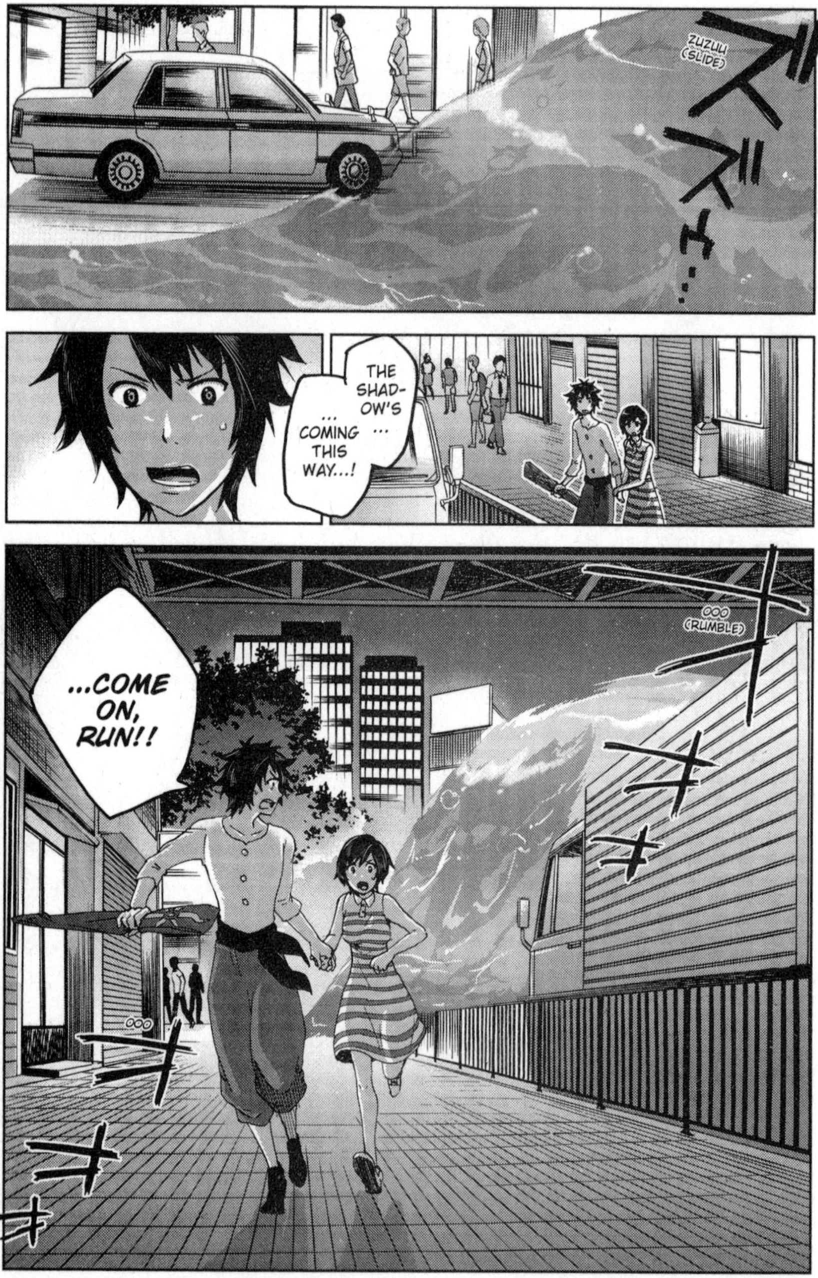
ZUZUU (SLIDE)
THE SHADOW'S ... COMING THIS WAY...!
OOO (RUMBLE)
...COME ON, RUN!!
OOO

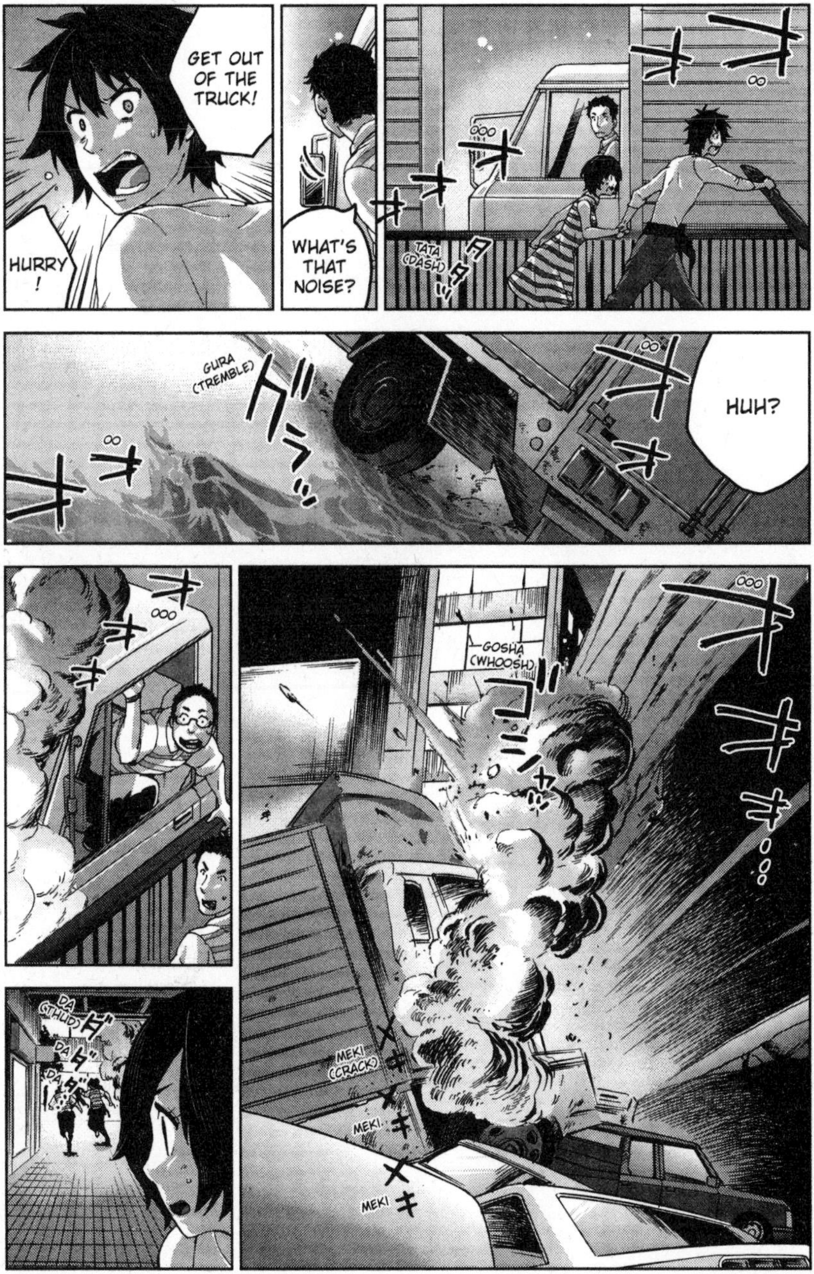
TATA (DASH)
WHAT'S THAT NOISE?
GET OUT OF THE TRUCK!
HURRY!
HUH?
GURA (TREMBLE)
GOSHA (WHOOSH)
MEKI (CRACK)
MEKI
MEKI
DA (THUD)
DA
DA

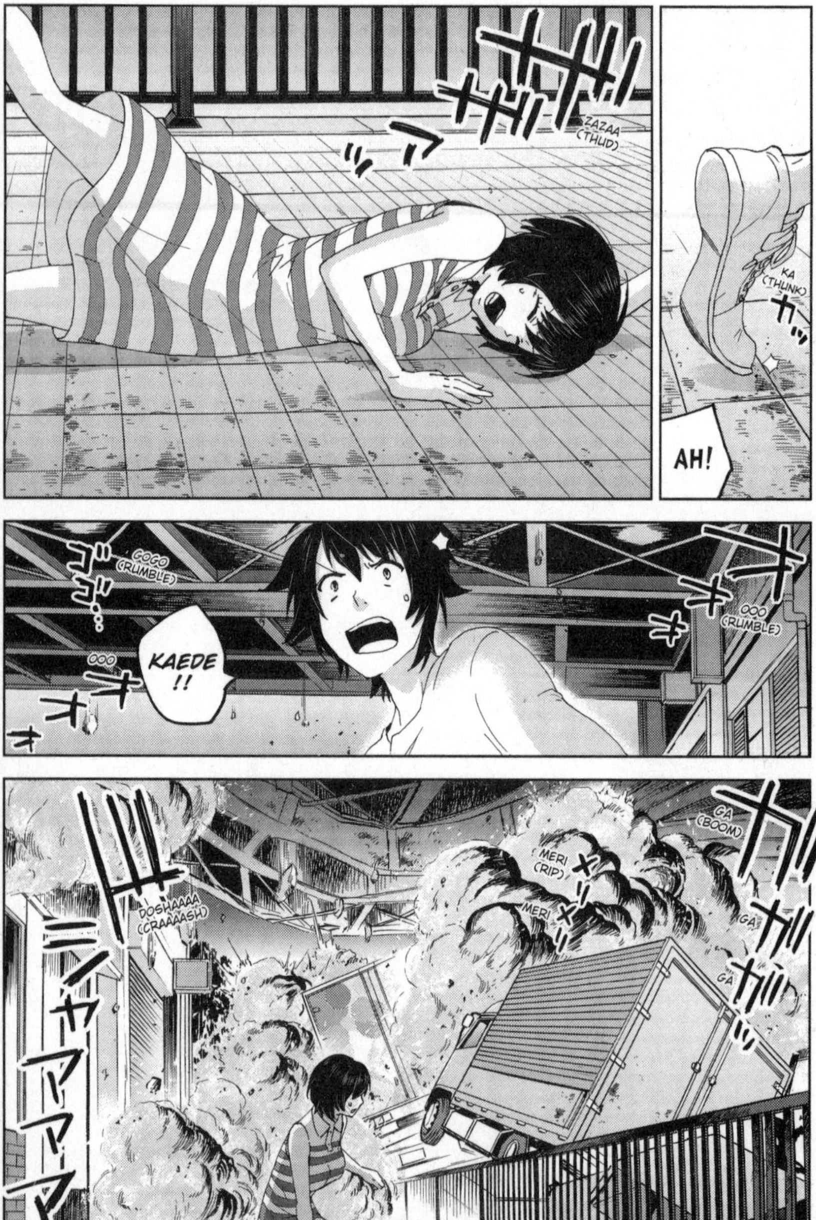
KA (THUNK)
AH!
ZAZAA (THUD)
OOO (RUMBLE)
KAEDE!!
GOGO (RUMBLE)
OOO
GA (BOOM)
GA
GA
MERI (RIP)
MERI
DOSHAAAA (CRAAAASH)

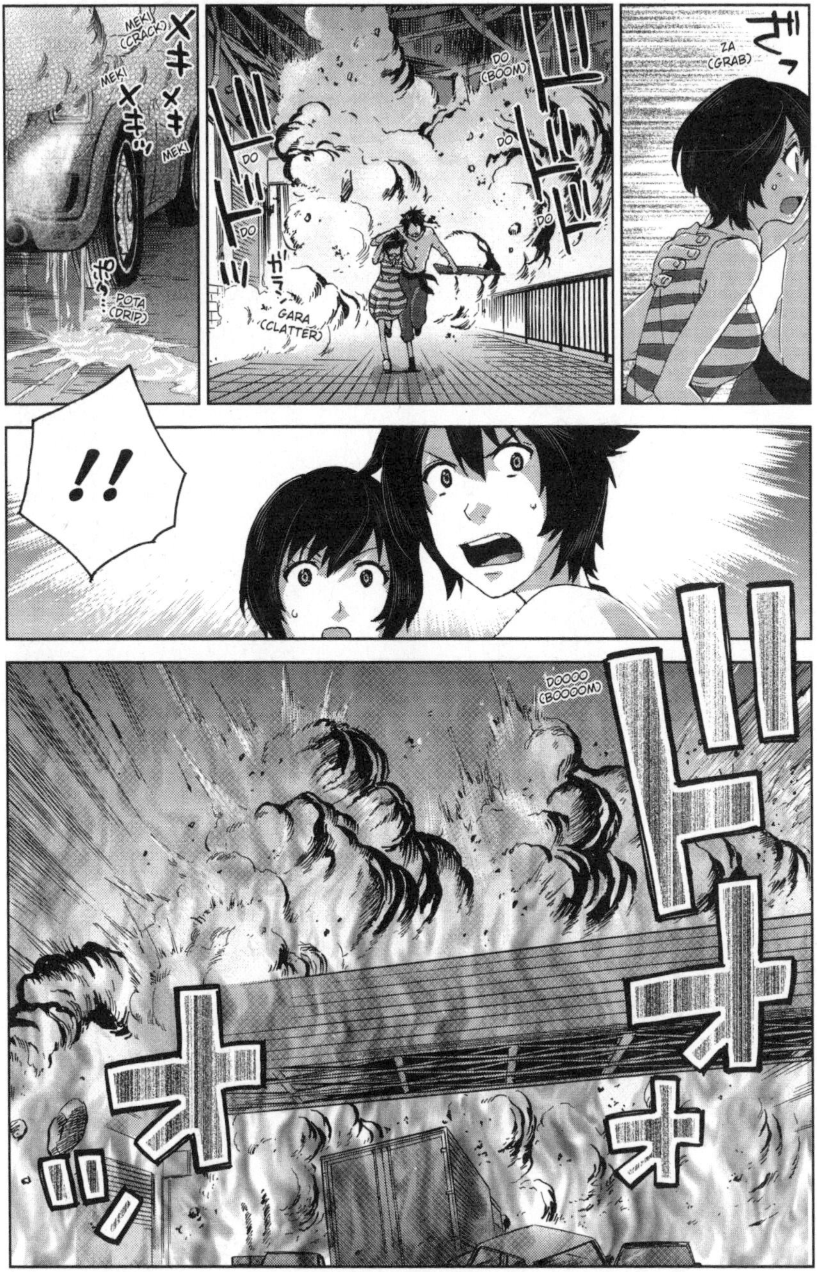

ZA (GRAB)
DO (BOOM)
DO
DO
DO
GARA (CLATTER)
MEKI (CRACK)
MEKI
MEKI
POTA (DRIP)
!!
DOOOO (BOOOOM)

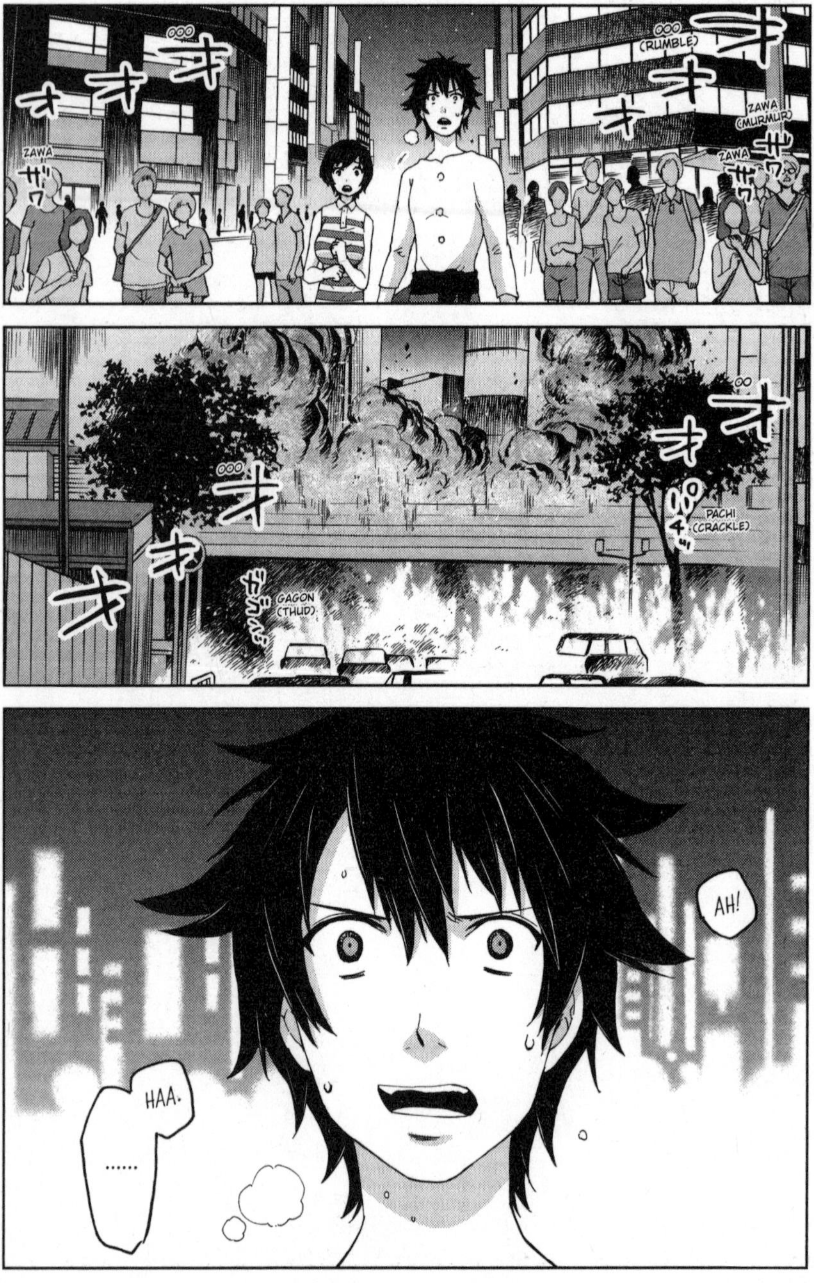
OOO (RUMBLE)
ZAWA (MURMUR)
ZAWA
OOO
ZAWA
OO
PACHI (CRACKLE)
OOO
GAGON (THUD)
AH!
HAA.
......

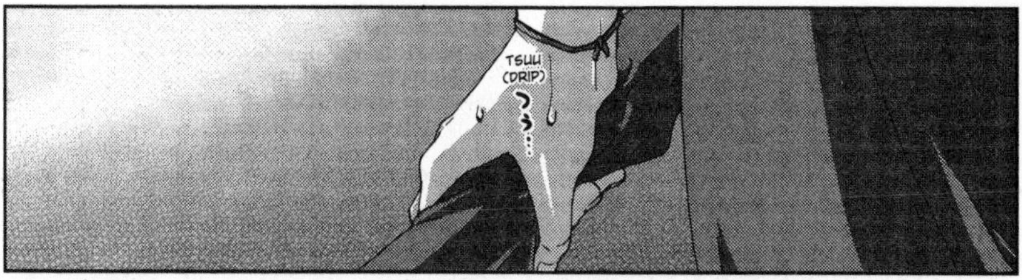
TSUU (DRIP)

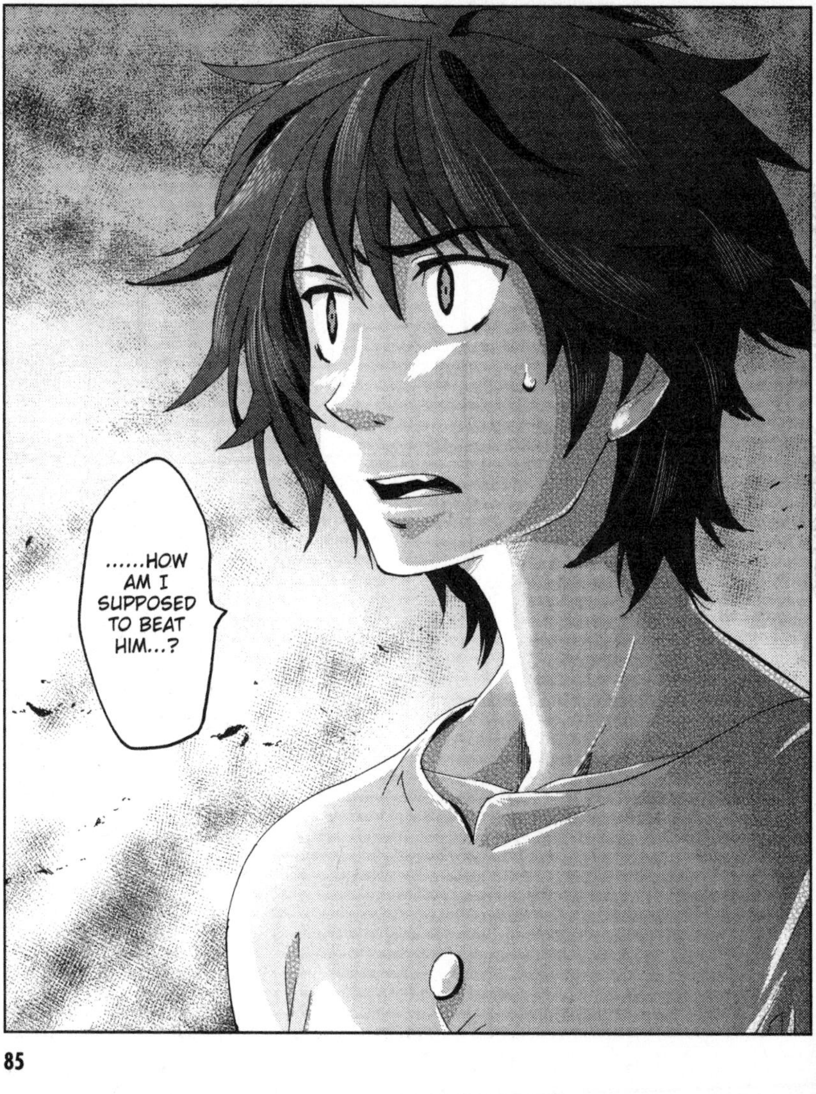
......HOW AM I SUPPOSED TO BEAT HIM...?

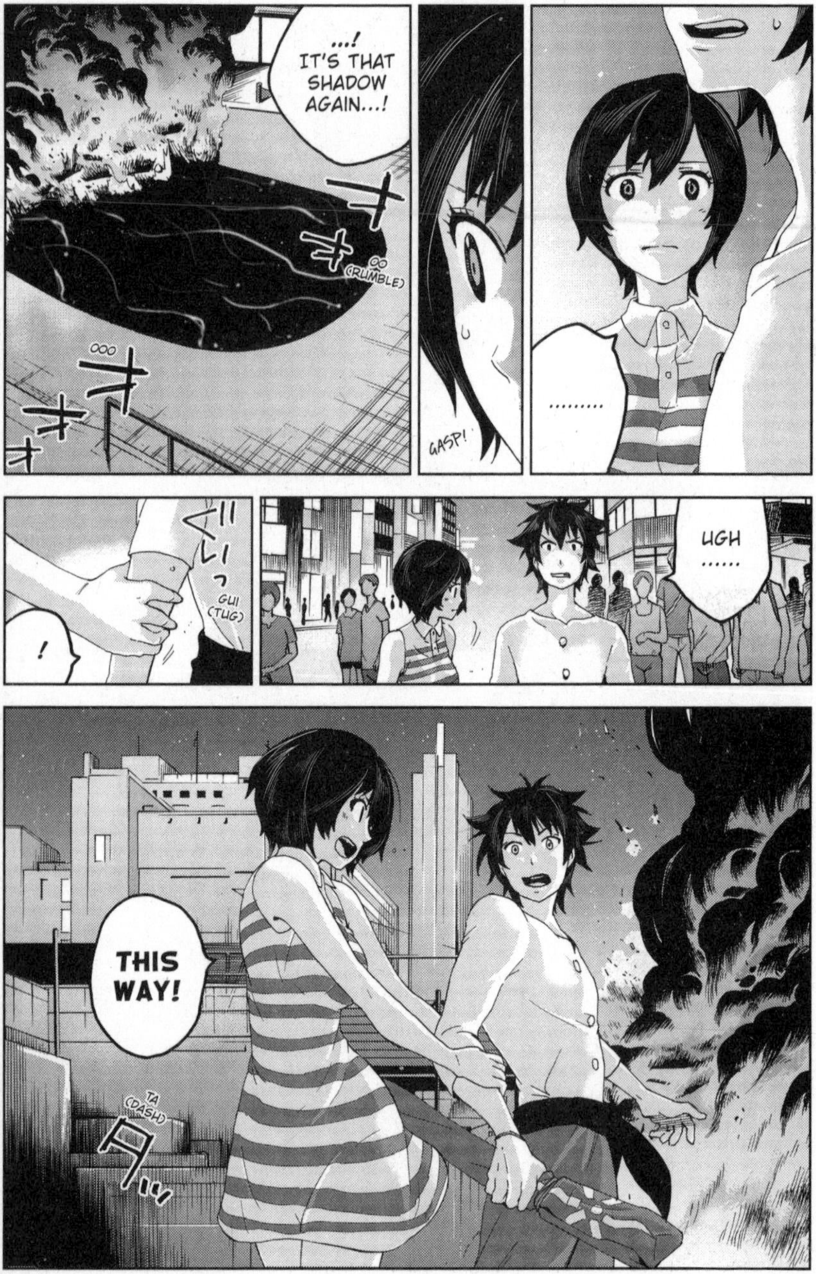
....
GASP!
...! IT'S THAT SHADOW AGAIN...!
OO (RUMBLE)
OOO
UGH ......
GUI (TUG)
!
THIS WAY!
TA (DASH)

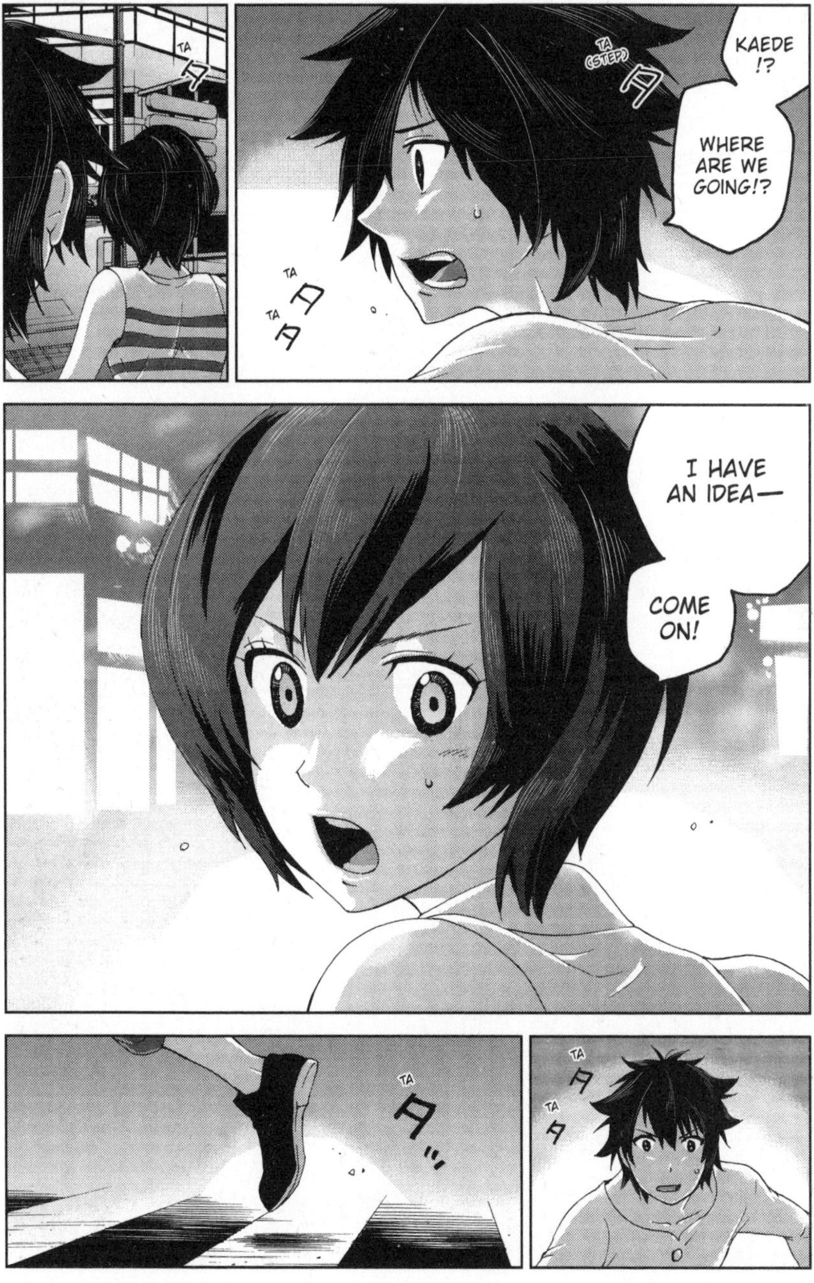
TA (STEP)
KAEDE!?
WHERE ARE WE GOING!?
TA
TA
TA
I HAVE AN IDEA—
COME ON!
TA
TA
TA

SIGN: BANK

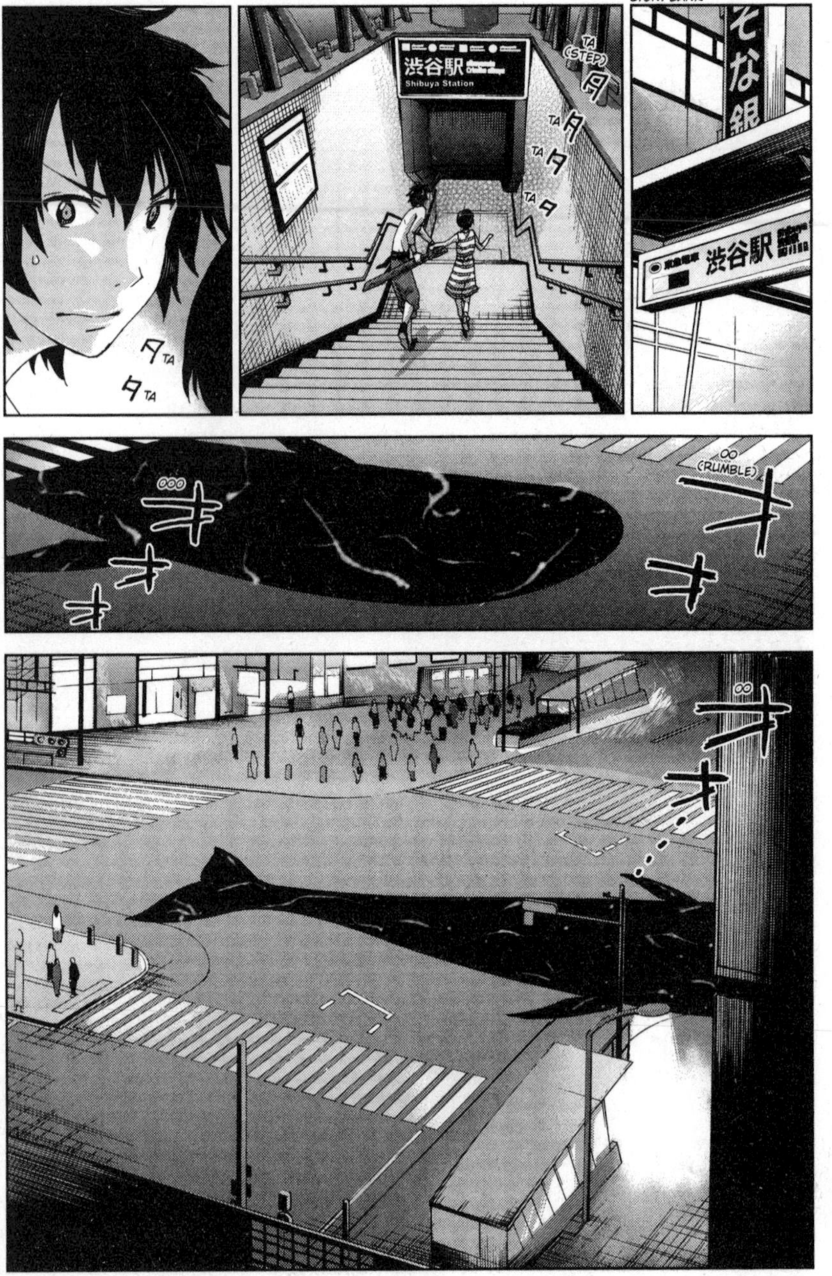

そな銀
渋谷駅
渋谷駅
Shibuya Station
TA (STEP)
TA
TA
TA
TA
TA
∞ (RUMBLE)
ooo
∞

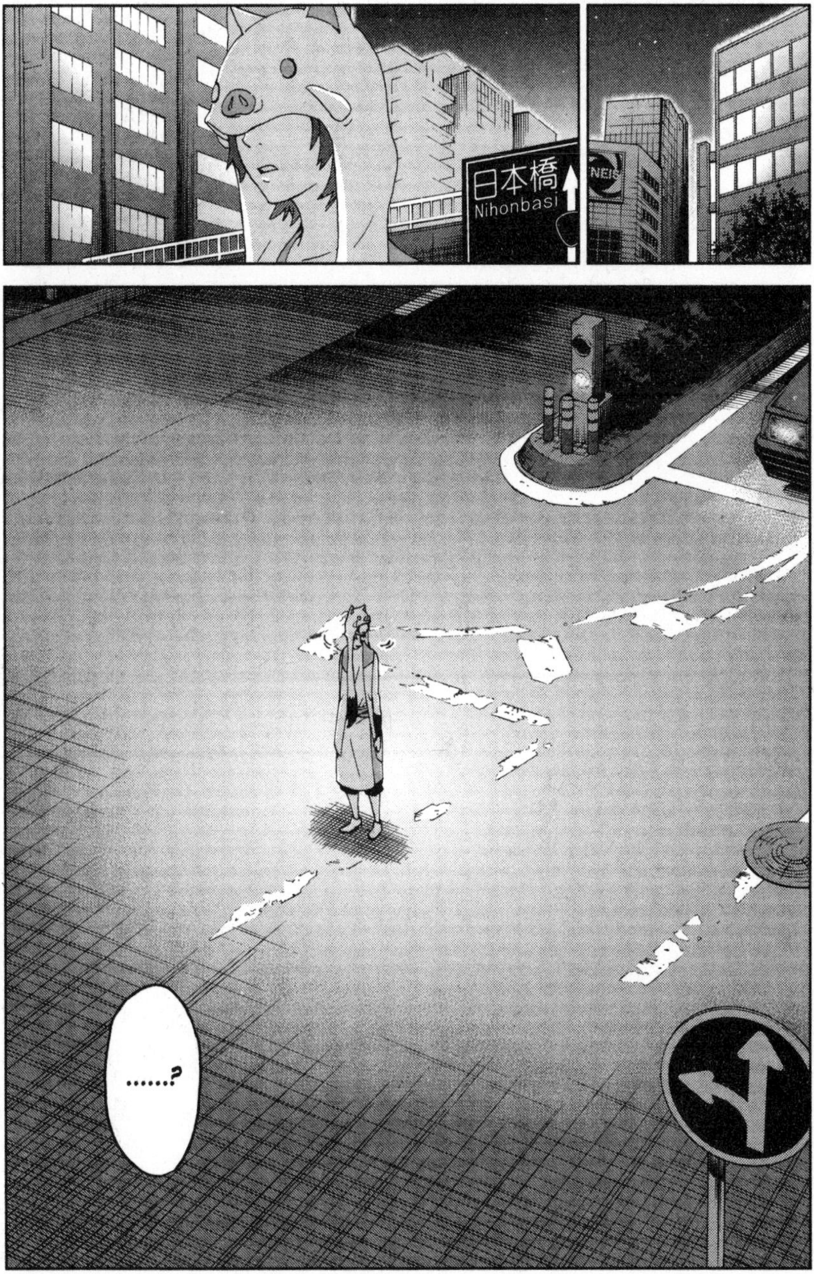
日本橋
Nihonbasi
......?

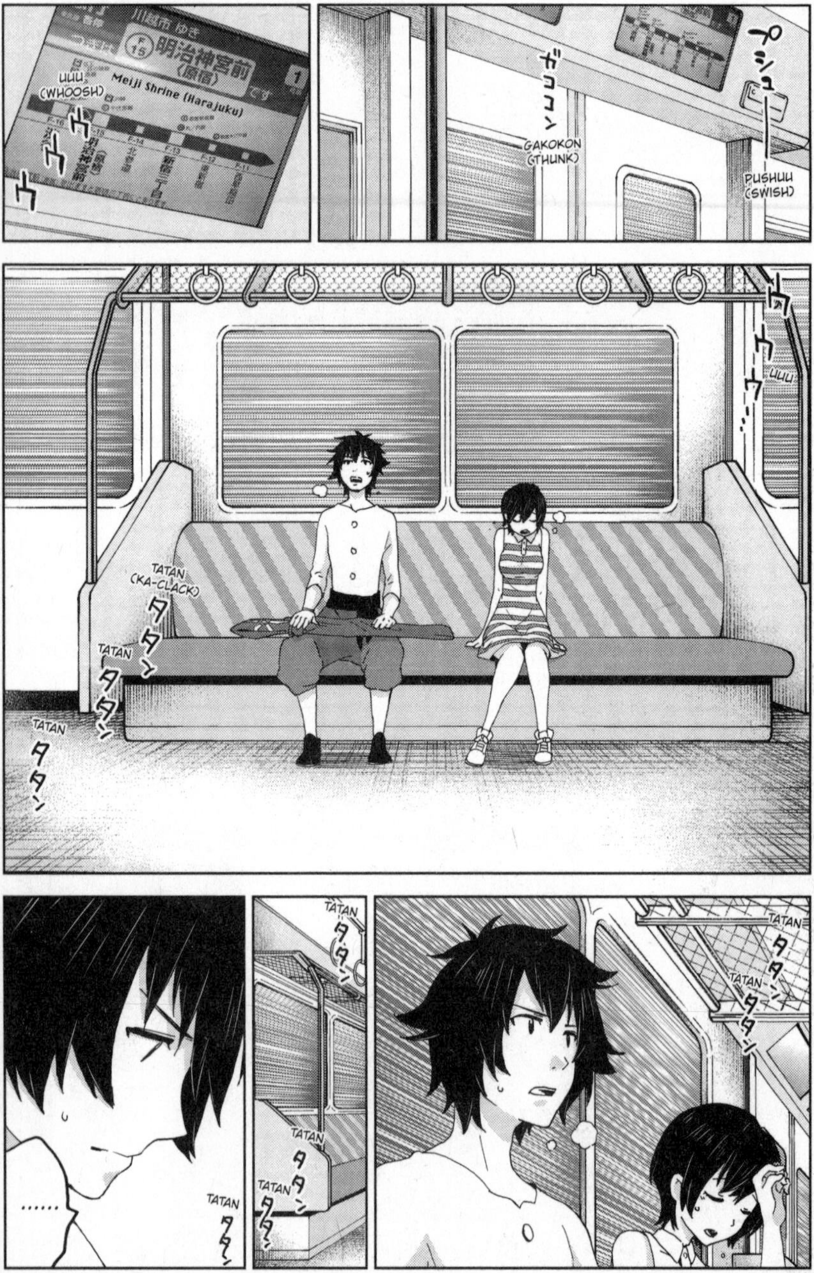
プシュー
PUSHUU (SWISH)
ガココン
GAKOKON (THUNK)
明治神宮前 (原宿)
Meiji Shrine (Harajuku)
UUU (WHOOSH)
ウウウ
ウウウ…
UUU
TATAN (KA-CLACK)
タタン
TATAN
タタン
TATAN
タタン
TATAN
タタン
TATAN
タタン
TATAN
タタン
TATAN
タタン
TATAN
タタン
TATAN
タタン
……

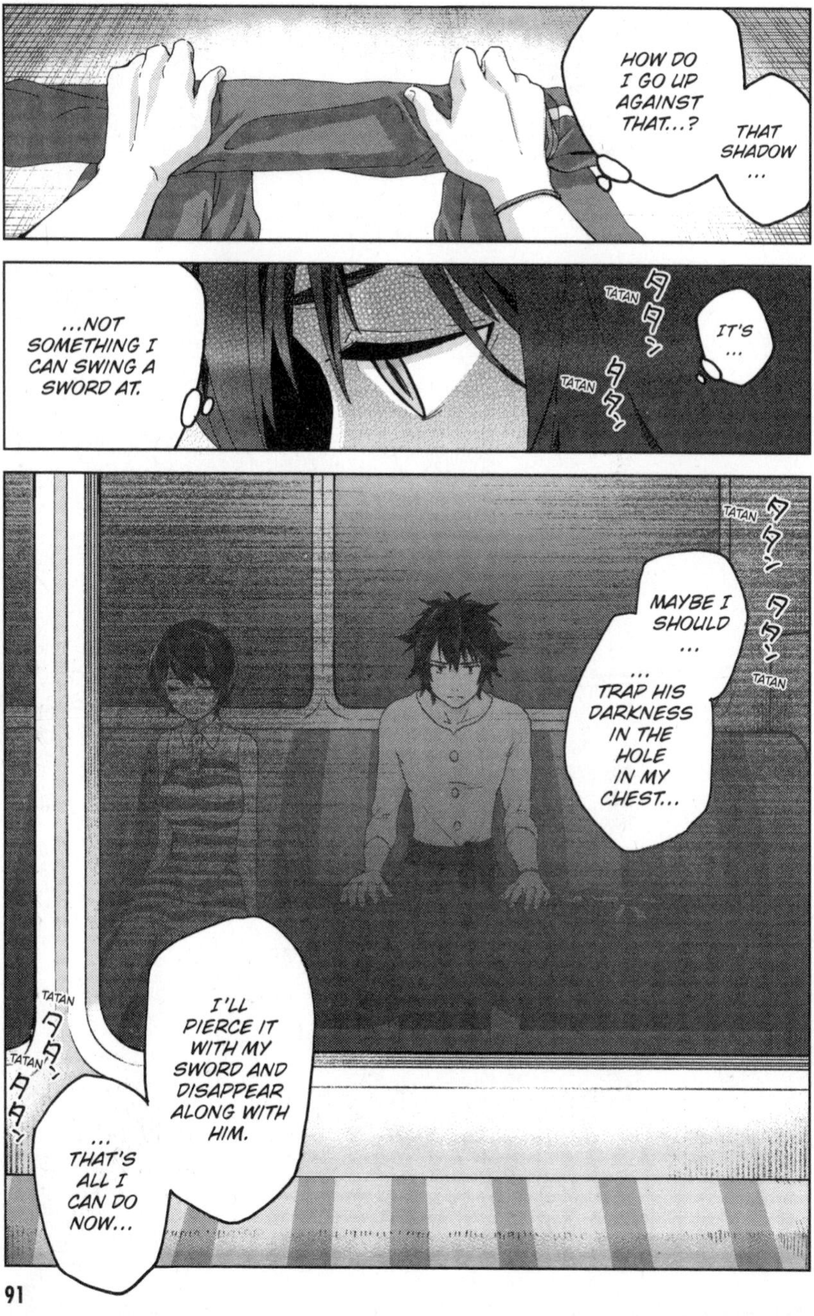
THAT SHADOW ...
HOW DO I GO UP AGAINST THAT...?
IT'S ...
タタン TATAN
タタン TATAN
...NOT SOMETHING I CAN SWING A SWORD AT.
タタン TATAN
タタン TATAN
MAYBE I SHOULD ...
... TRAP HIS DARKNESS IN THE HOLE IN MY CHEST...
I'LL PIERCE IT WITH MY SWORD AND DISAPPEAR ALONG WITH HIM.
... THAT'S ALL I CAN DO NOW...
タタン TATAN
タタン TATAN

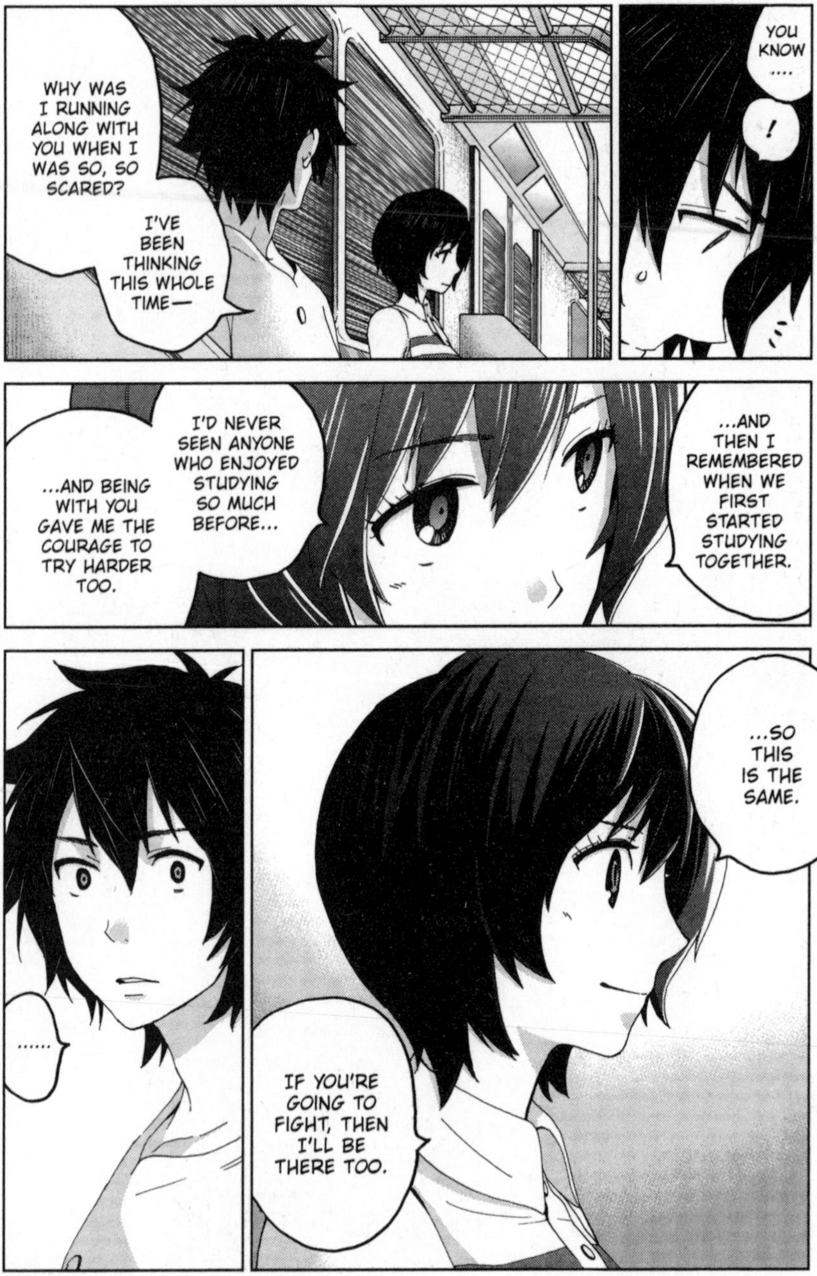
YOU KNOW ....
!
I'VE BEEN THINKING THIS WHOLE TIME—
WHY WAS I RUNNING ALONG WITH YOU WHEN I WAS SO, SO SCARED?
...AND THEN I REMEMBERED WHEN WE FIRST STARTED STUDYING TOGETHER.
I'D NEVER SEEN ANYONE WHO ENJOYED STUDYING SO MUCH BEFORE...
...AND BEING WITH YOU GAVE ME THE COURAGE TO TRY HARDER TOO.
...SO THIS IS THE SAME.
IF YOU'RE GOING TO FIGHT, THEN I'LL BE THERE TOO.
......

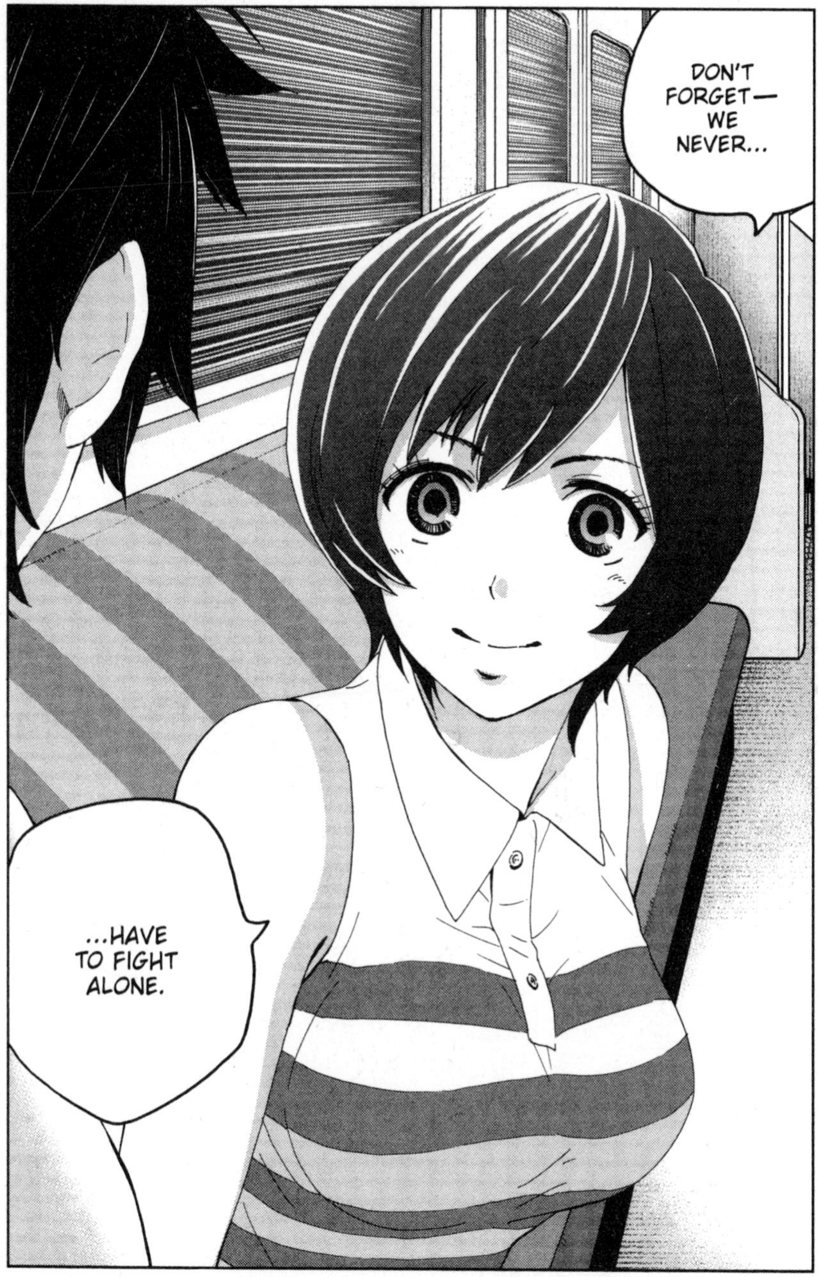
DON'T FORGET—WE NEVER...
...HAVE TO FIGHT ALONE.

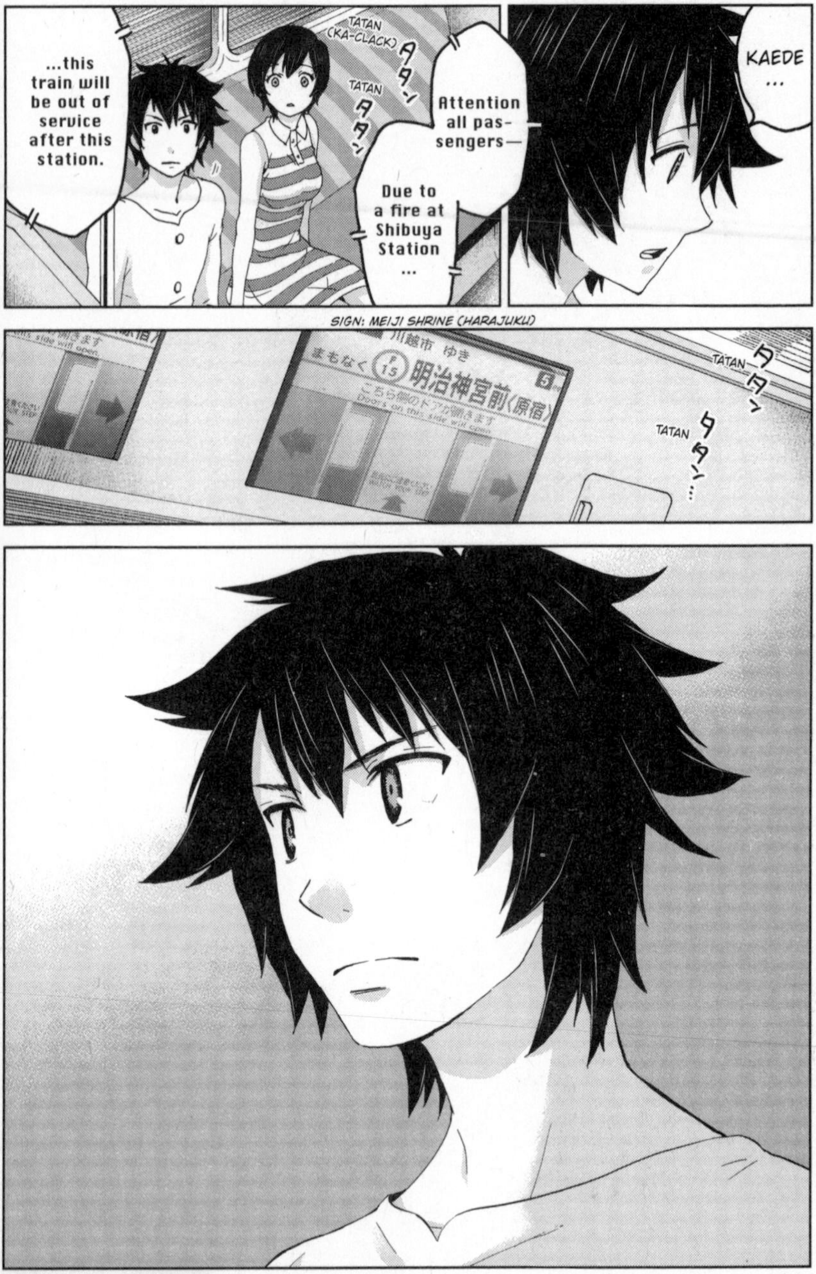
KAEDE ...
TATAN (KA-CLACK) タタン
TATAN タタン
Attention all passengers—
Due to a fire at Shibuya Station ...
...this train will be out of service after this station.
SIGN: MEIJI SHRINE (HARAJUKU)
川越市 ゆき
まもなく
明治神宮前〈原宿〉
こちら側のドアが開きます
Doors on this side will open.
TATAN— タタン
TATAN タタン...

CHAPTER 17 END

BUUU
(WHOOSH)

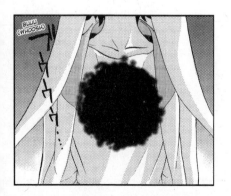

THE BOY & THE BEAST

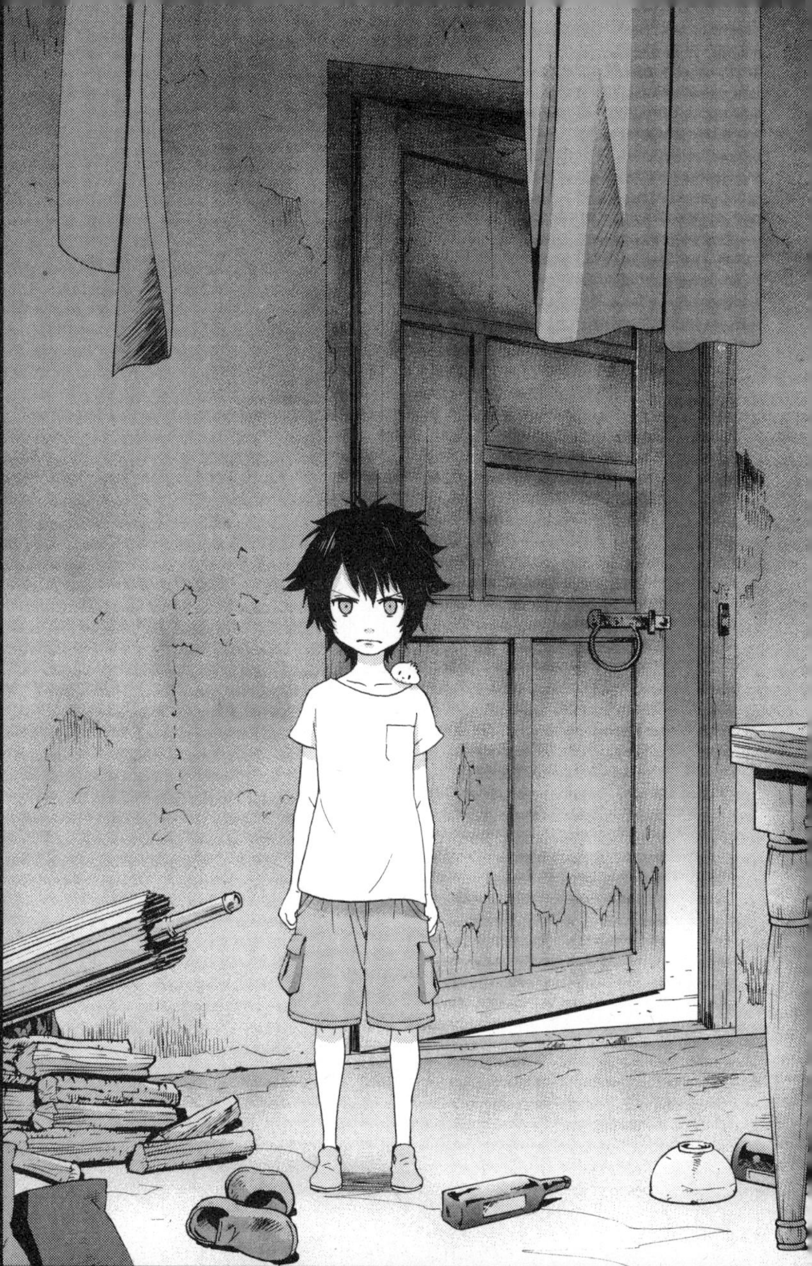

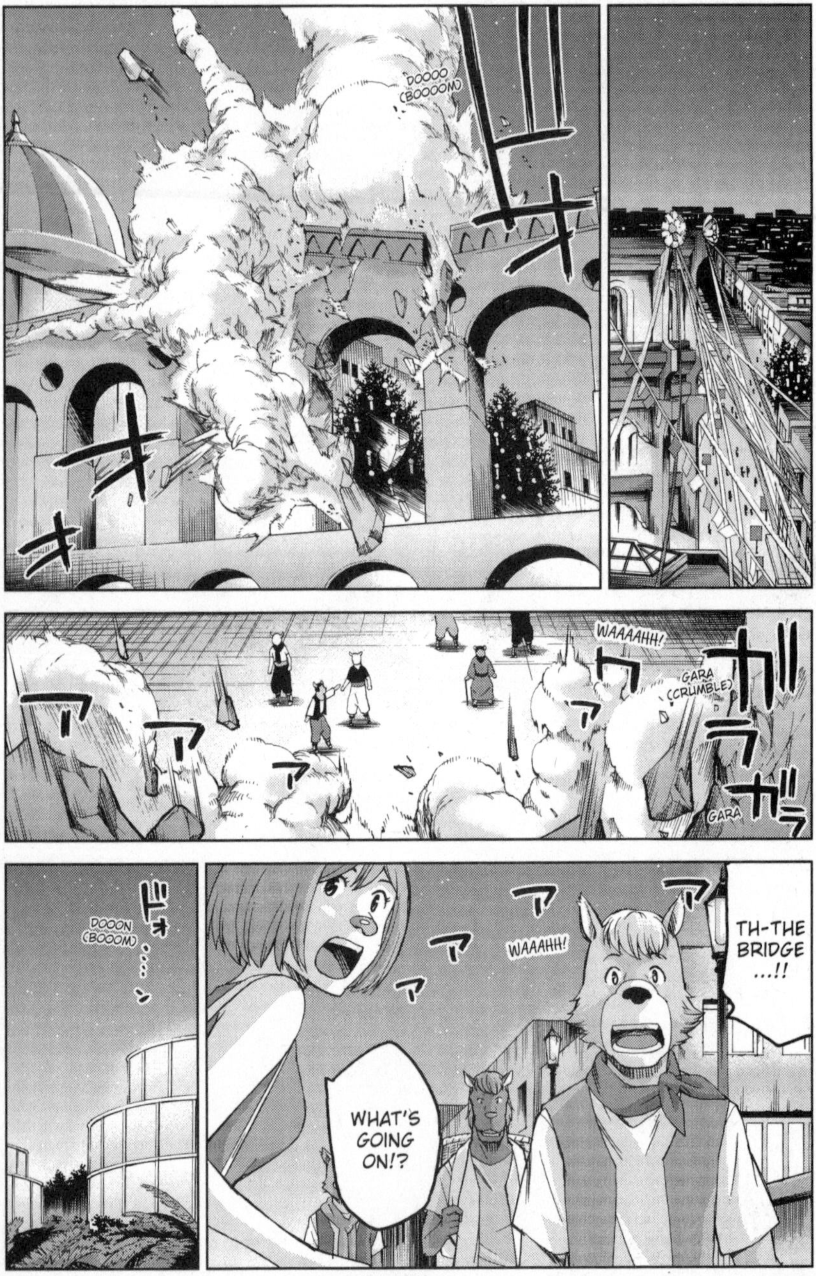
DOOOO (BOOOOM)
WAAAAHH!
GARA (CRUMBLE)
GARA
TH-THE BRIDGE ...!!
WAAAHH!
WHAT'S GOING ON!?
DOOON (BOOOM)

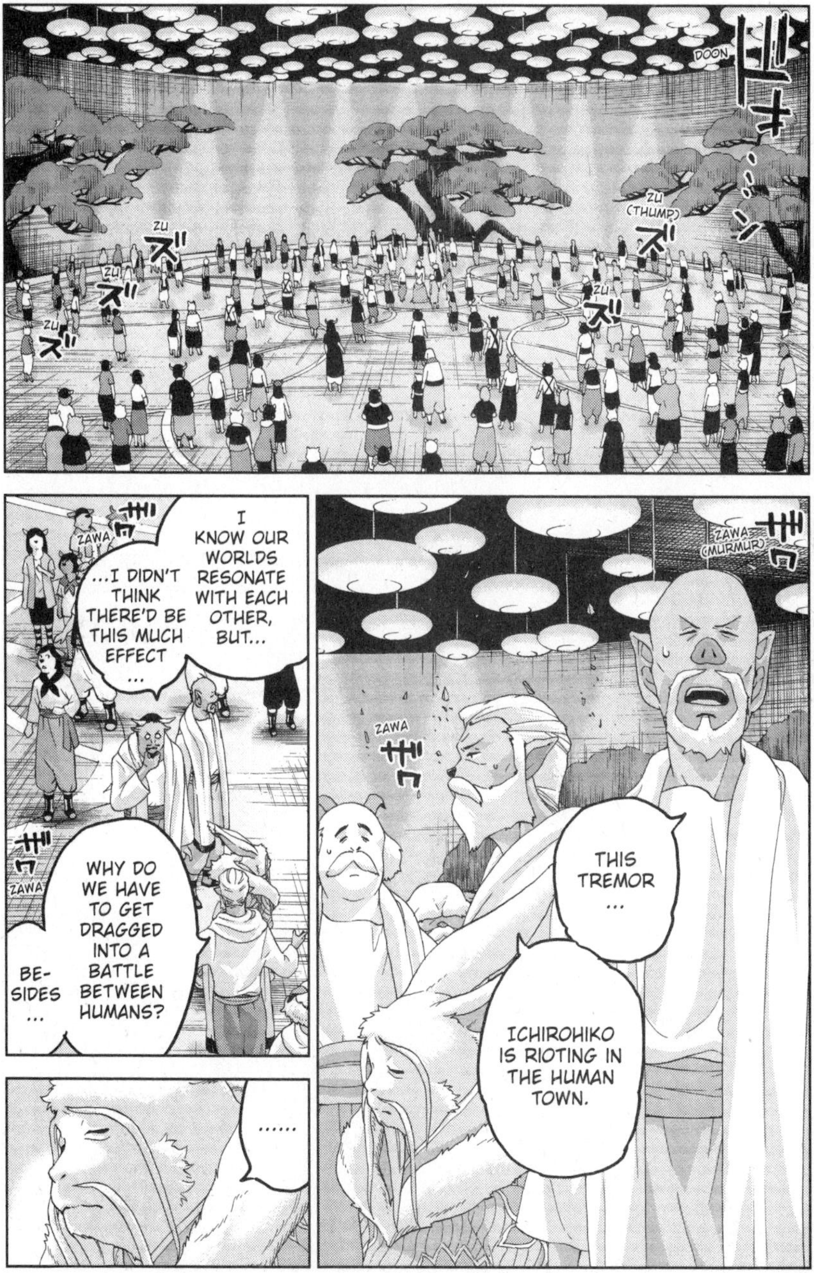
DOON
ZU (THUMP)
ZU
ZU
ZU
ZU
ZAWA (MURMUR)
ZAWA
THIS TREMOR ...
ICHIROHIKO IS RIOTING IN THE HUMAN TOWN.
ZAWA
I KNOW OUR WORLDS RESONATE WITH EACH OTHER, BUT...
...I DIDN'T THINK THERE'D BE THIS MUCH EFFECT ...
ZAWA
WHY DO WE HAVE TO GET DRAGGED INTO A BATTLE BETWEEN HUMANS?
BE-SIDES ...
......

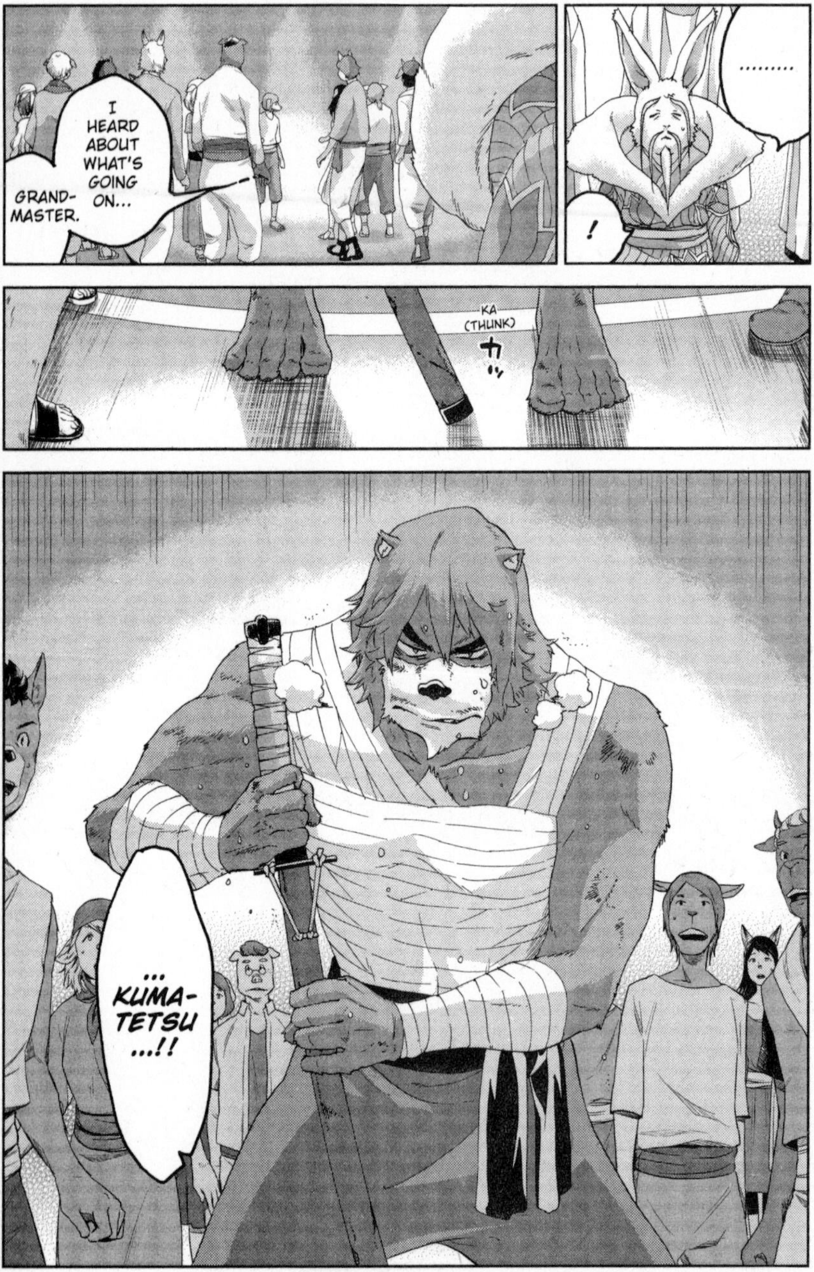
....
!
I HEARD ABOUT WHAT'S GOING ON...
GRAND-MASTER.
KA (THUNK)
カッ
...KUMA-TETSU...!!

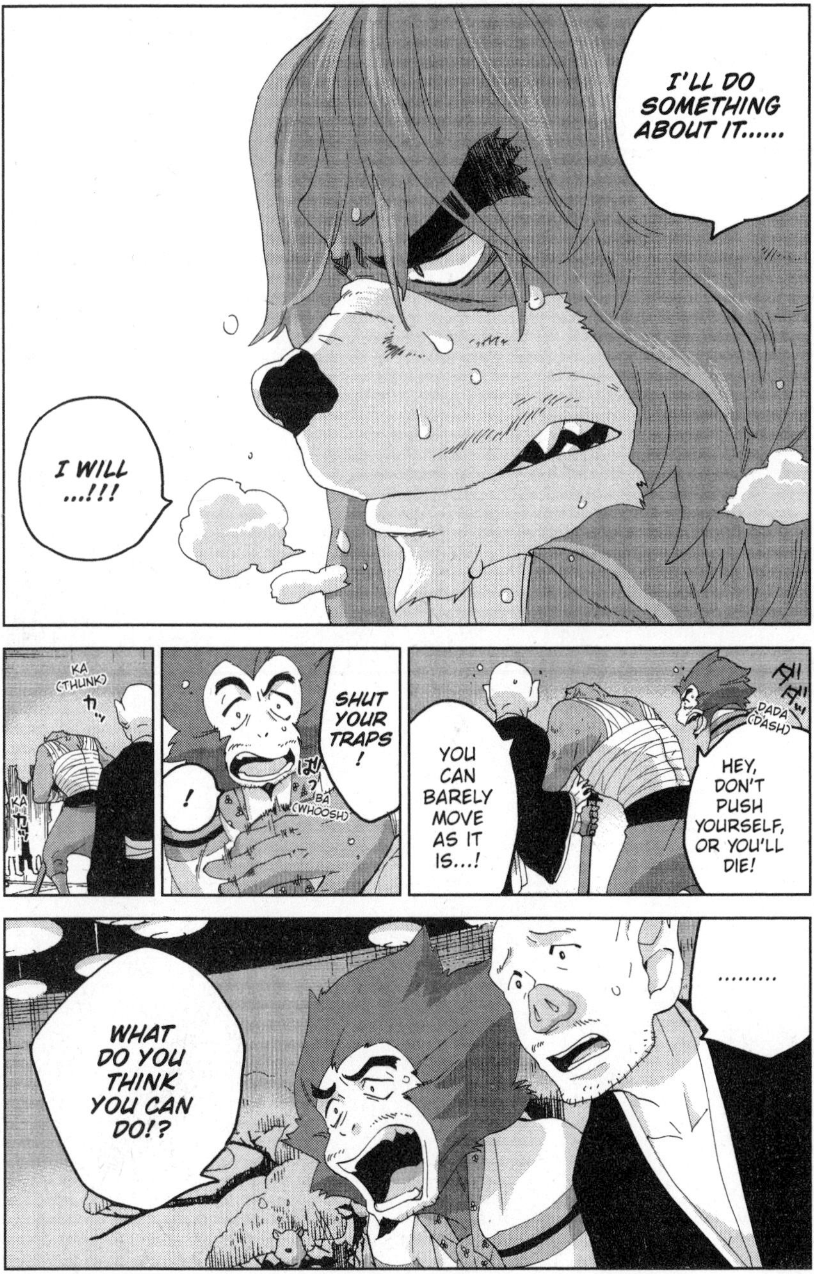
I'LL DO SOMETHING ABOUT IT......
I WILL ...!!!
DADA (DASH)
HEY, DON'T PUSH YOURSELF, OR YOU'LL DIE!
YOU CAN BARELY MOVE AS IT IS...!
SHUT YOUR TRAPS!
BA (WHOOSH)
!
KA (THUNK)
KA
....
WHAT DO YOU THINK YOU CAN DO!?

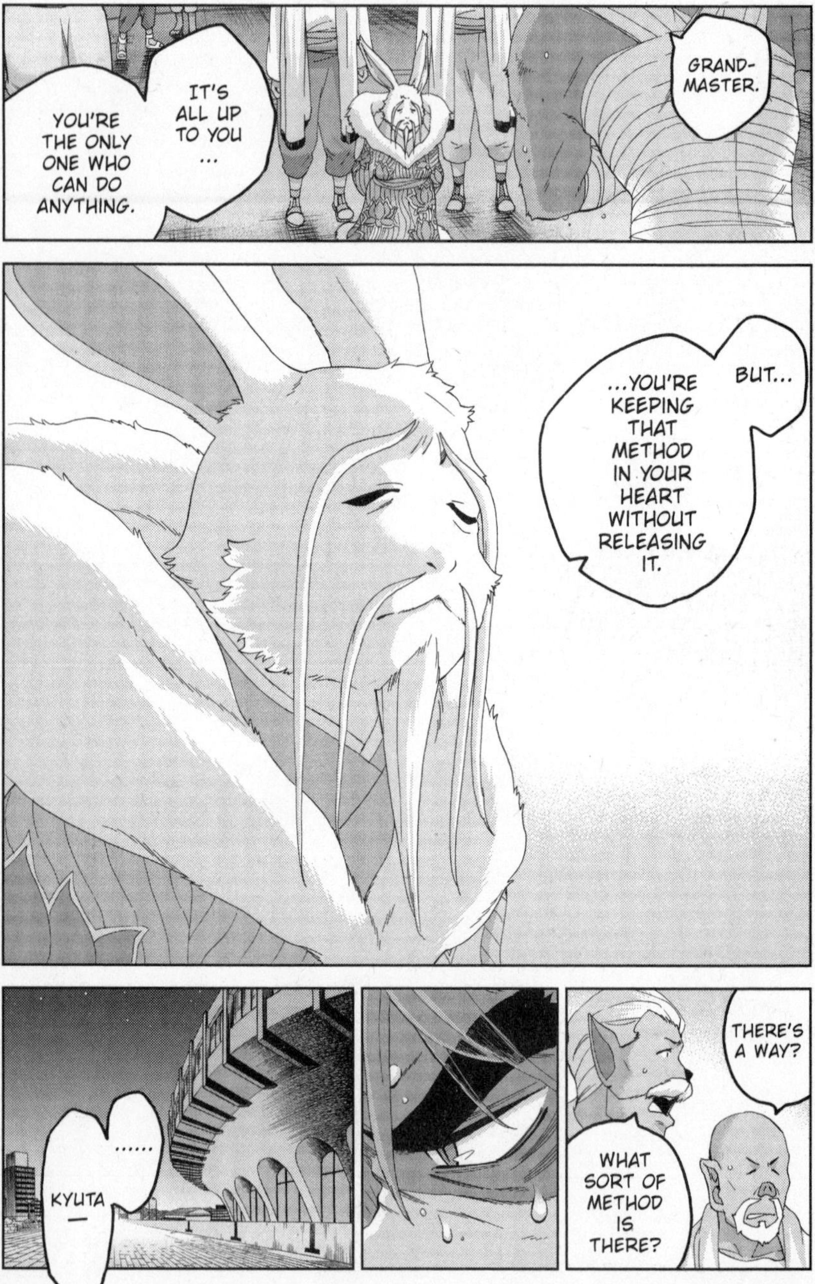
GRAND-MASTER.
IT'S ALL UP TO YOU ...
YOU'RE THE ONLY ONE WHO CAN DO ANYTHING.
BUT...
...YOU'RE KEEPING THAT METHOD IN YOUR HEART WITHOUT RELEASING IT.
THERE'S A WAY?
WHAT SORT OF METHOD IS THERE?
......
KYUTA —

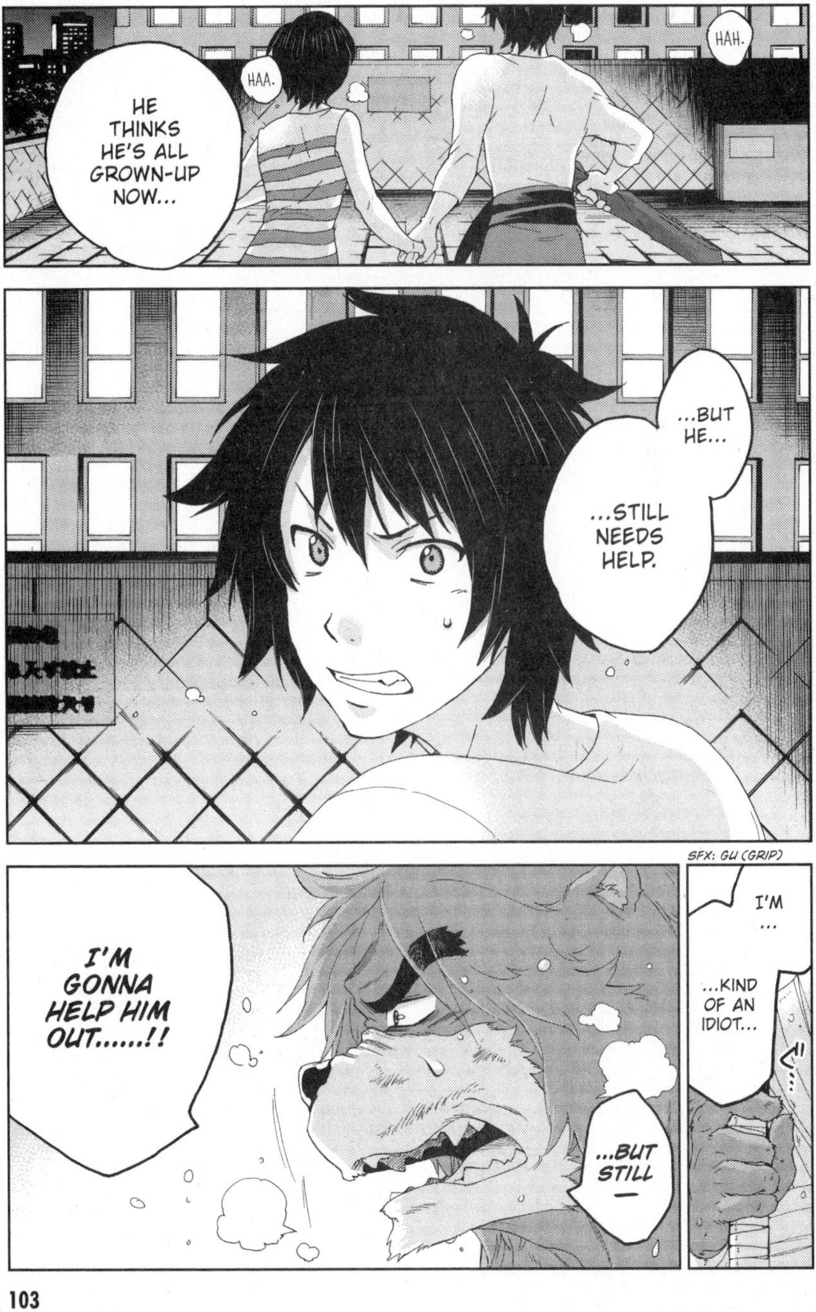
HAH.
HAA.
HE THINKS HE'S ALL GROWN-UP NOW...
...BUT HE...
...STILL NEEDS HELP.
SFX: GU (GRIP)
I'M ...
...KIND OF AN IDIOT...
...BUT STILL —
I'M GONNA HELP HIM OUT......!!

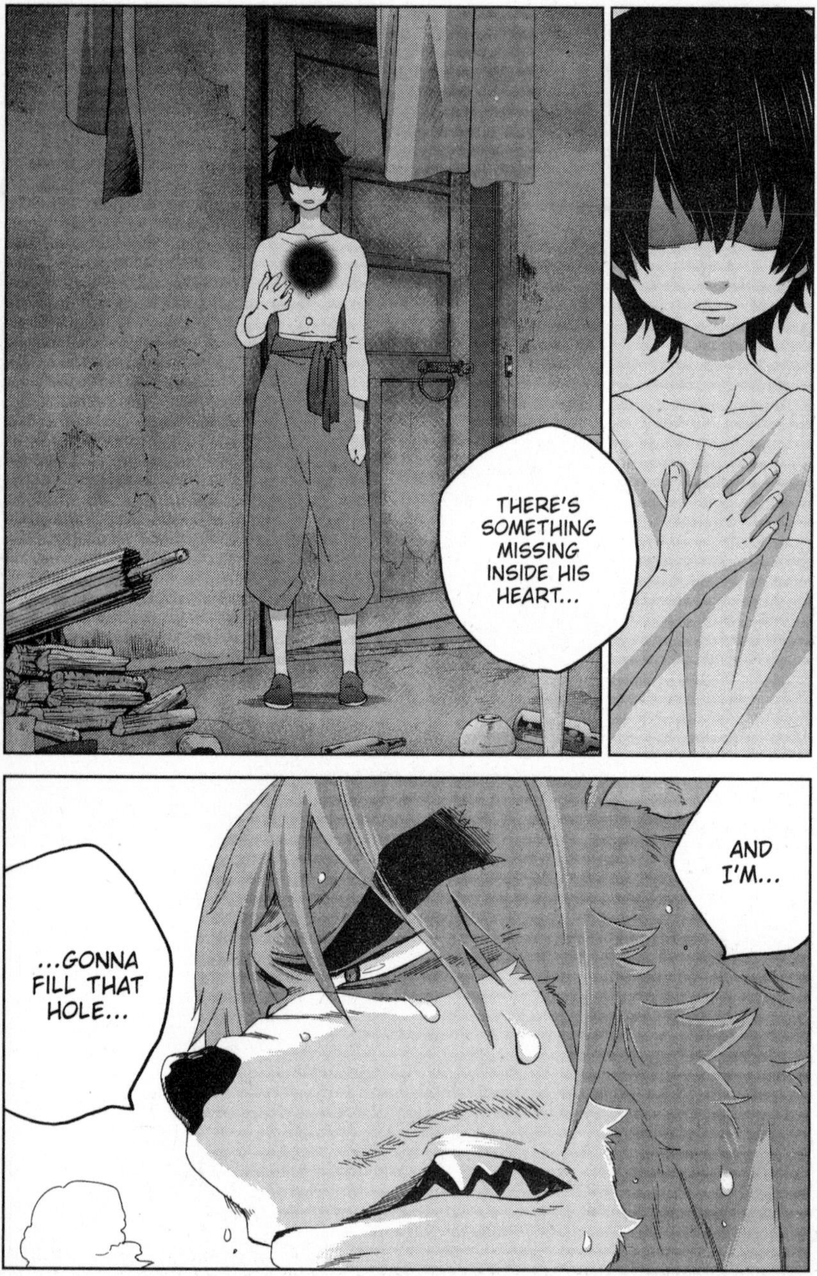
THERE'S SOMETHING MISSING INSIDE HIS HEART...
AND I'M...
...GONNA FILL THAT HOLE...

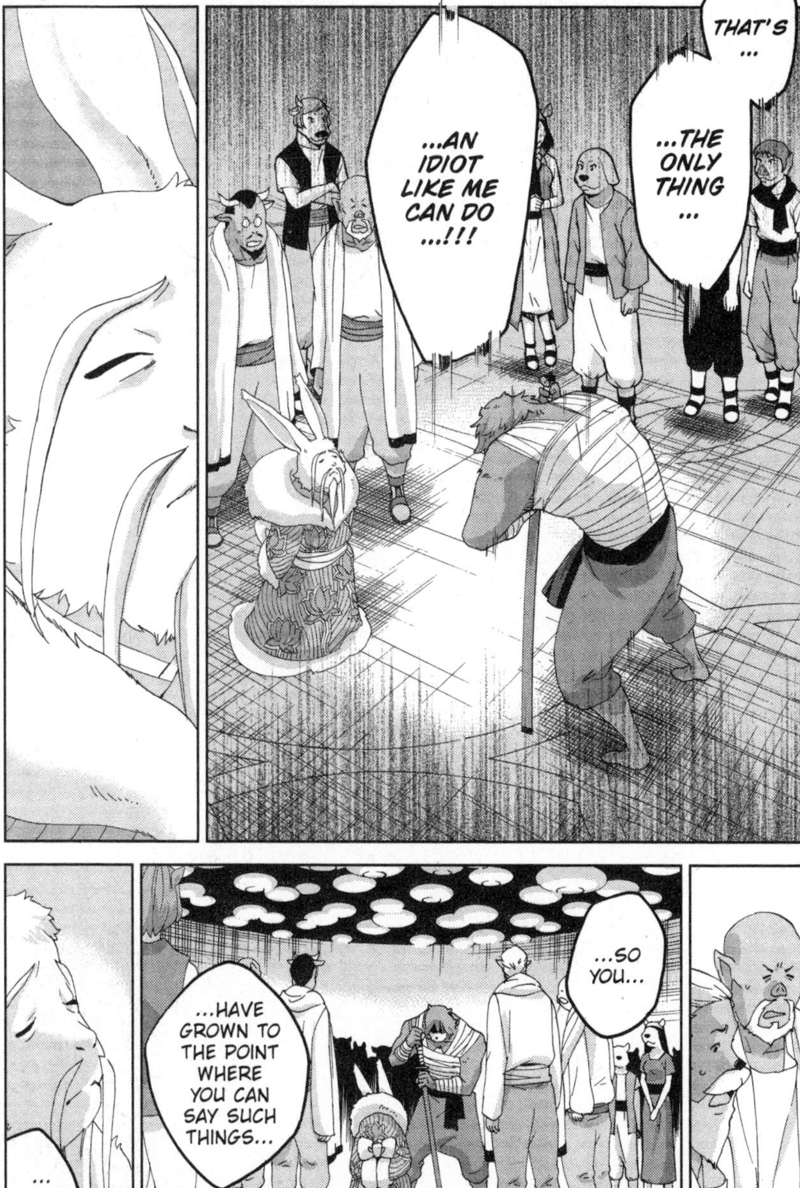
THAT'S ...
...THE ONLY THING ...
...AN IDIOT LIKE ME CAN DO ...!!!
...SO YOU...
...HAVE GROWN TO THE POINT WHERE YOU CAN SAY SUCH THINGS...
... HAVE YOU?

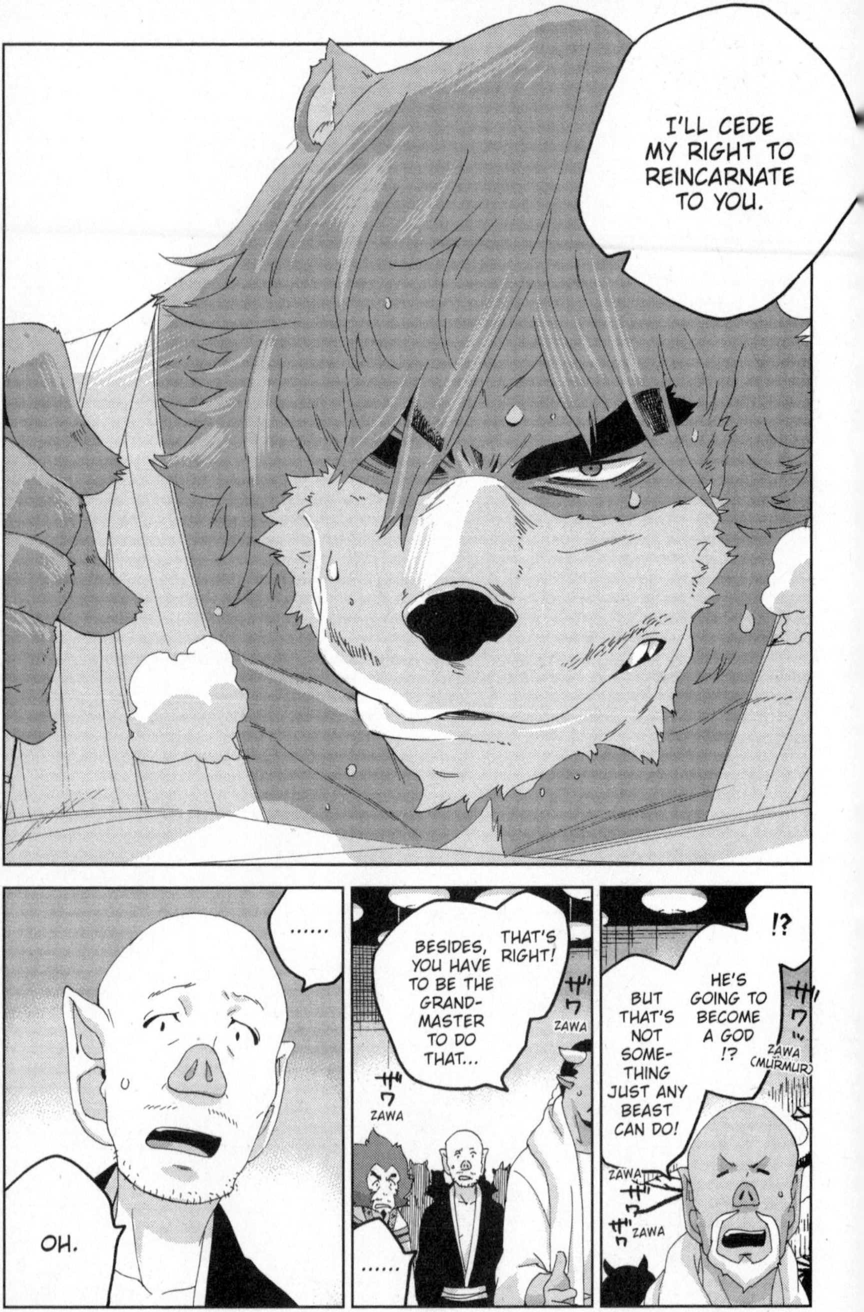
I'LL CEDE MY RIGHT TO REINCARNATE TO YOU.
!?
HE'S GOING TO BECOME A GOD !?
BUT THAT'S NOT SOMETHING JUST ANY BEAST CAN DO!
ザワッ
ZAWA (MURMUR)
ザワ
ZAWA
ZAWA
THAT'S RIGHT!
BESIDES, YOU HAVE TO BE THE GRANDMASTER TO DO THAT...
ザワ
ZAWA
ザワ
ZAWA
......
......
OH.

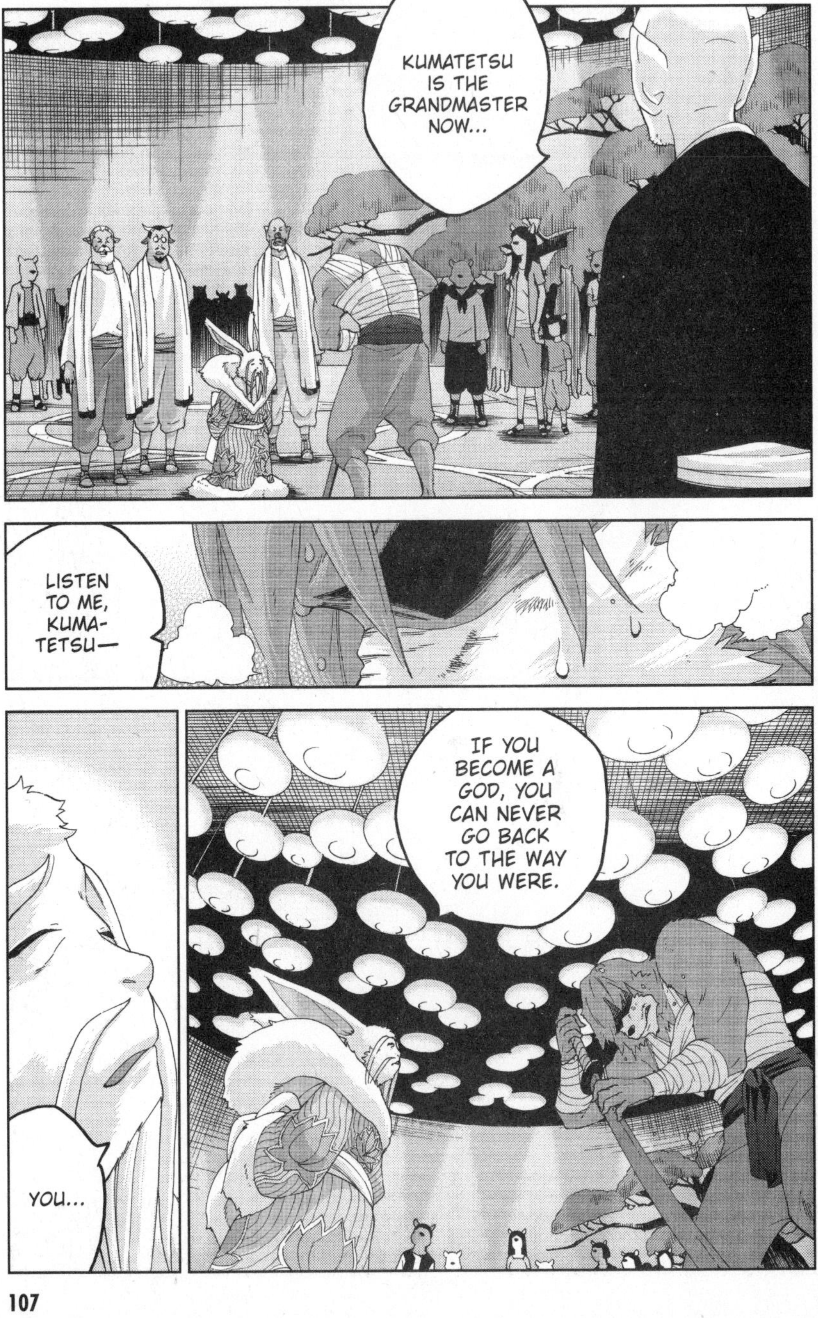
KUMATETSU IS THE GRANDMASTER NOW...
LISTEN TO ME, KUMA-TETSU—
IF YOU BECOME A GOD, YOU CAN NEVER GO BACK TO THE WAY YOU WERE.
YOU...

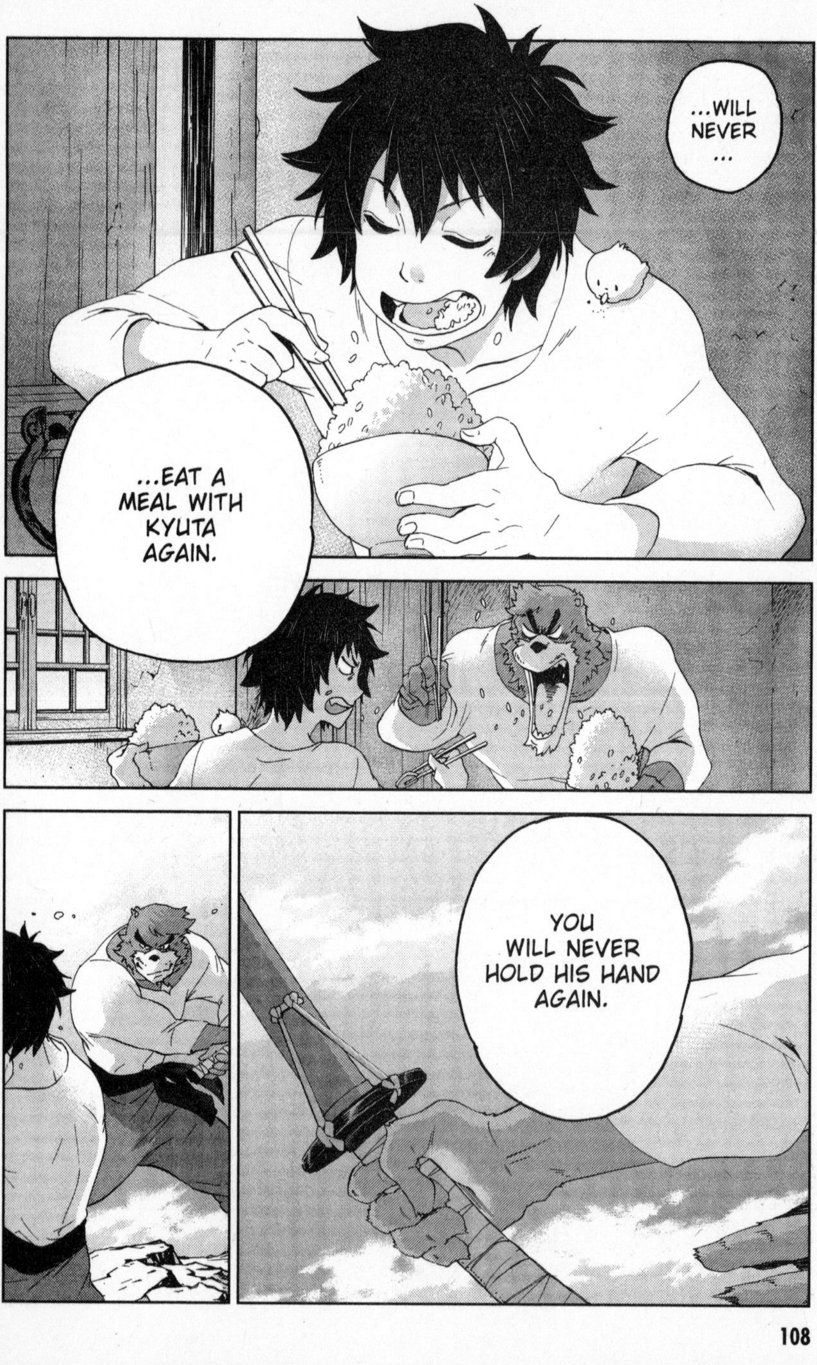
...WILL NEVER ...
...EAT A MEAL WITH KYUTA AGAIN.
YOU WILL NEVER HOLD HIS HAND AGAIN.

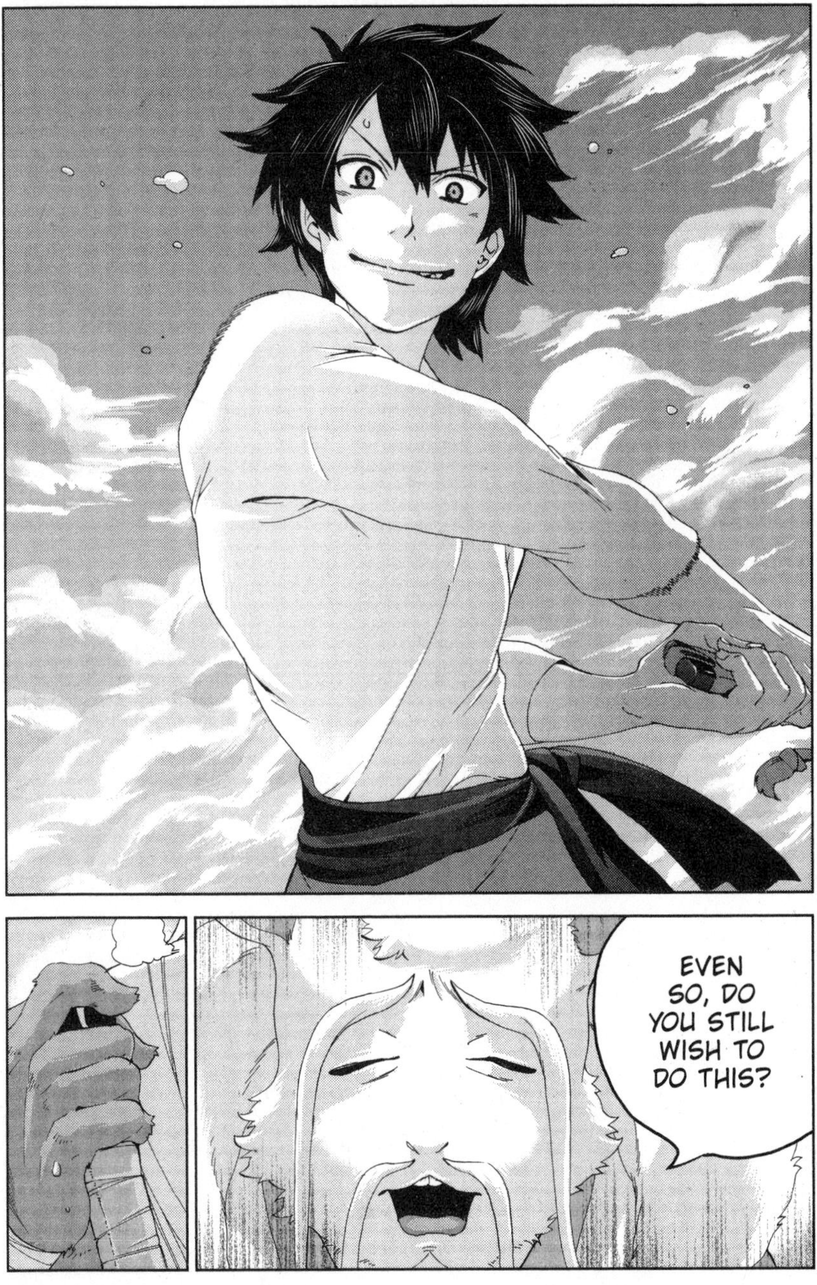
EVEN SO, DO YOU STILL WISH TO DO THIS?

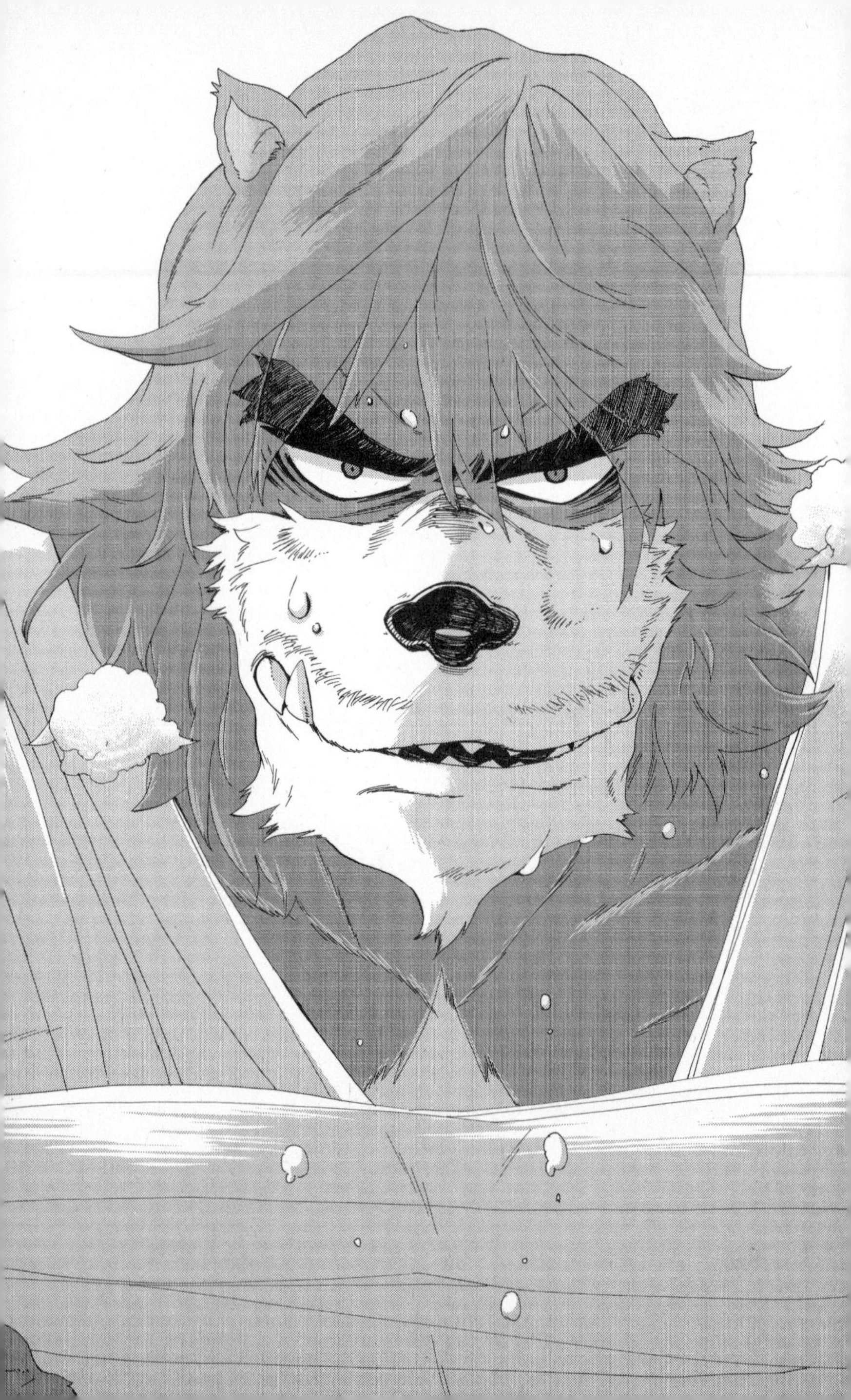

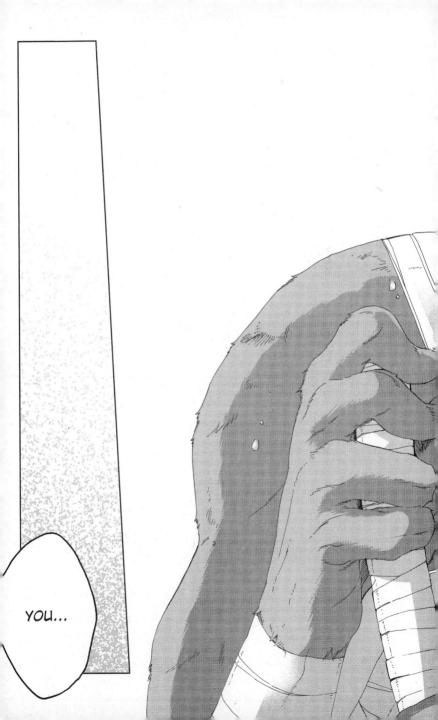

YOU...

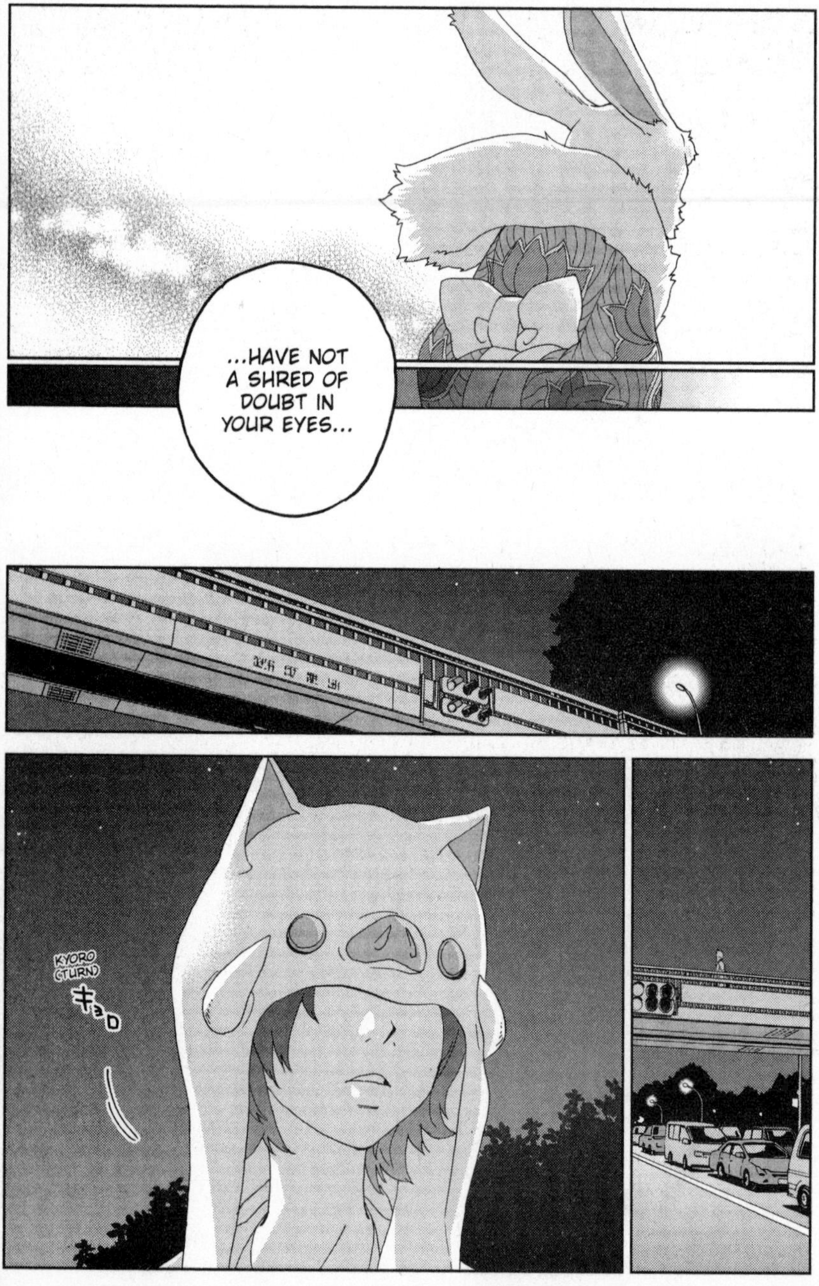
...HAVE NOT A SHRED OF DOUBT IN YOUR EYES...
KYORO (TURN)
キョロ

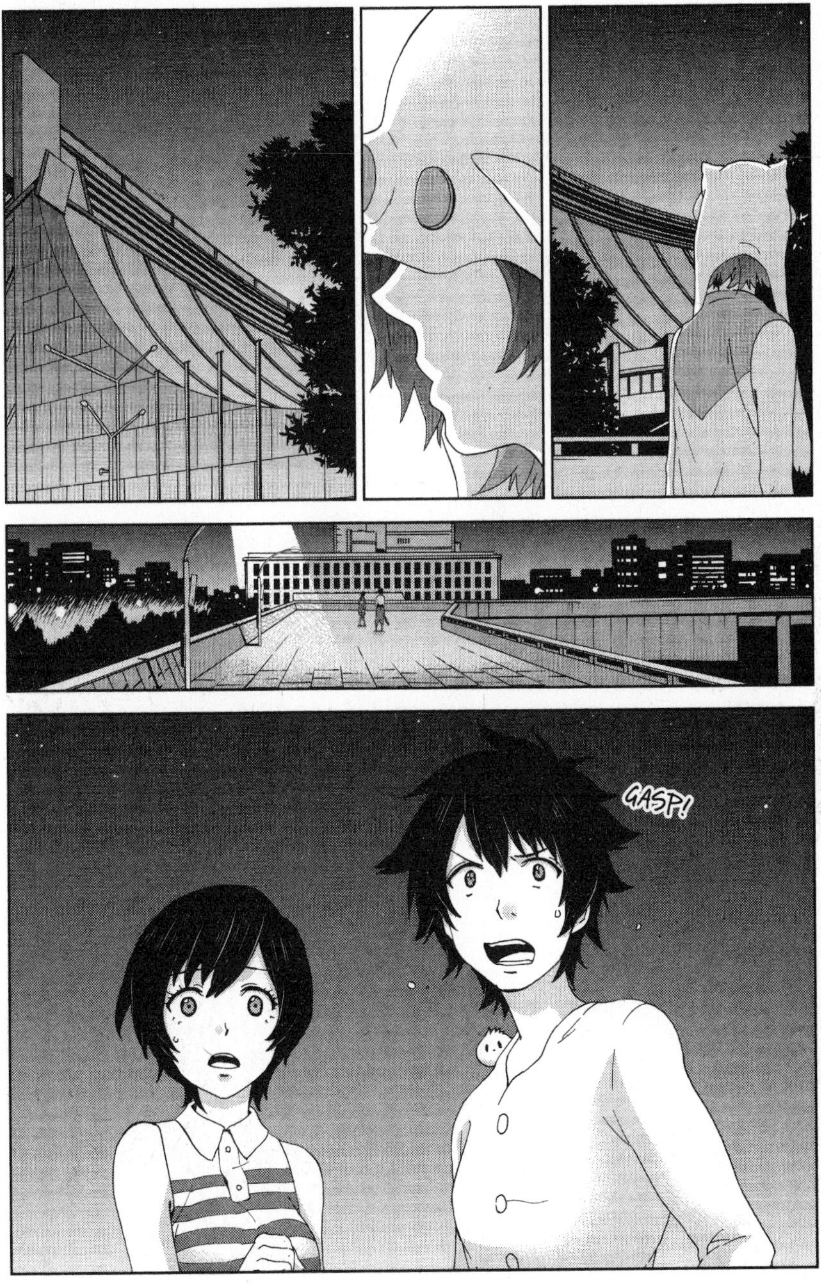
GASP!

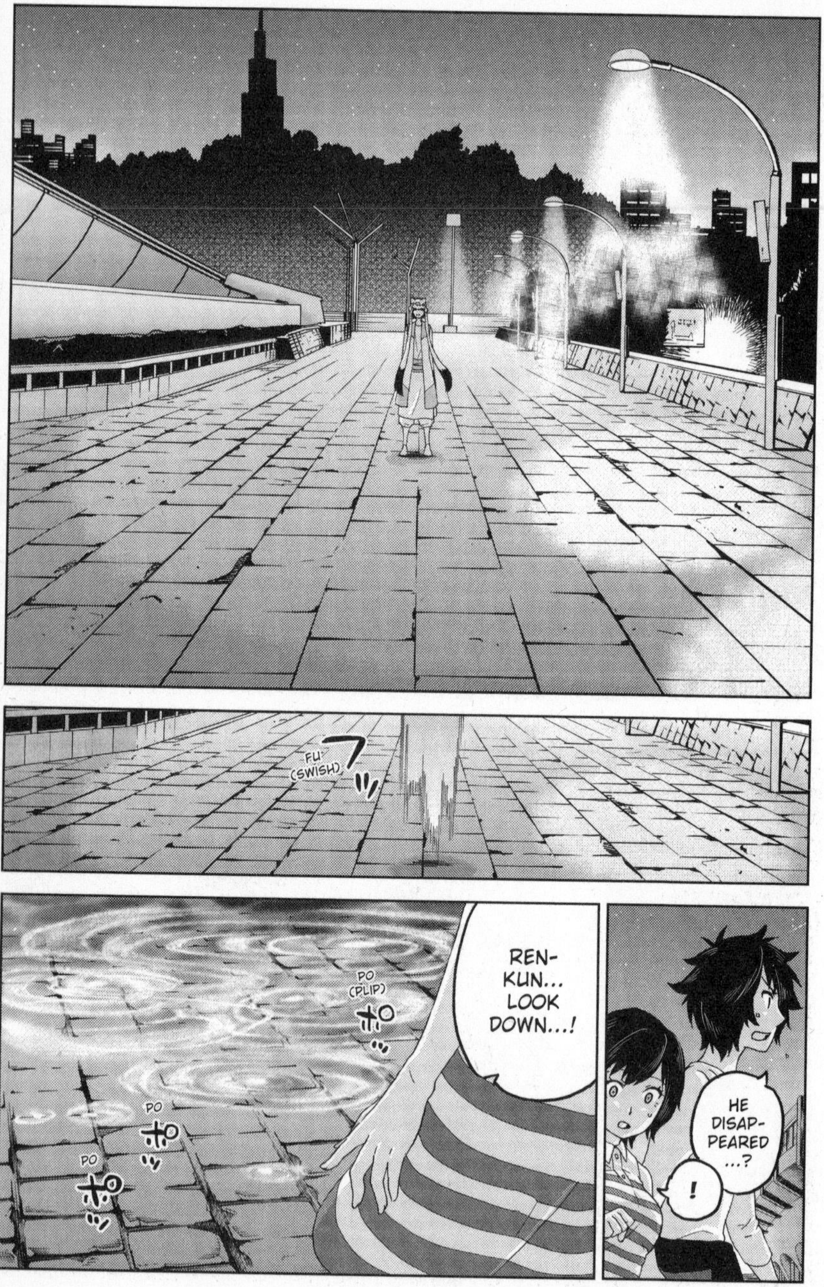
FU (SWISH)
HE DISAPPEARED...?
!
REN-KUN... LOOK DOWN...!
PO (PLIP)
PO
PO

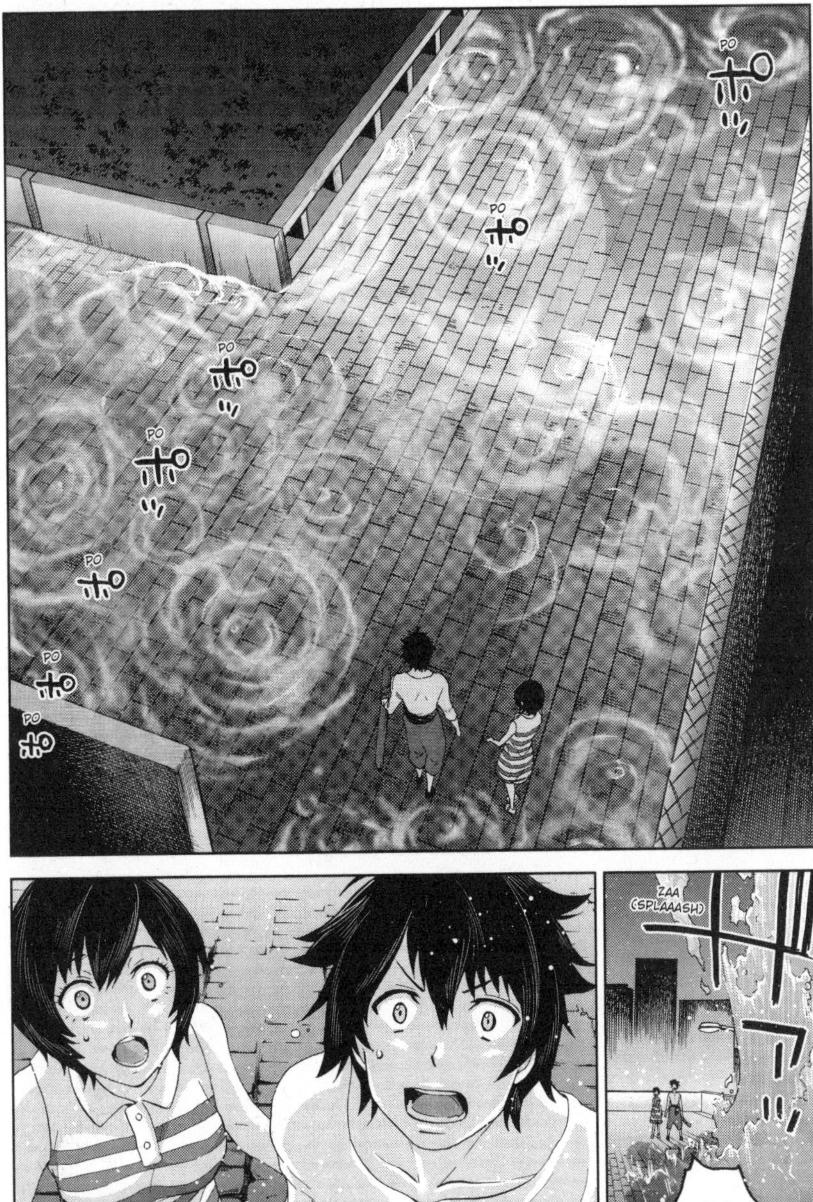
PO
ポッ
PO
ポッ
PO
ポッ
PO
ポッ
PO
ポ
PO
ポ
PO
ポ
ZAA (SPLAAASH)
ザアァッ
!!

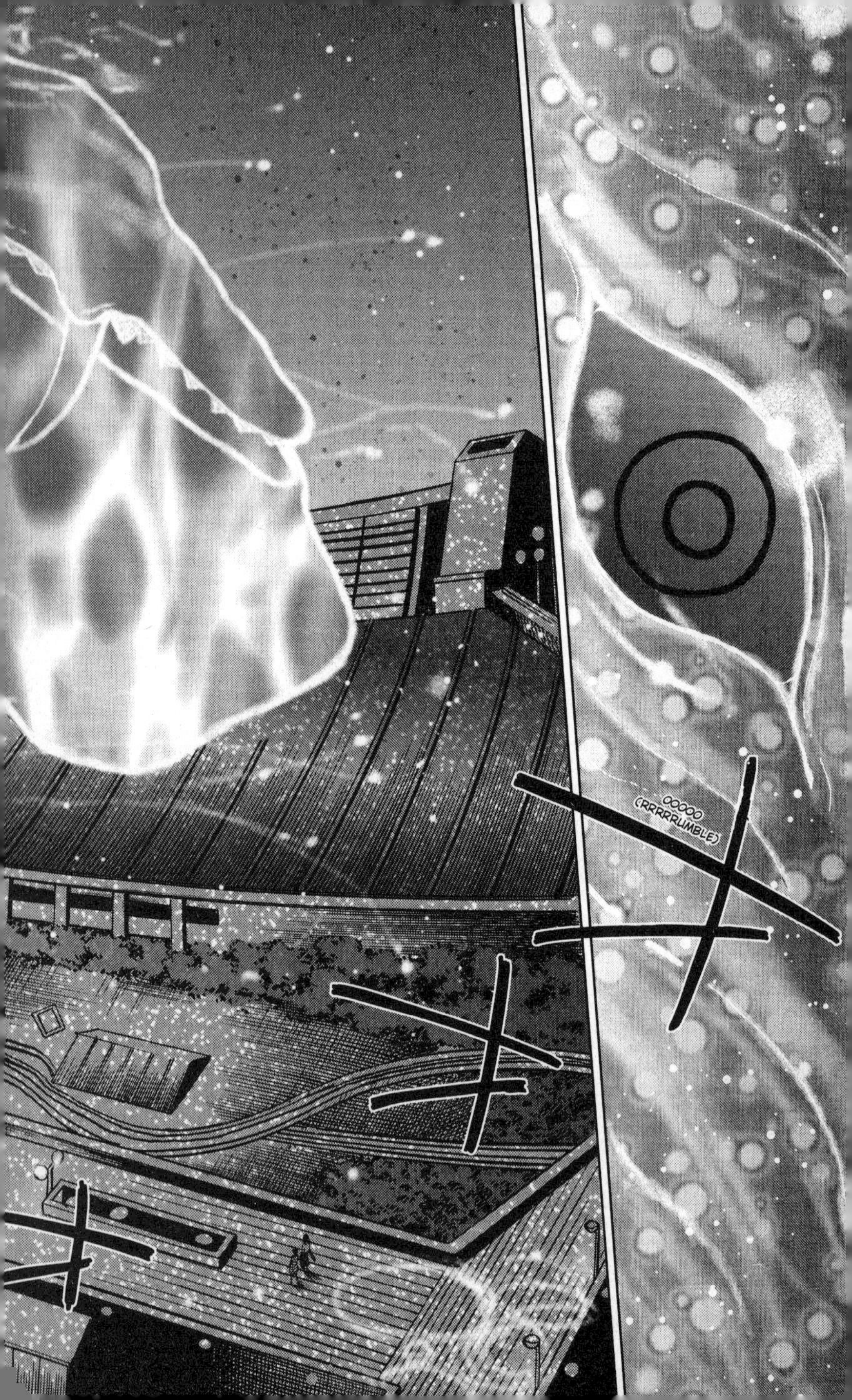
OOOOO
(RRRRRUMBLE)

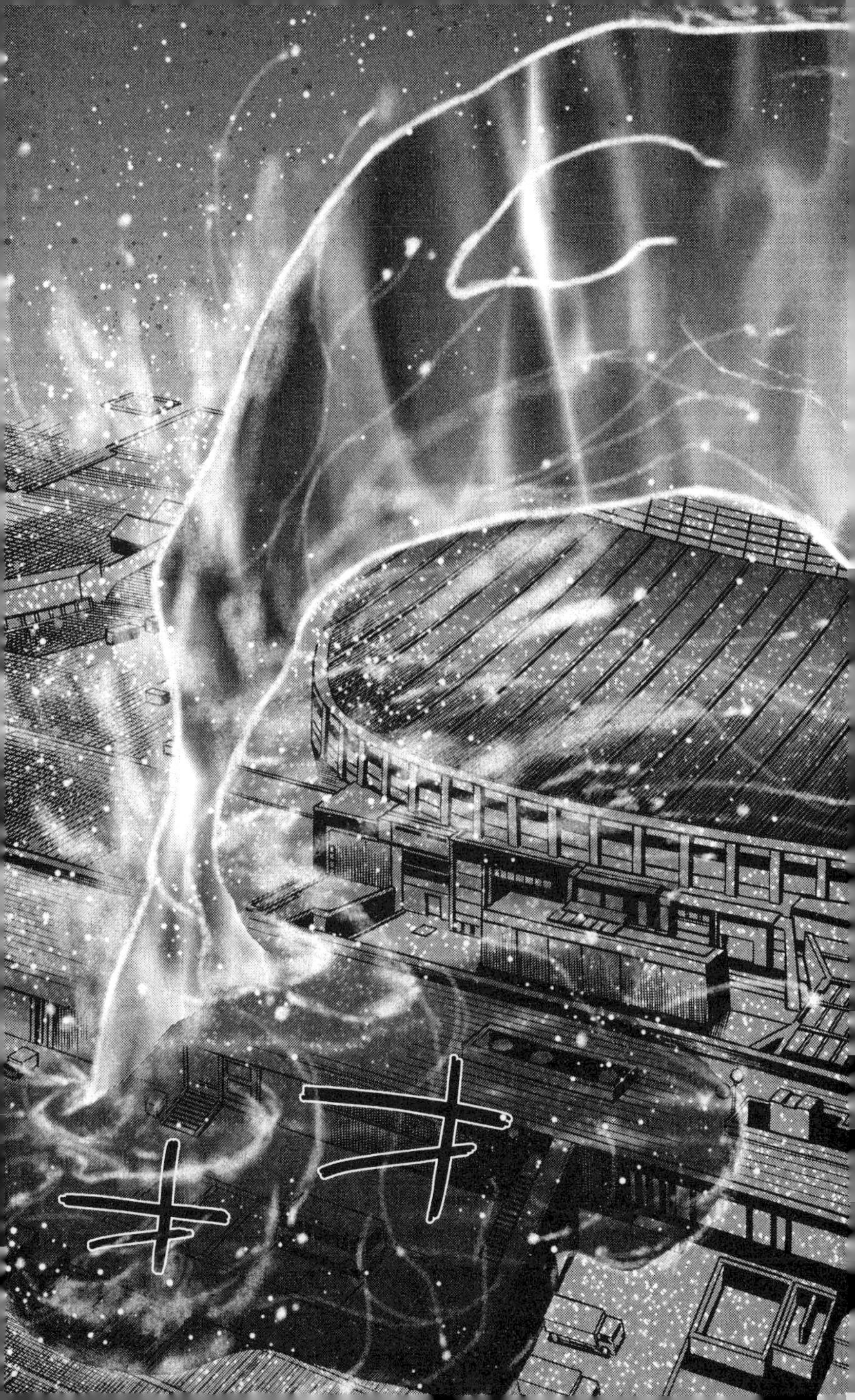
キキ

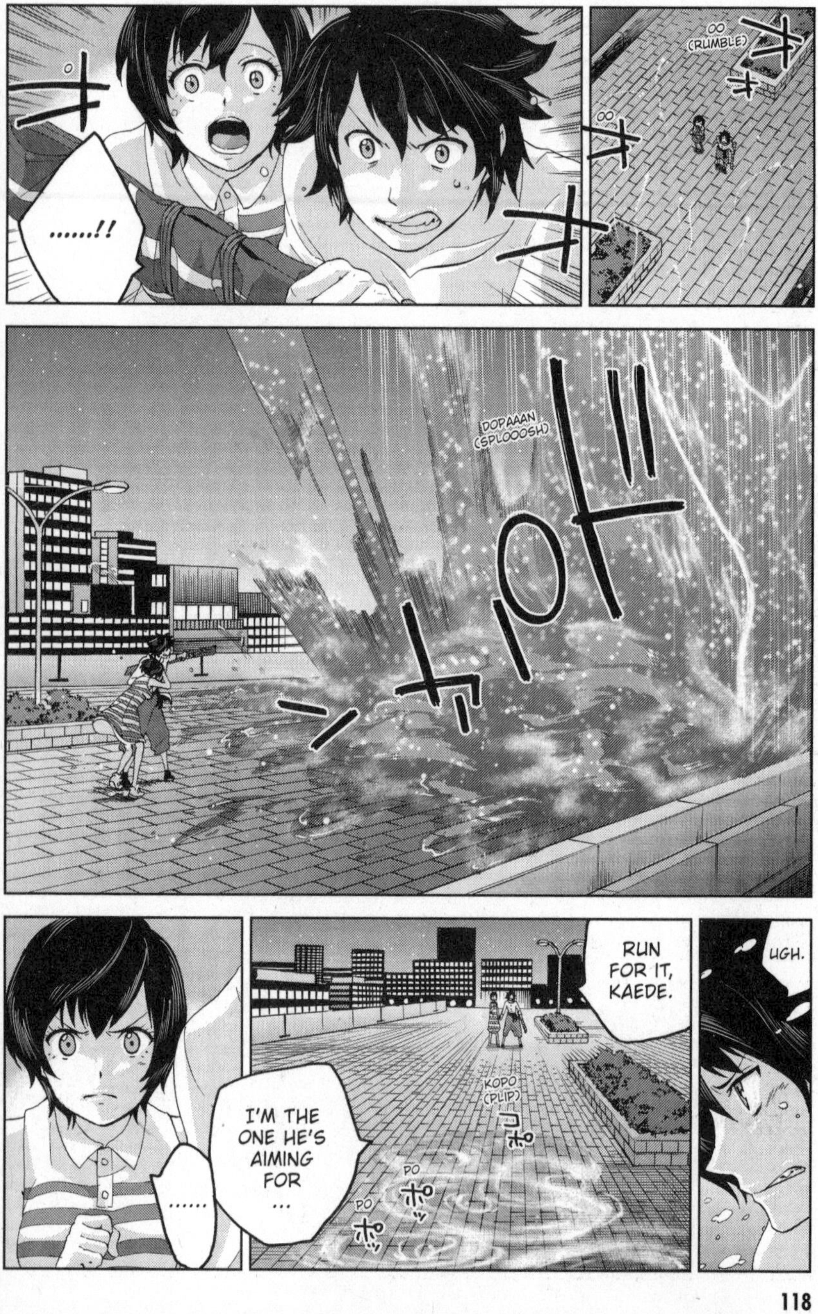
OO (RUMBLE)
OO
......!!
DOPAAAN (SPLOOOSH)
UGH.
RUN FOR IT, KAEDE.
KOPO (PLIP)
PO
PO
I'M THE ONE HE'S AIMING FOR ...
......

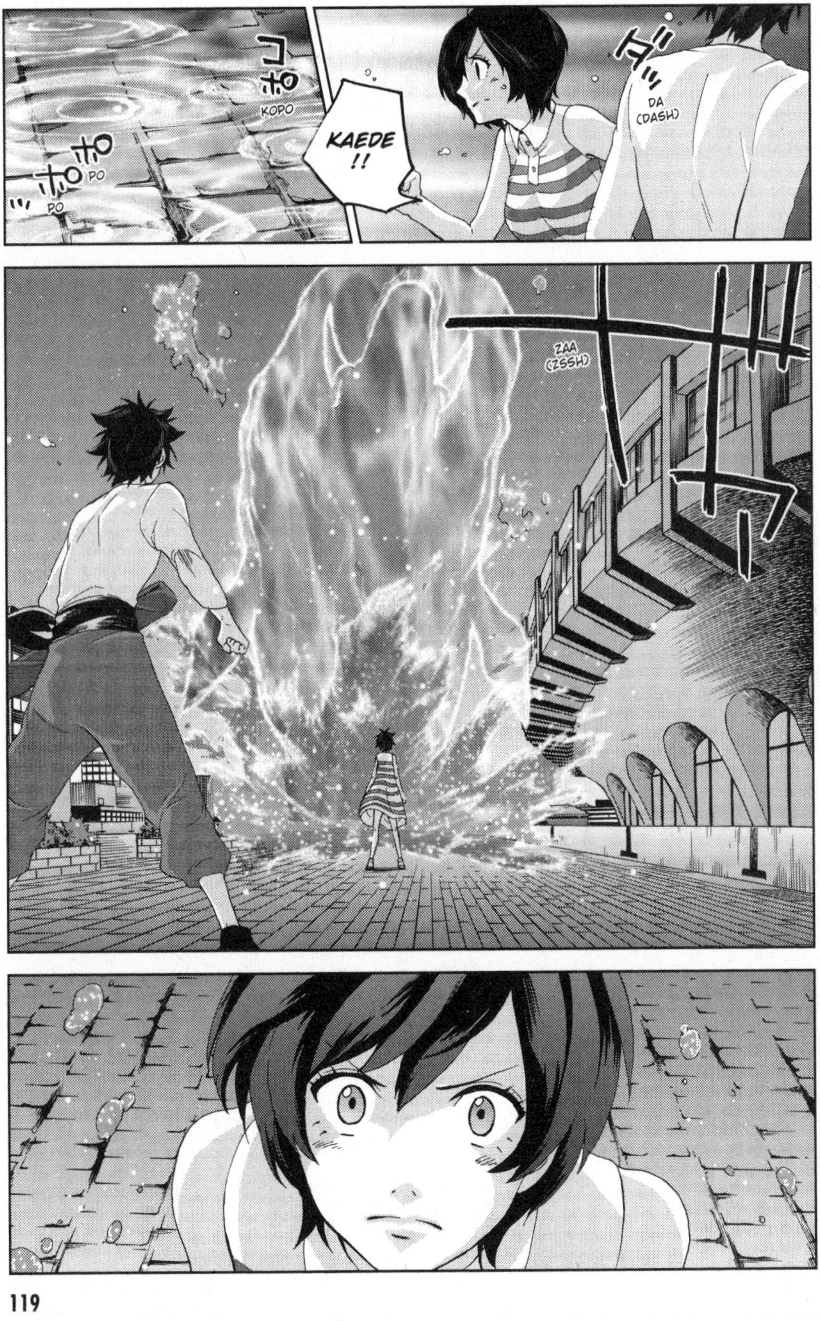
ダッ
DA (DASH)
KAEDE !!
コポ
KOPO
ポポッ
PO
PO
ZAA (ZSSH)

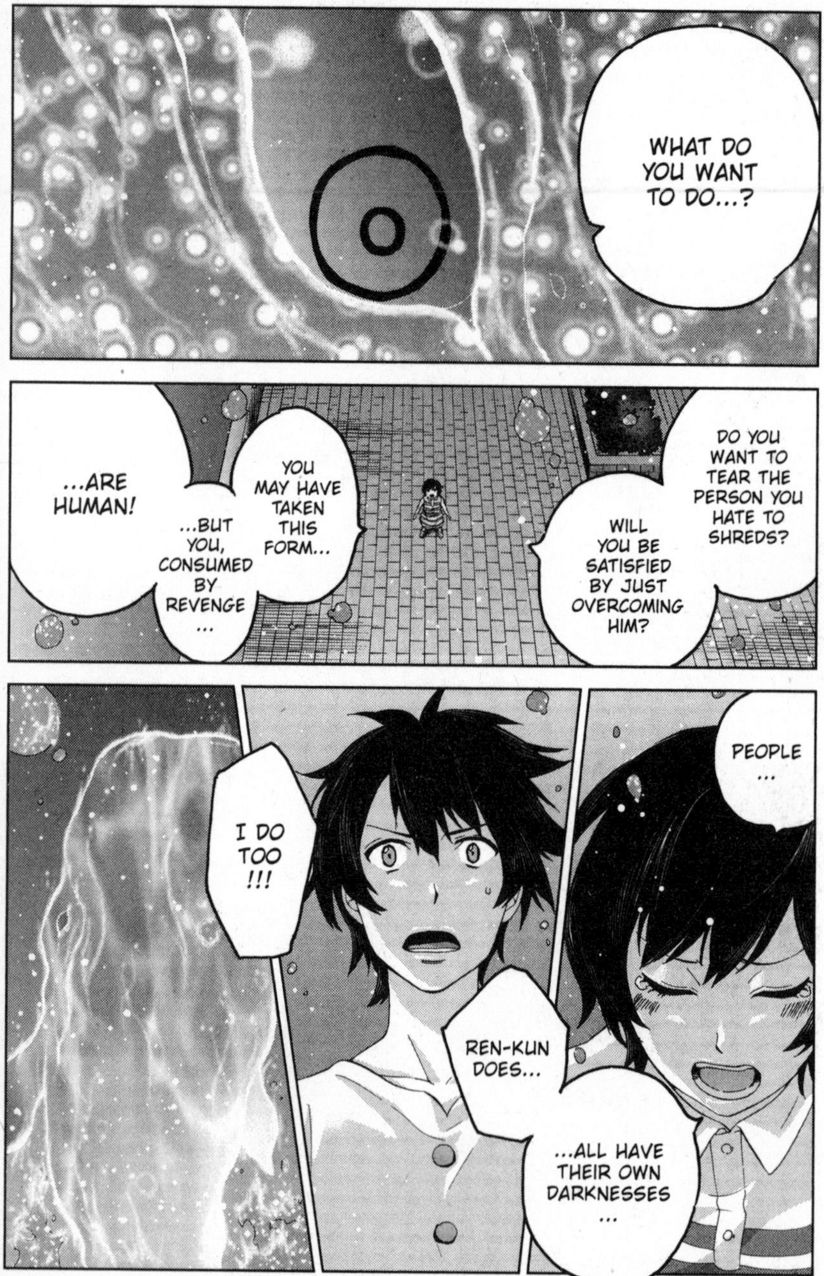
WHAT DO YOU WANT TO DO...?
DO YOU WANT TO TEAR THE PERSON YOU HATE TO SHREDS?
WILL YOU BE SATISFIED BY JUST OVERCOMING HIM?
YOU MAY HAVE TAKEN THIS FORM...
...BUT YOU, CONSUMED BY REVENGE ...
...ARE HUMAN!
PEOPLE ...
REN-KUN DOES...
I DO TOO !!!
...ALL HAVE THEIR OWN DARKNESSES ...

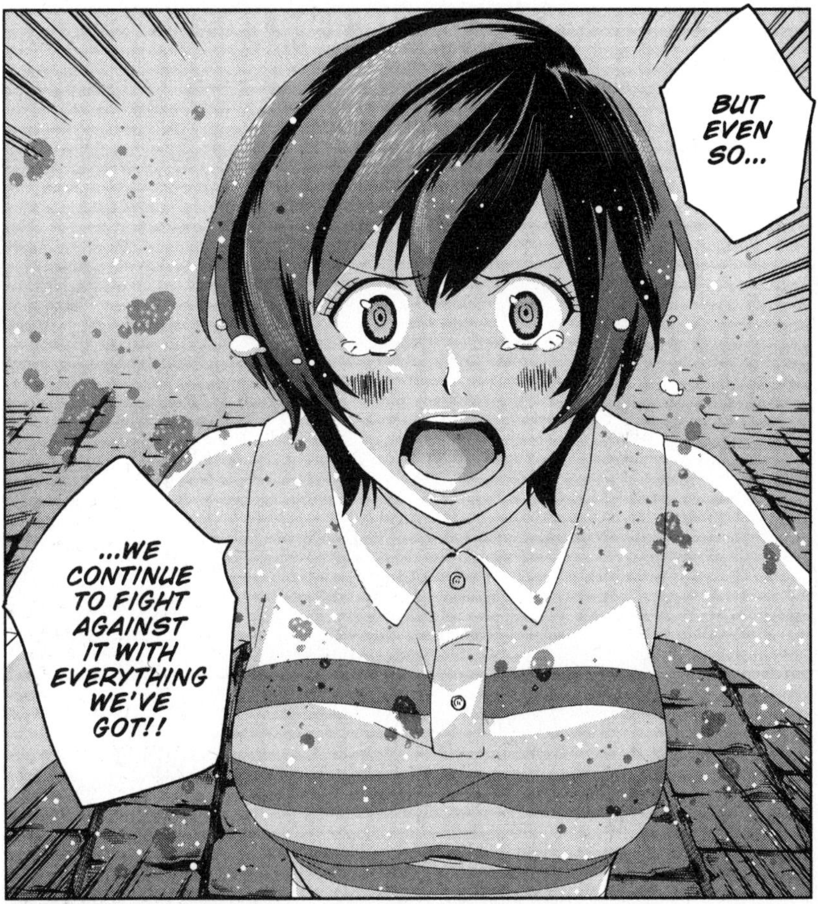
BUT EVEN SO...
...WE CONTINUE TO FIGHT AGAINST IT WITH EVERYTHING WE'VE GOT!!

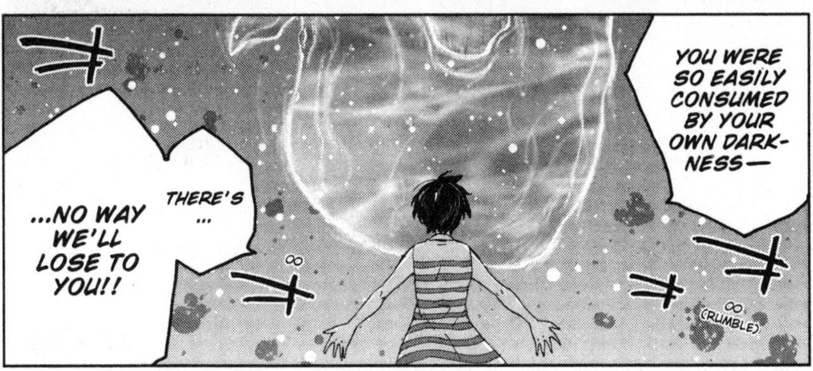
YOU WERE SO EASILY CONSUMED BY YOUR OWN DARK-NESS—
(RUMBLE)
THERE'S...
...NO WAY WE'LL LOSE TO YOU!!

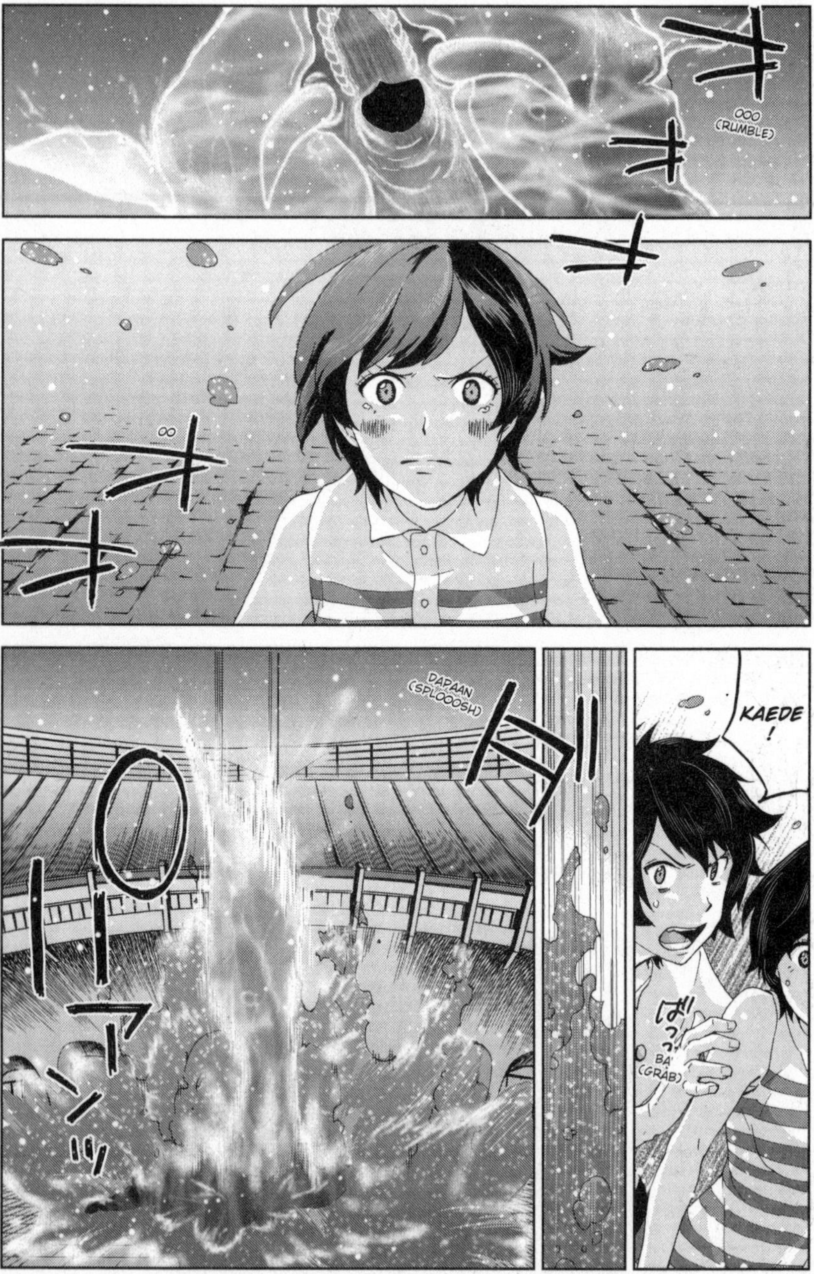
OOO
(RUMBLE)
KAEDE!
BA
(GRAB)
DAPAAN
(SPLOOOSH)

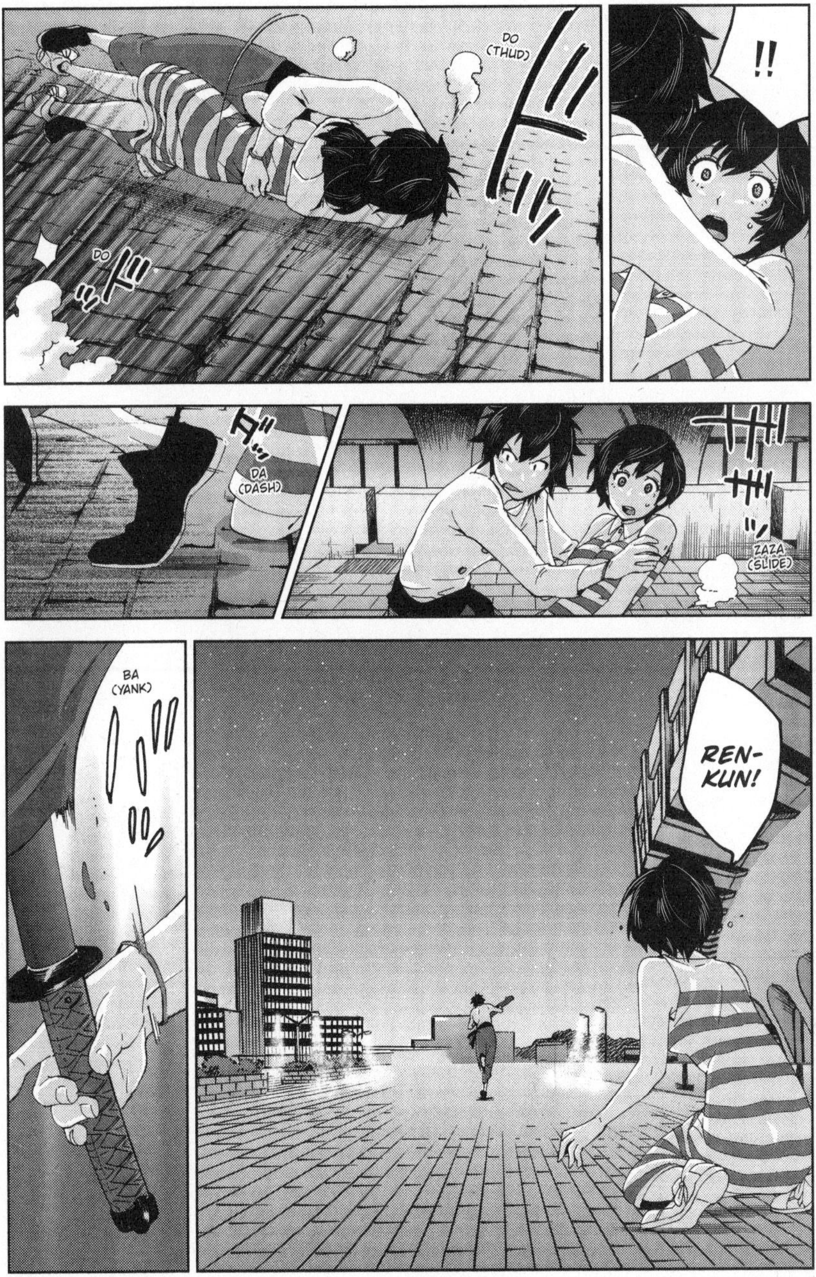
!!
DO (THUD)
DO
ZAZA (SLIDE)
DA (DASH)
REN-KUN!
BA (YANK)

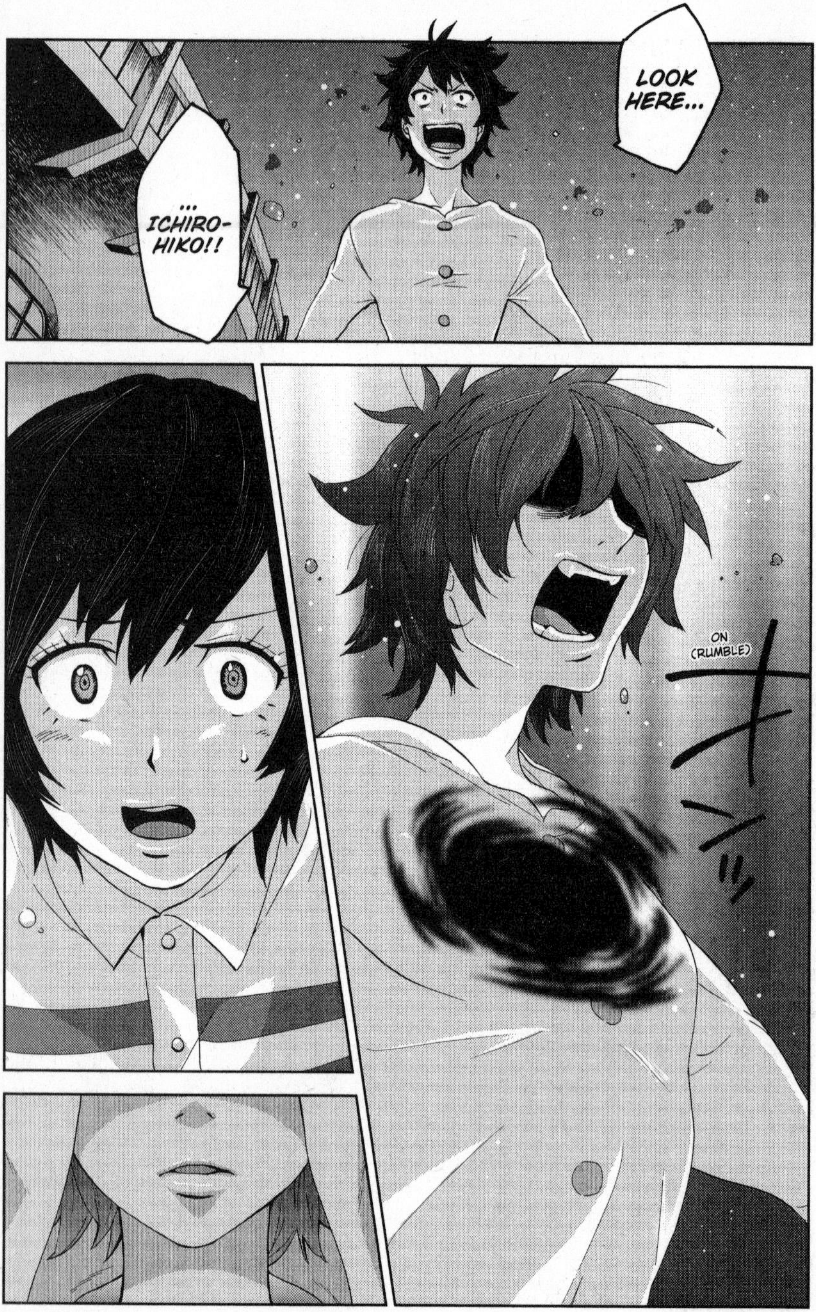
LOOK HERE...
... ICHIRO-HIKO!!
ON (RUMBLE)

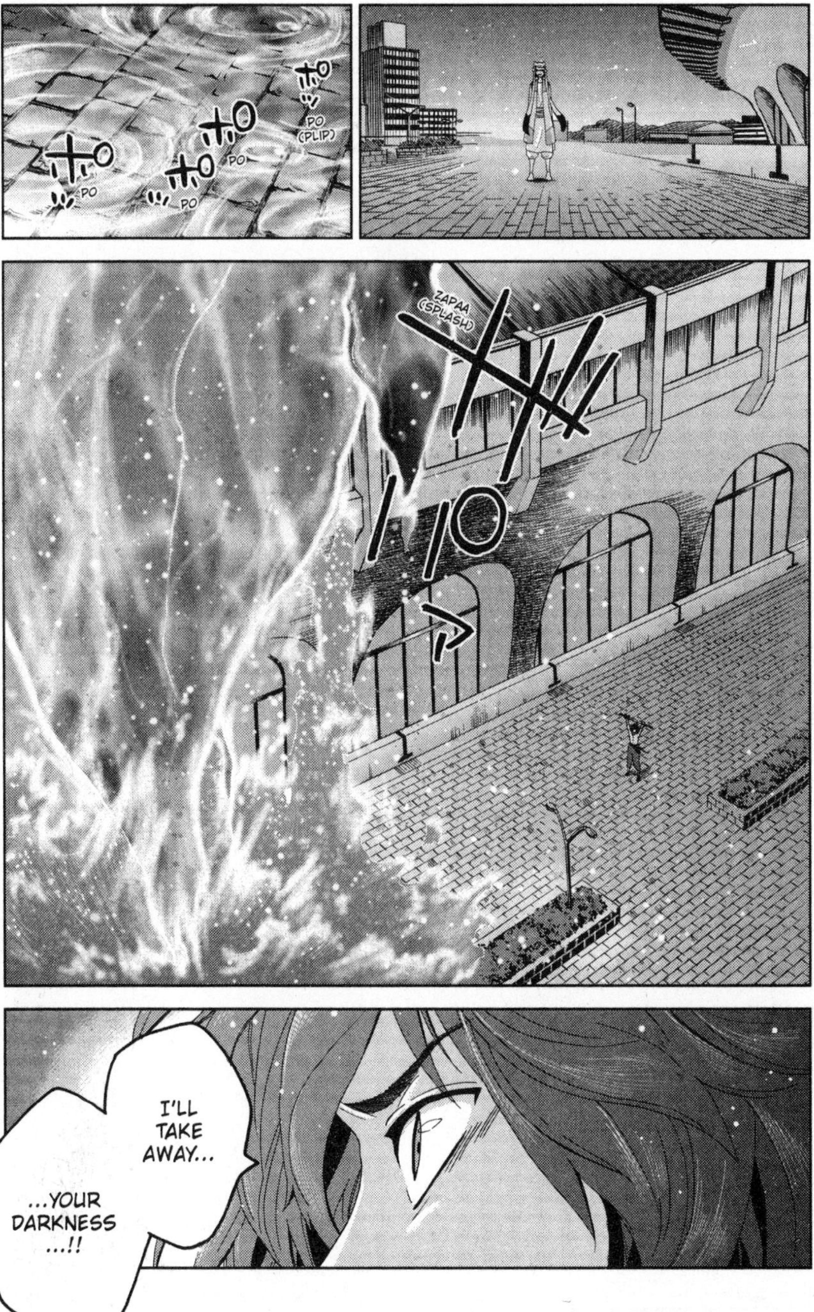
PO (PLIP)
PO
PO
PO
ZAPAA (SPLASH)
I'LL TAKE AWAY...
...YOUR DARKNESS ...!!

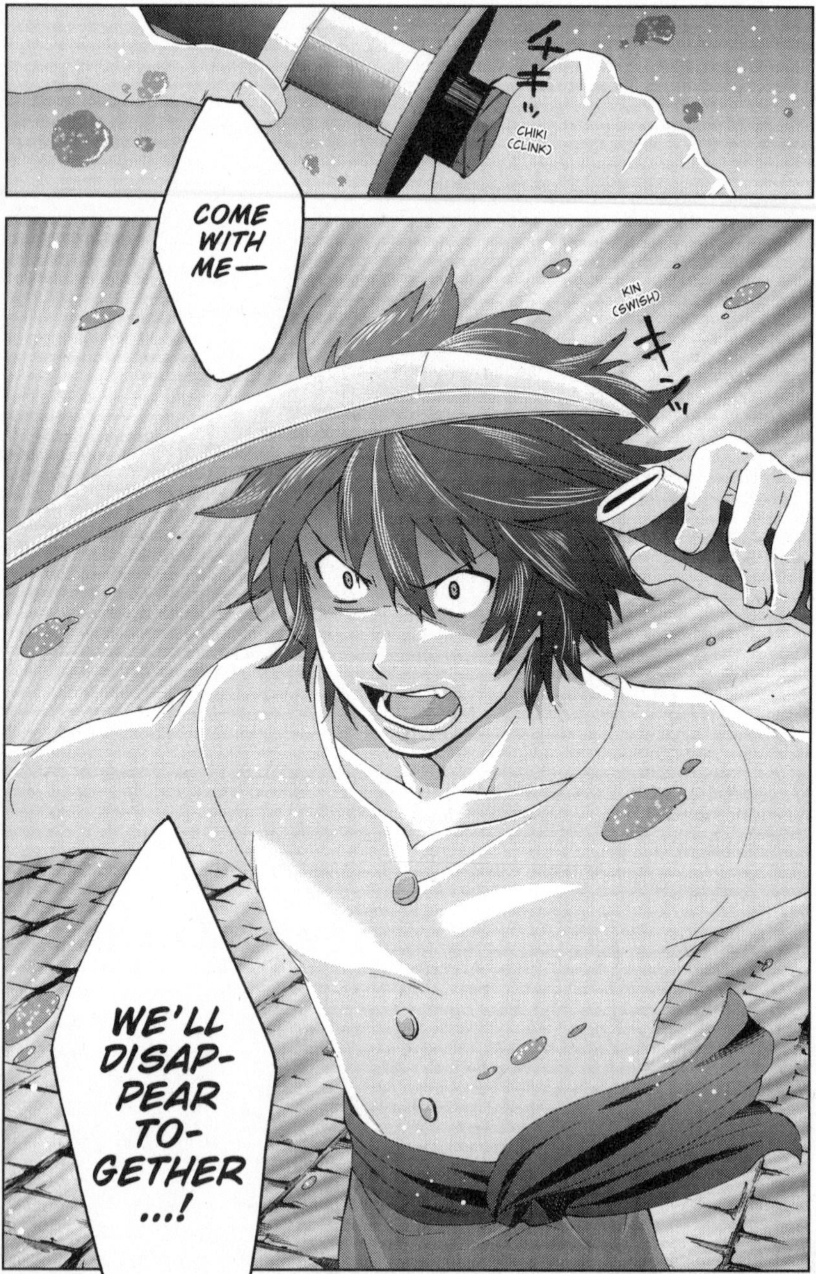
CHIKI (CLINK)
COME WITH ME—
KIN (SWISH)
WE'LL DISAP-PEAR TO-GETHER ...!

CHAPTER 18 END

THE BOY & THE BEAST

I'LL TRAP HIS DARKNESS...

...PIERCE IT WITH MY SWORD AND DISAPPEAR WITH HIM...!!

...REN-KUN, YOU'RE NOT GOING TO—!?

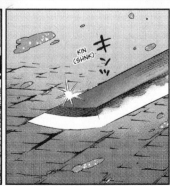

KIN (SHNK)

SIGNS: UOGASHI / WORLD'S BEST—

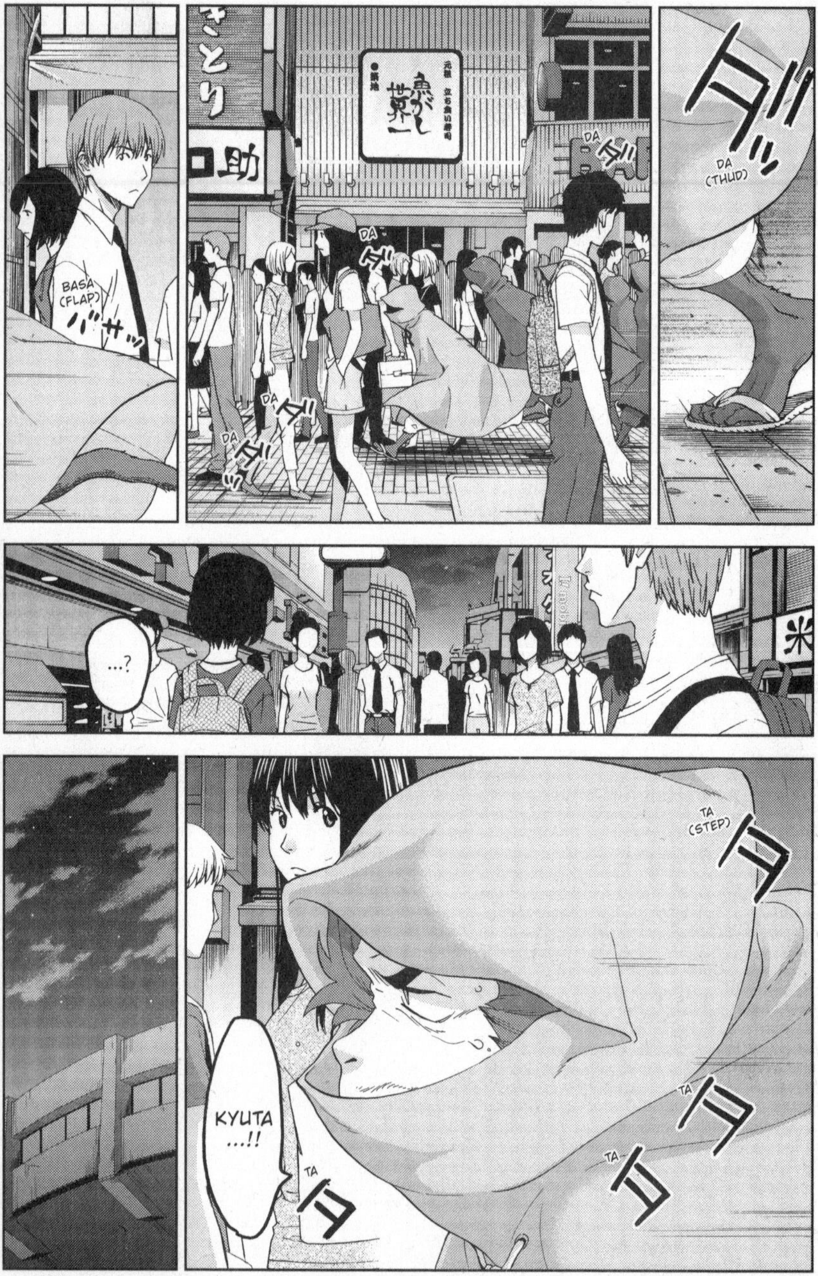
DA (THUD)
DA
DA
DA
DA
BASA (FLAP)
...?
TA (STEP)
TA
TA
KYUTA ...!!
TA

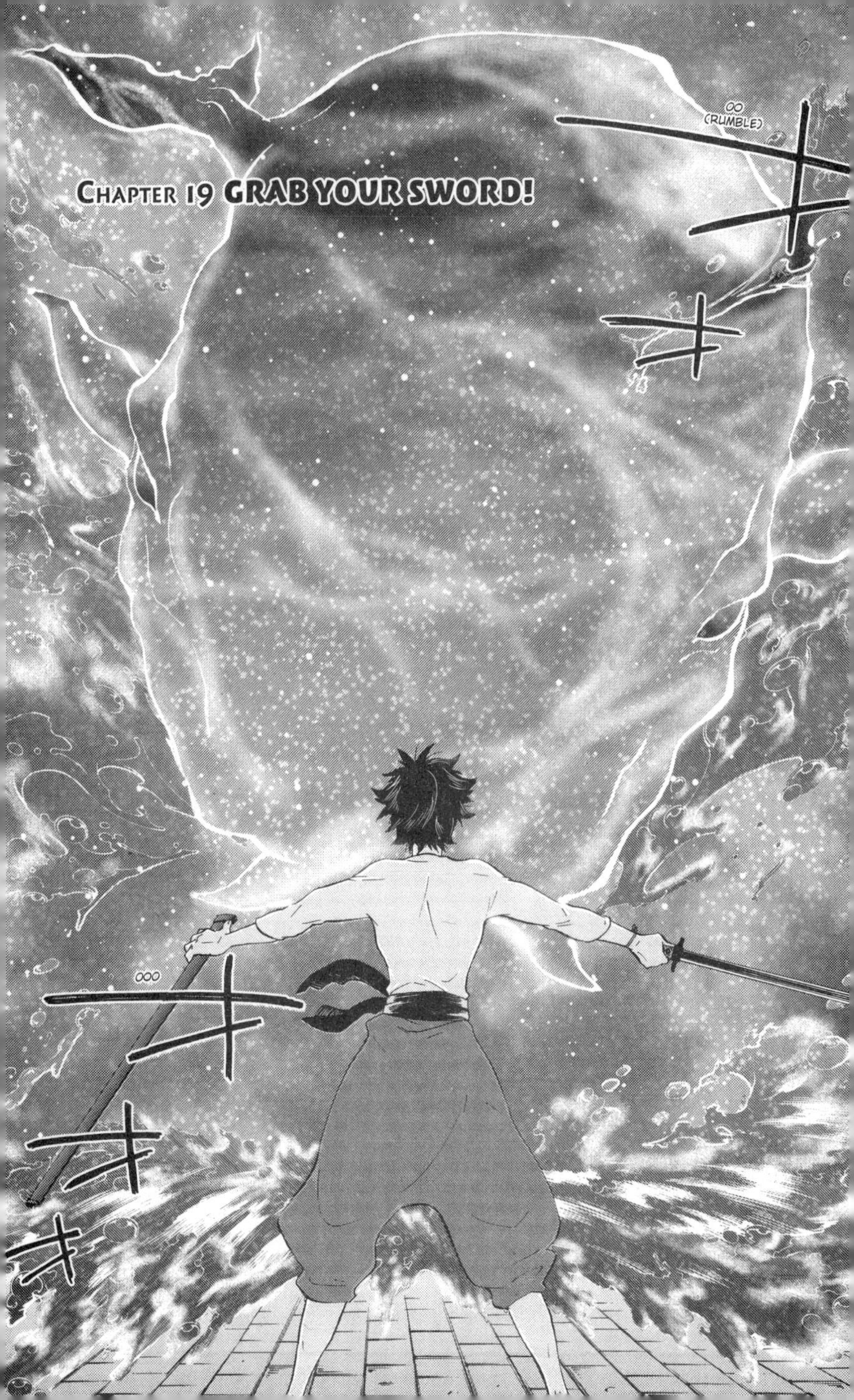
OO (RUMBLE)
Chapter 19 Grab Your Sword!
OOO

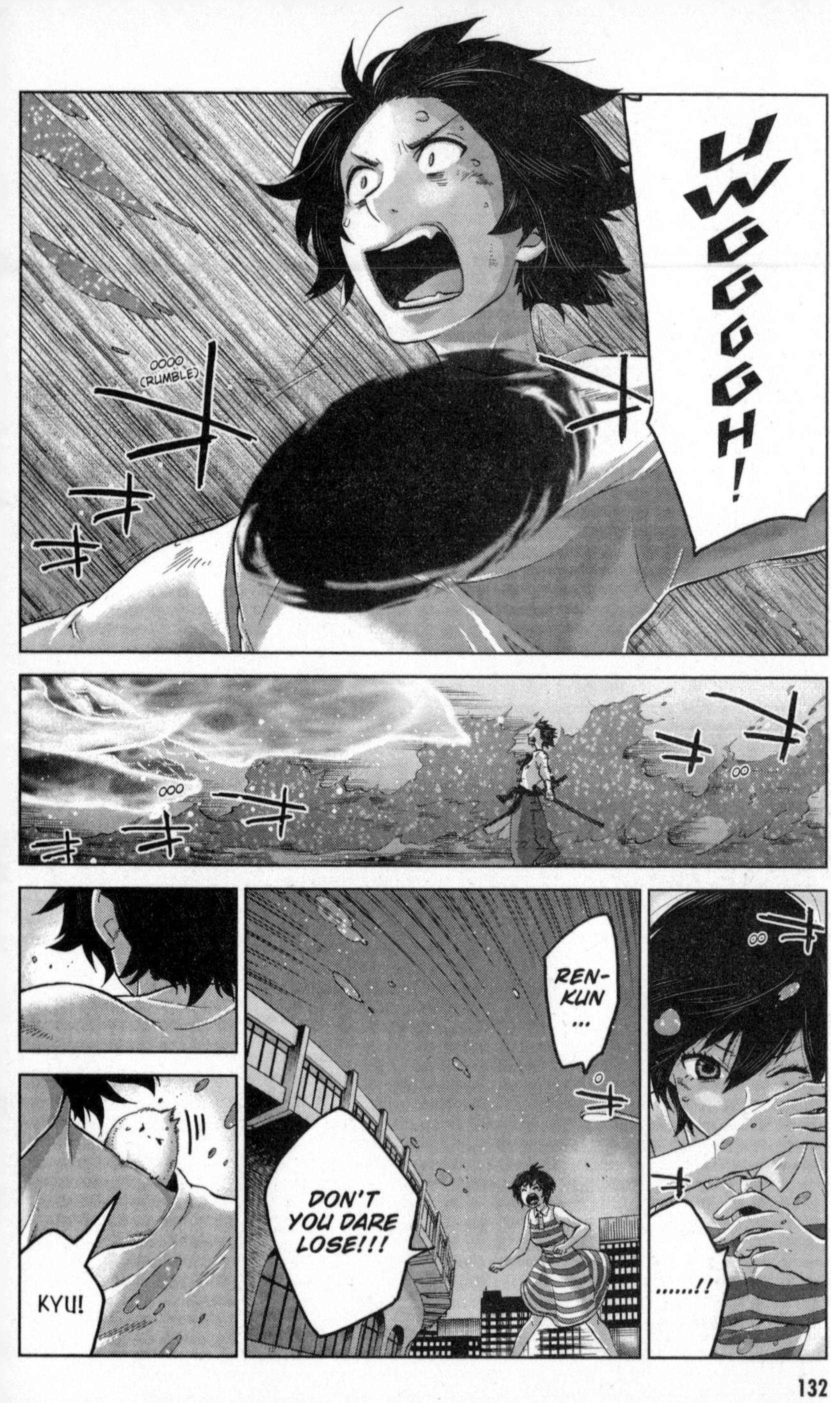
UWOOOOH!
OOOO (RUMBLE)
OOO
......!!
REN-KUN ...
DON'T YOU DARE LOSE!!!
KYU!

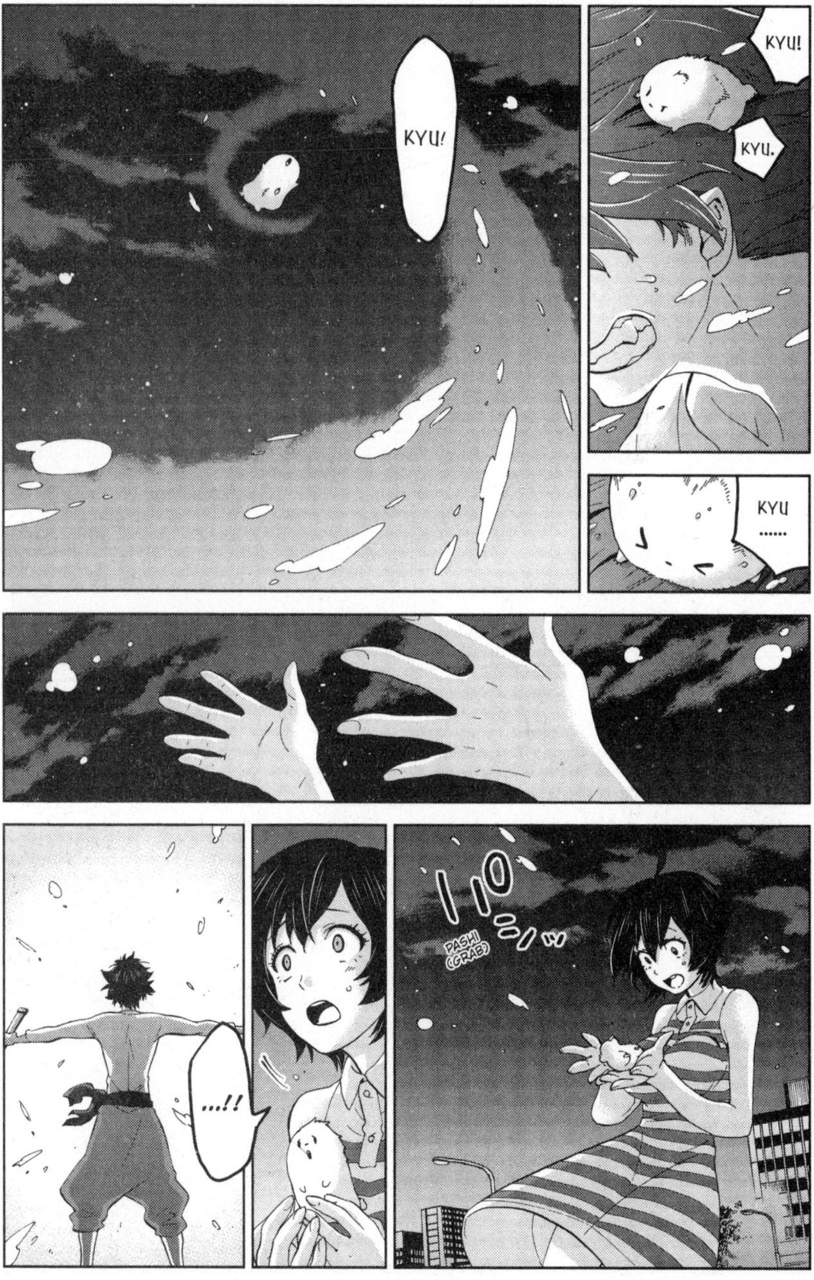
KYU!
KYU.
KYU ......
KYU!
PASHI (GRAB)
...!!

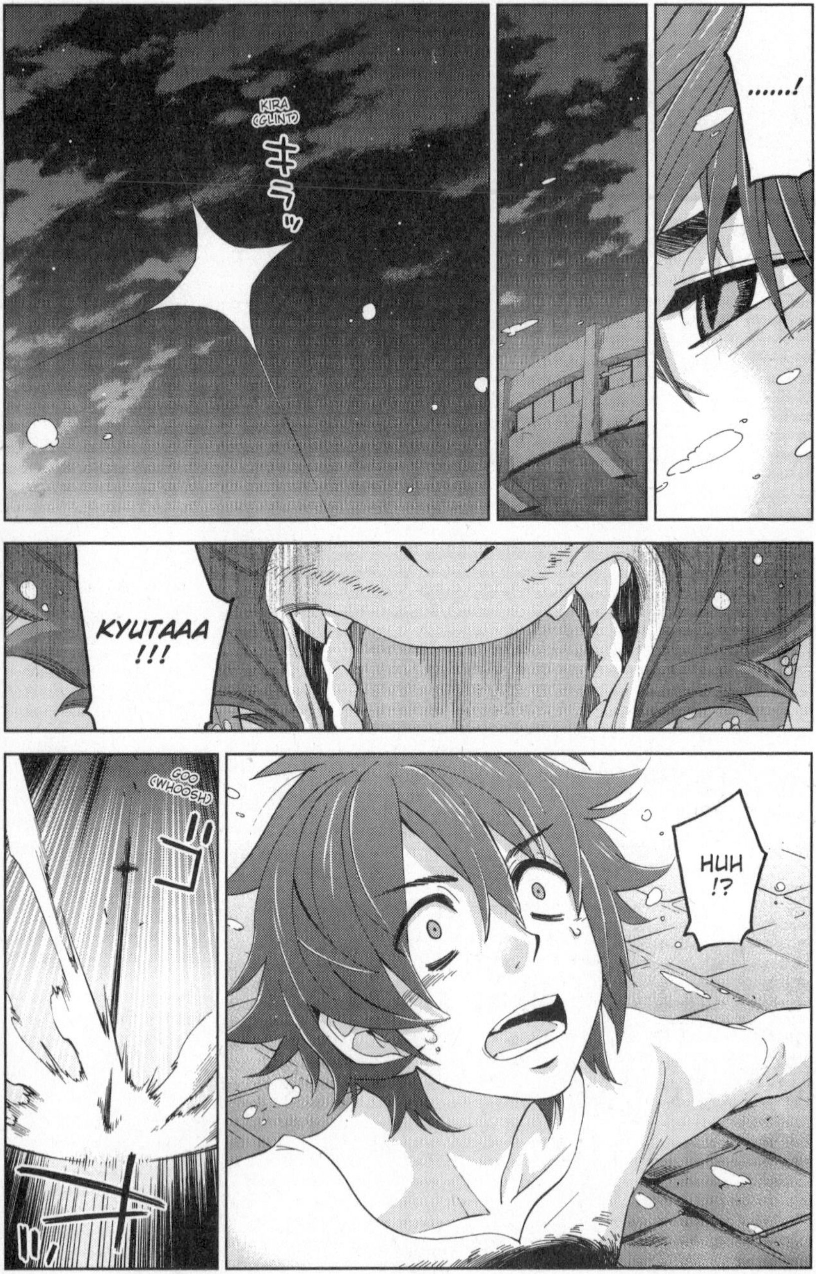
......!
KIRA (GLINT)
キラッ
KYUTAAA !!!
HUH !?
GOO (WHOOSH)
ゴッ

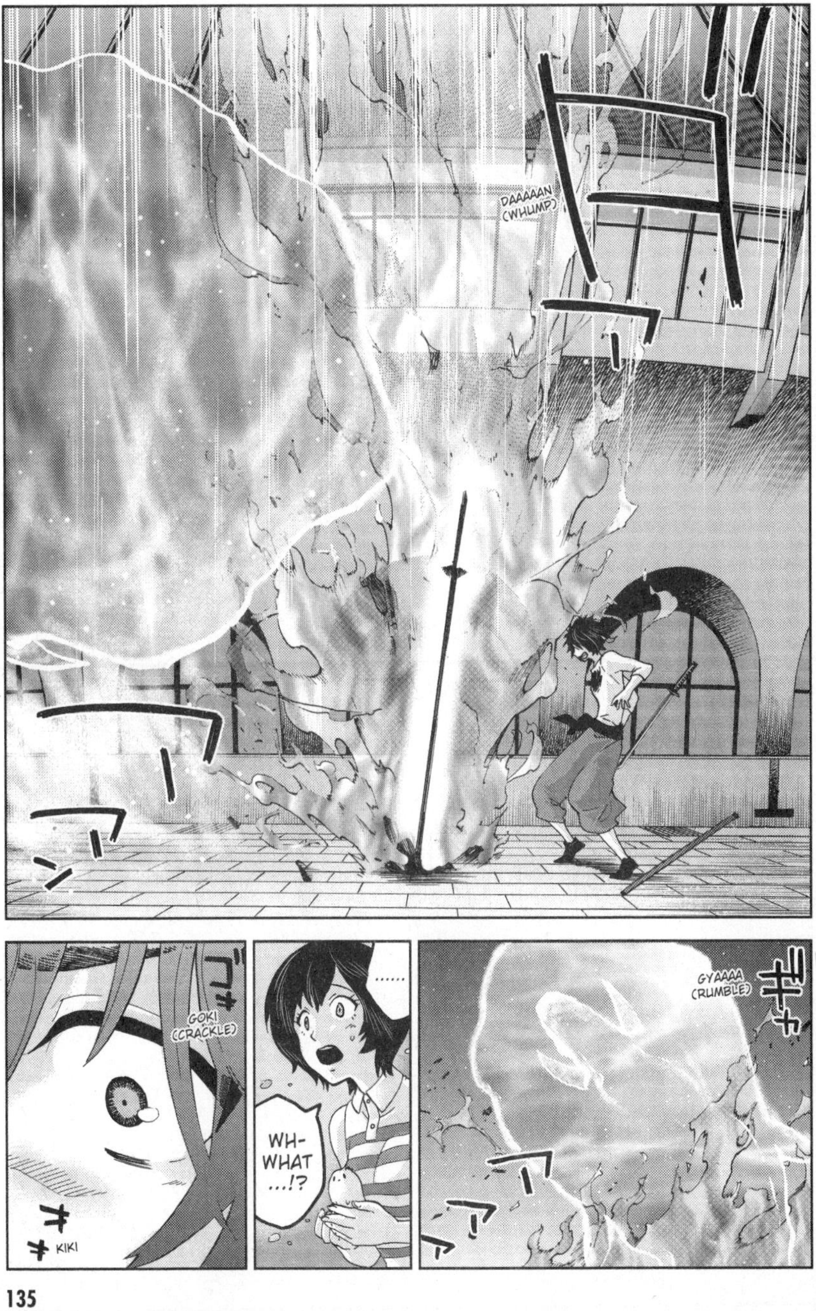
DAAAAAN (WHUMP)
GYAAAA (RUMBLE)
......
WH- WHAT ...!?
GOKI (CRACKLE)
KIKI

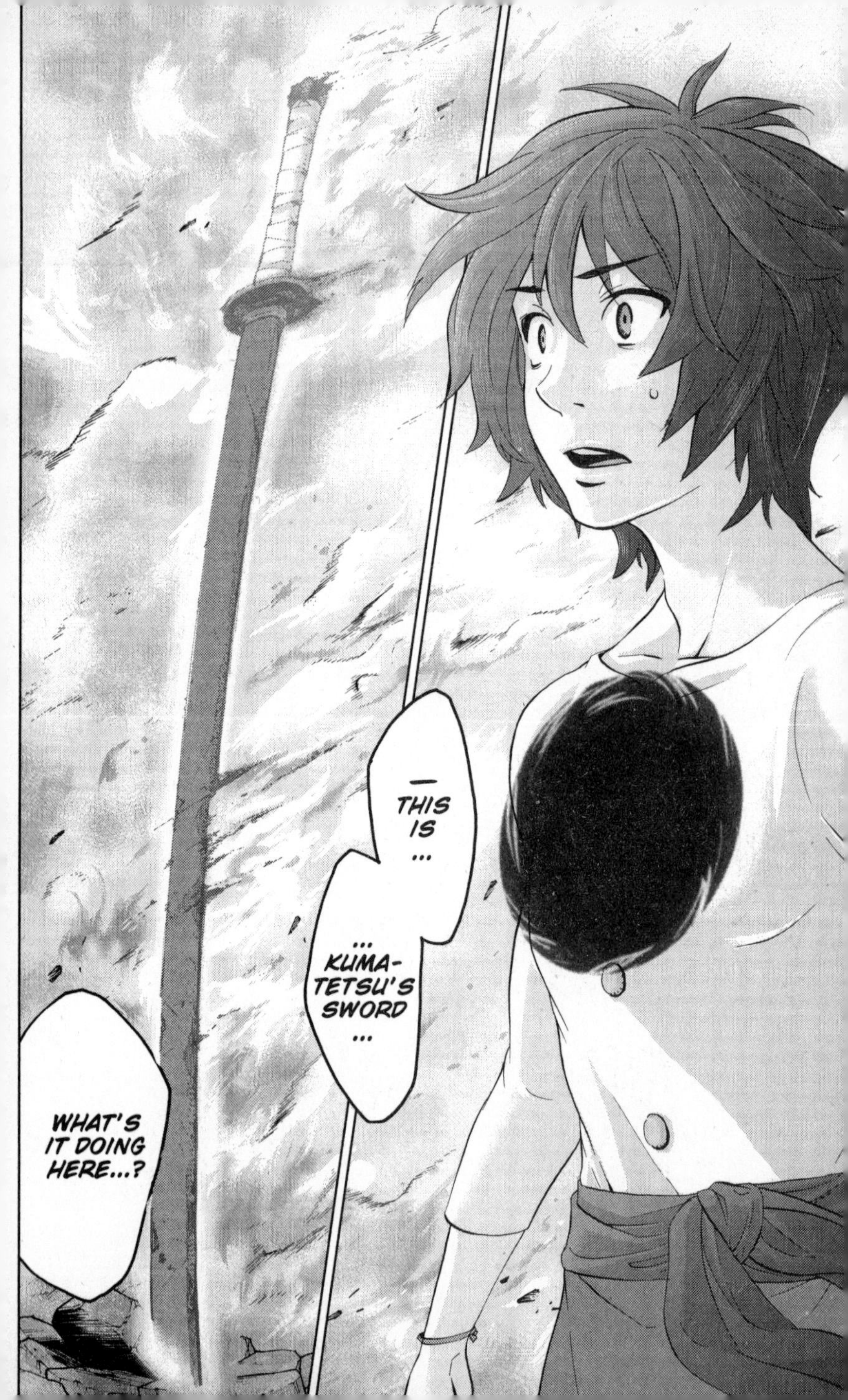
—THIS IS ...
... KUMA-TETSU'S SWORD ...
WHAT'S IT DOING HERE...?

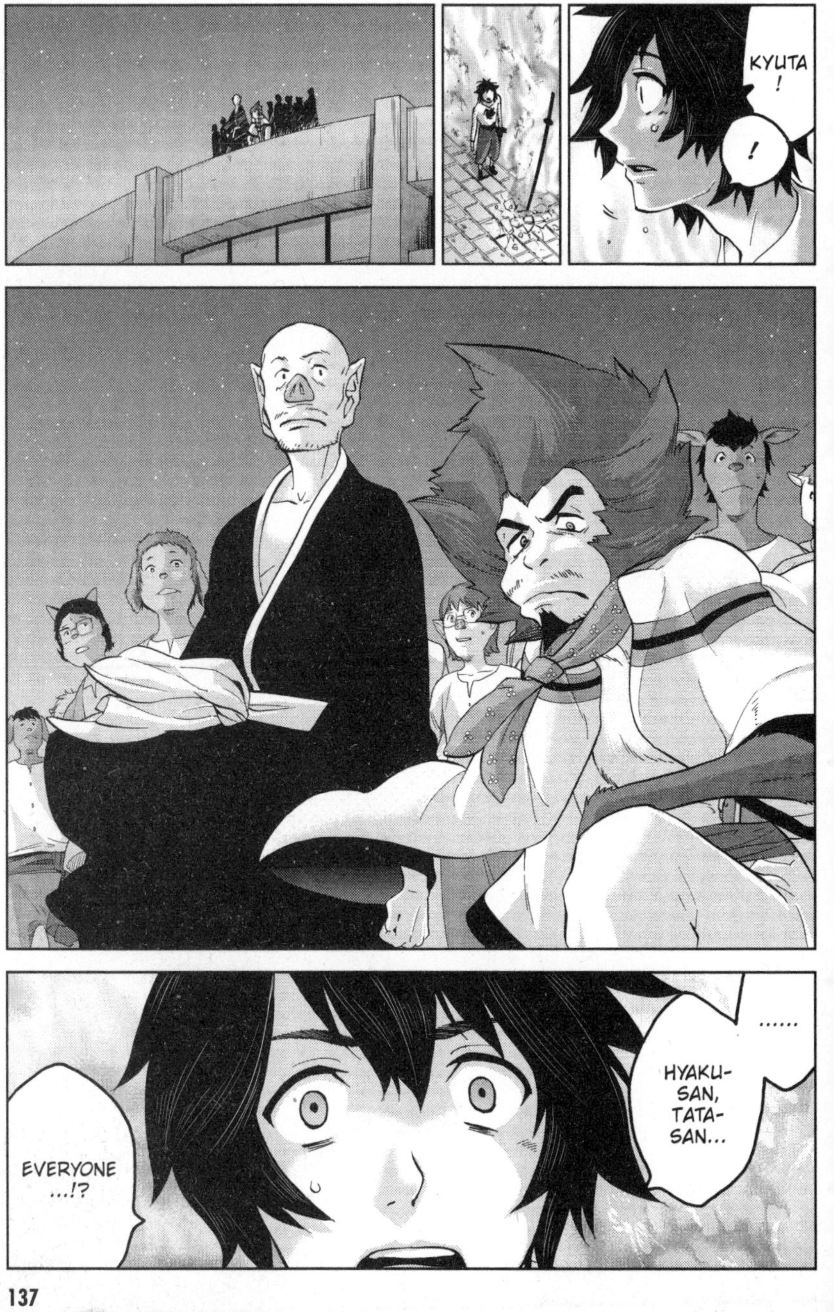
KYUTA!
!
......
HYAKU-SAN, TATA-SAN...
EVERYONE...!?

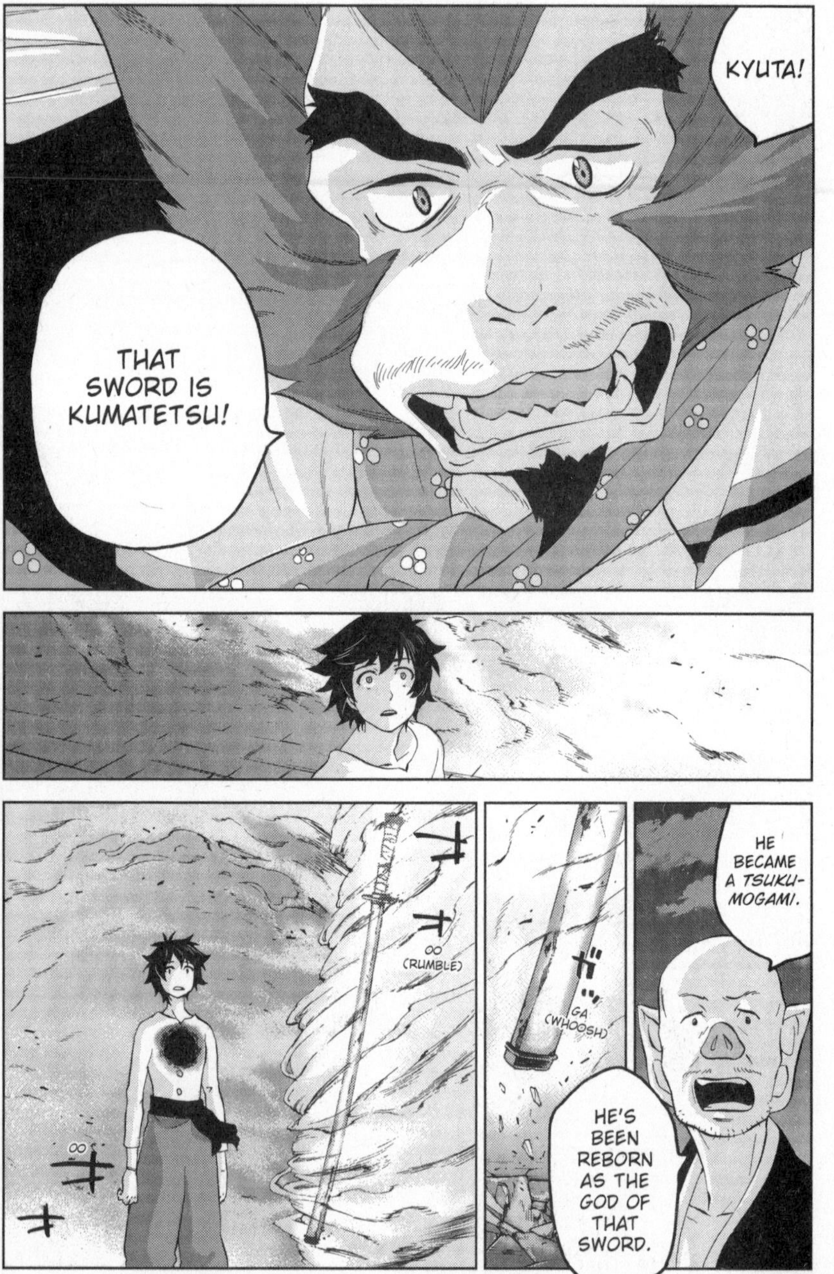
KYUTA!
THAT SWORD IS KUMATETSU!
HE BECAME A *TSUKUMOGAMI*.
HE'S BEEN REBORN AS THE GOD OF THAT SWORD.
GA (WHOOSH)
OO (RUMBLE)
OO

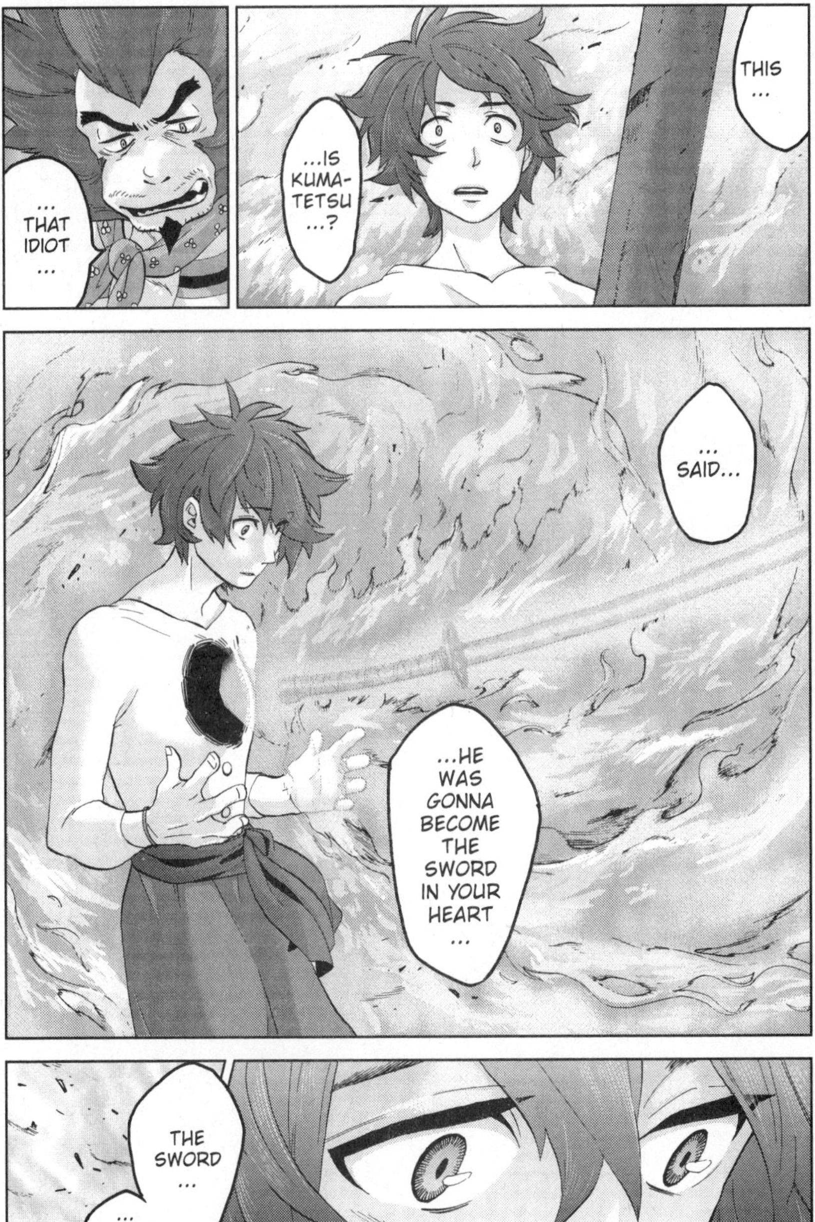
THIS ...
...IS KUMA-TETSU ...?
... THAT IDIOT ...
... SAID...
...HE WAS GONNA BECOME THE SWORD IN YOUR HEART ...
THE SWORD ...
... IN MY HEART ?

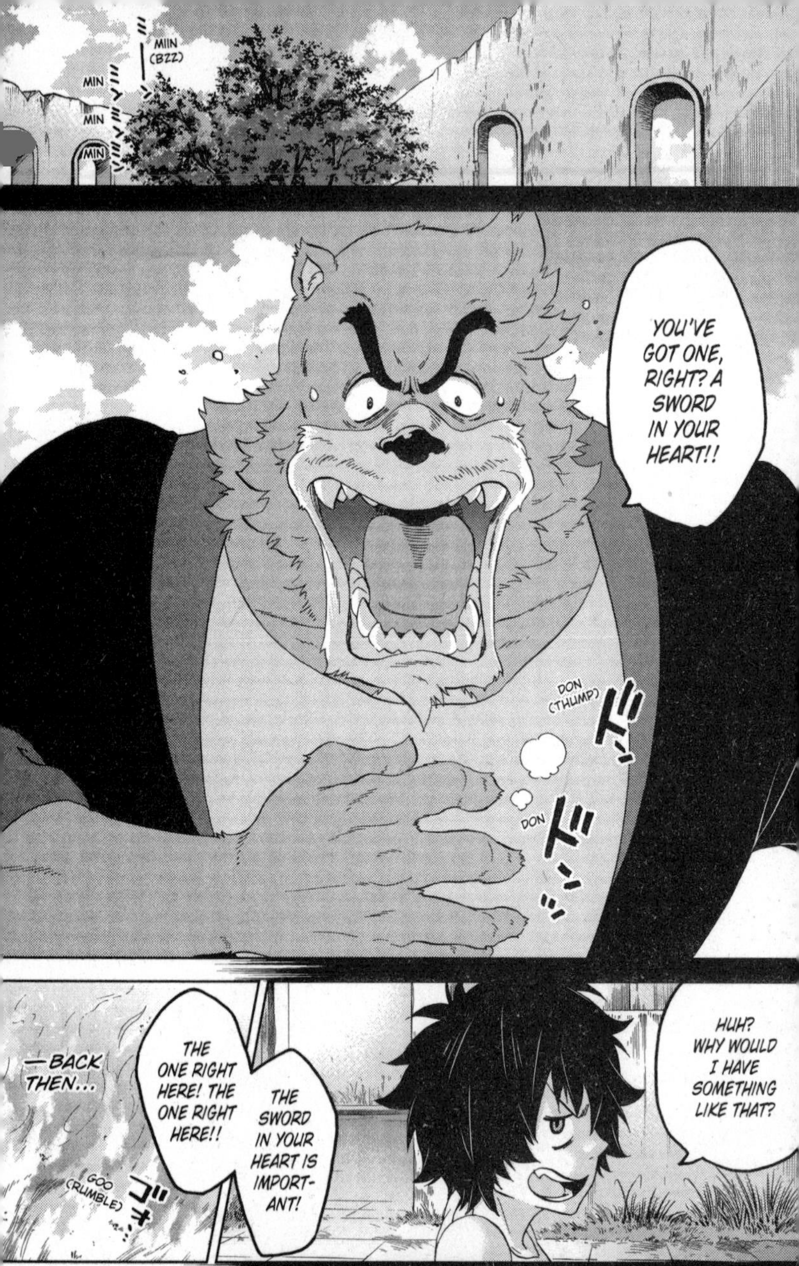
MIIN (BZZ)
MIN
MIN
MIN
YOU'VE GOT ONE, RIGHT? A SWORD IN YOUR HEART!!
DON (THUMP)
DON
HUH? WHY WOULD I HAVE SOMETHING LIKE THAT?
THE SWORD IN YOUR HEART IS IMPORT-ANT!
THE ONE RIGHT HERE! THE ONE RIGHT HERE!!
GOO (RUMBLE)
—BACK THEN...

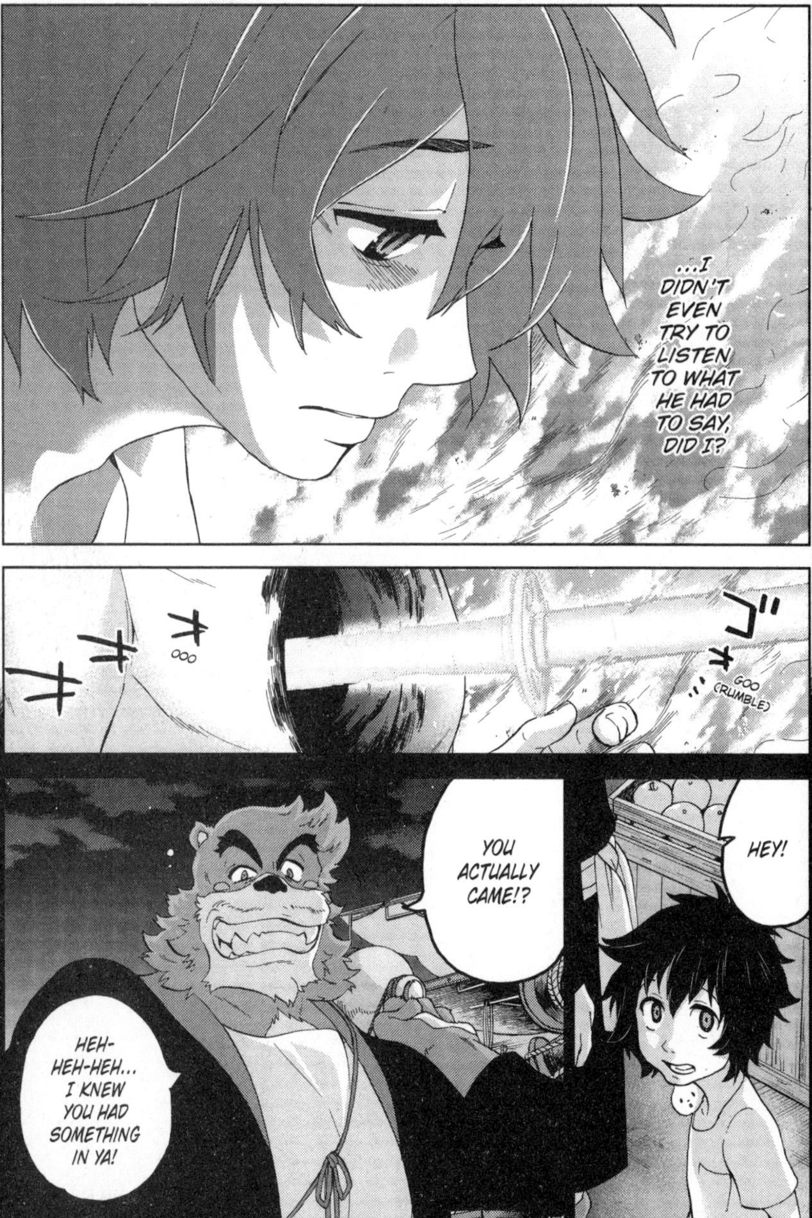
...I DIDN'T EVEN TRY TO LISTEN TO WHAT HE HAD TO SAY, DID I?
GOO (RUMBLE)
HEY!
YOU ACTUALLY CAME!?
HEH-HEH-HEH... I KNEW YOU HAD SOMETHING IN YA!

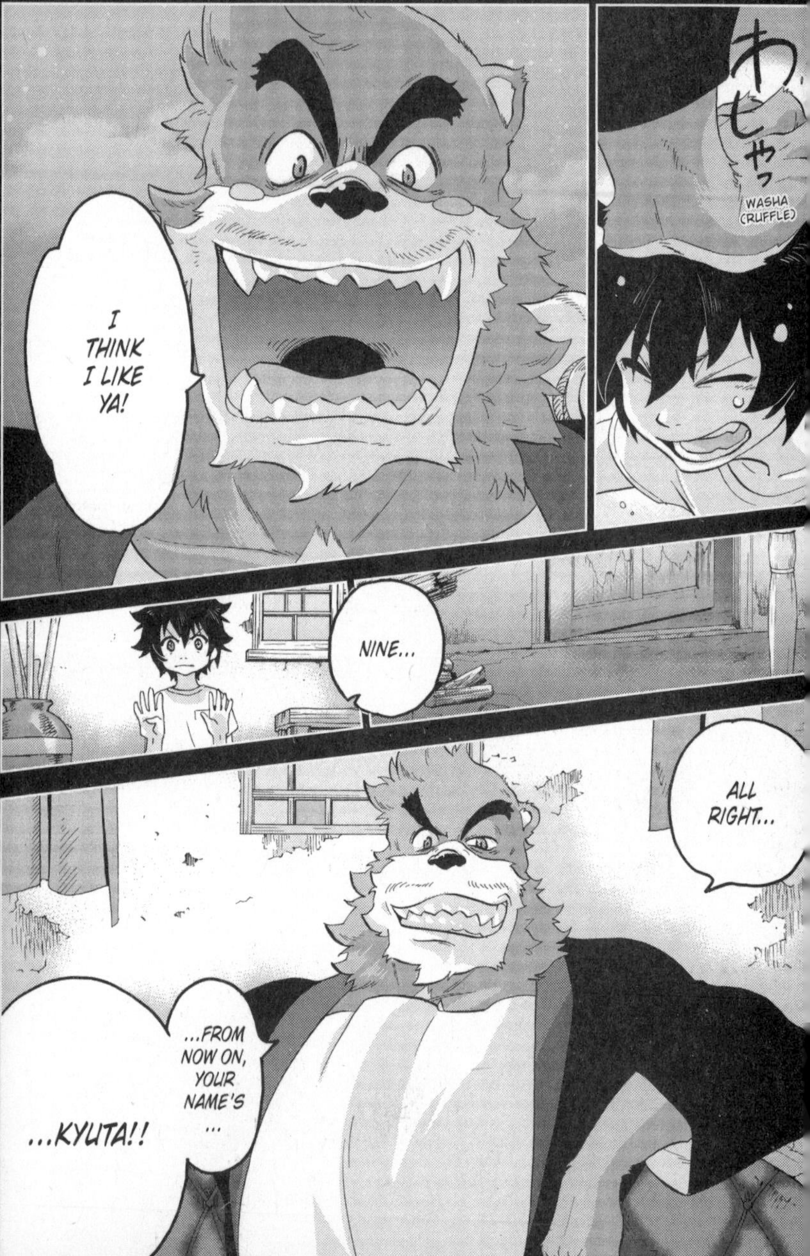
わしゃっ
WASHA (RUFFLE)
I THINK I LIKE YA!
NINE...
ALL RIGHT...
...FROM NOW ON, YOUR NAME'S ...
...KYUTA!!

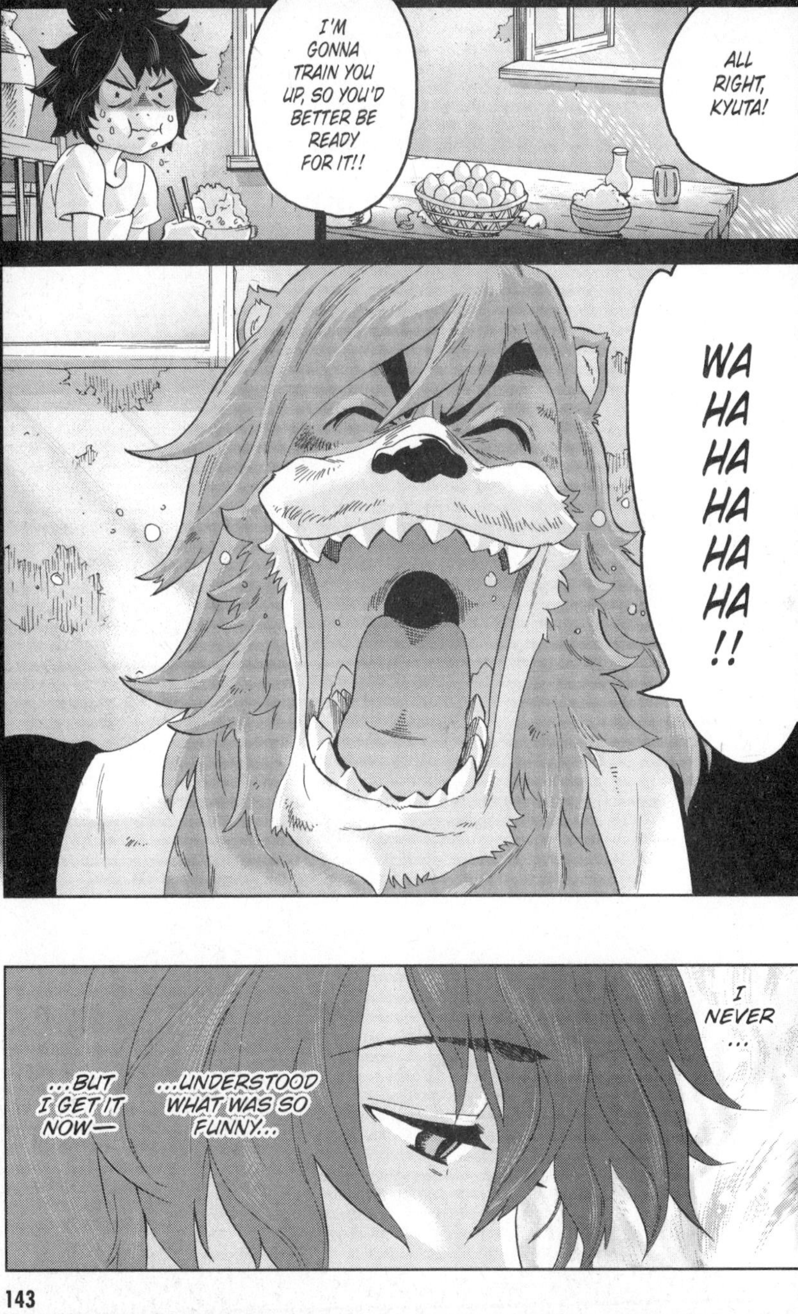
ALL RIGHT, KYUTA!
I'M GONNA TRAIN YOU UP, SO YOU'D BETTER BE READY FOR IT!!
WA HA HA HA HA HA!!
I NEVER...
...UNDERSTOOD WHAT WAS SO FUNNY...
...BUT I GET IT NOW—

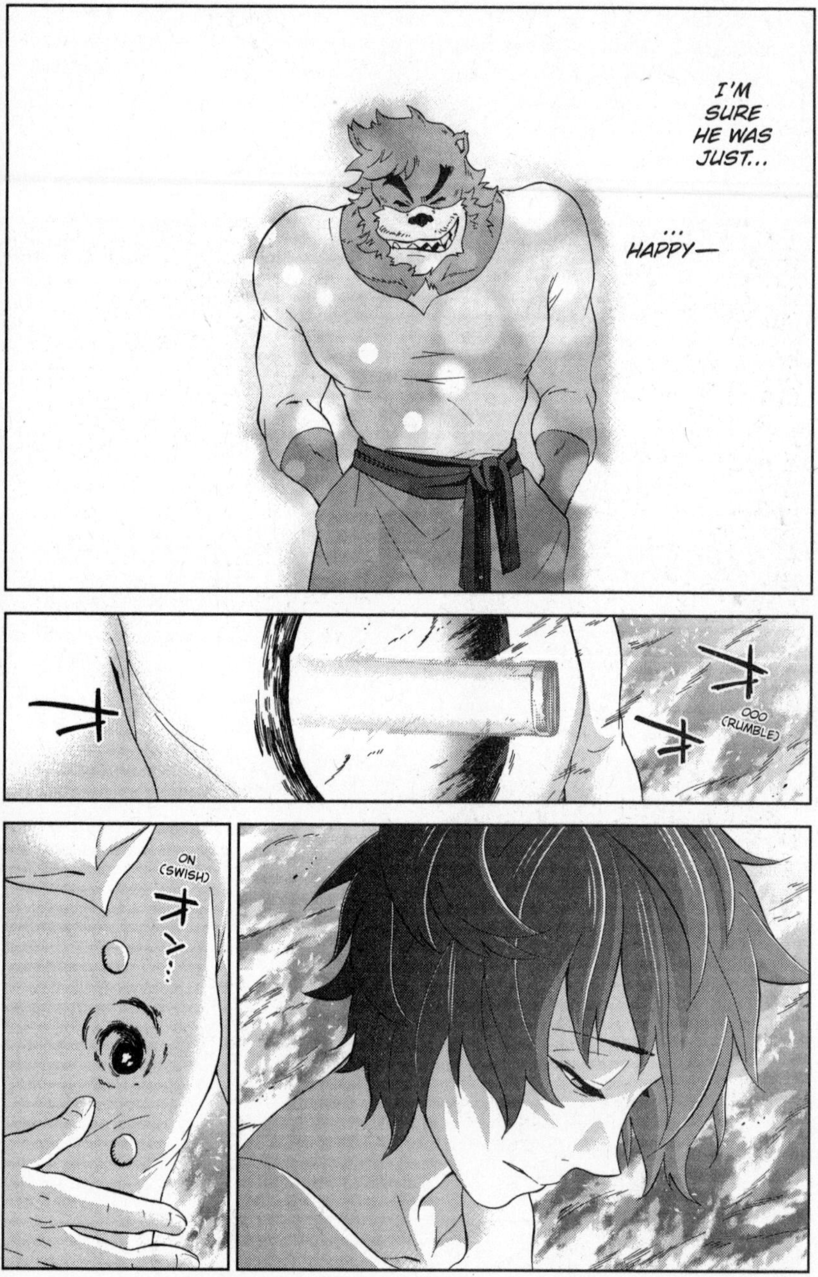
I'M SURE HE WAS JUST...
...HAPPY—
OOO (RUMBLE)
ON (SWISH)
オン...

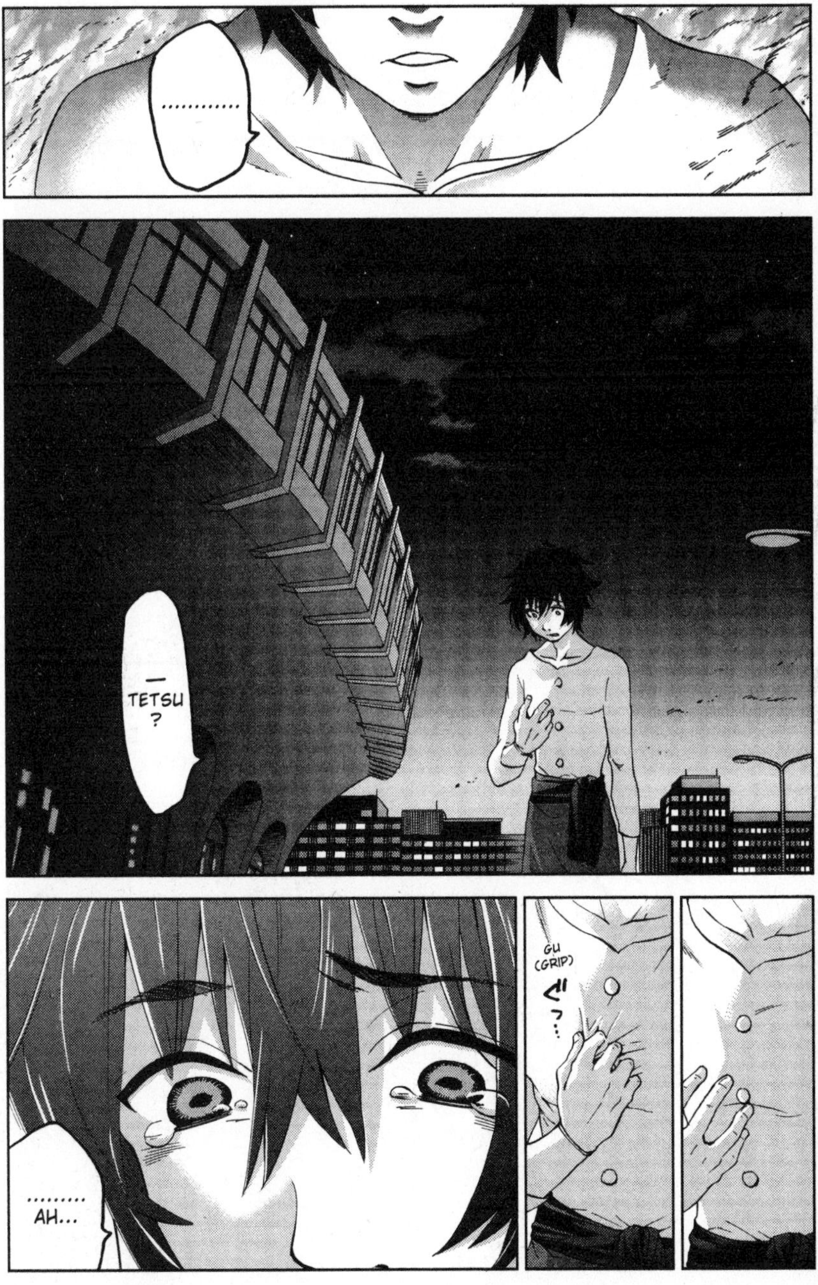
....
— TETSU ?
GU (GRIP)
ぐっ…
....
AH...

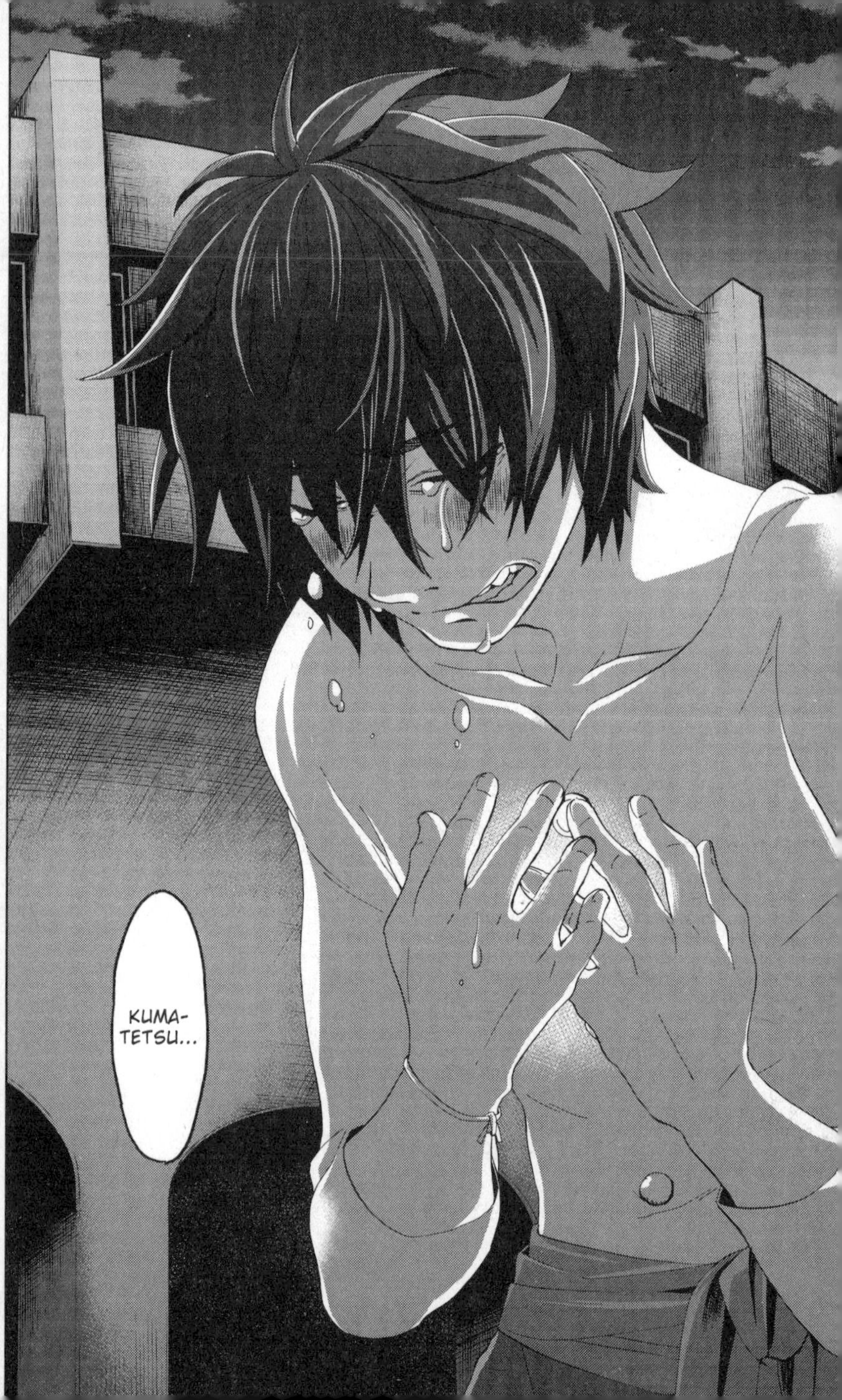
KUMA-TETSU...

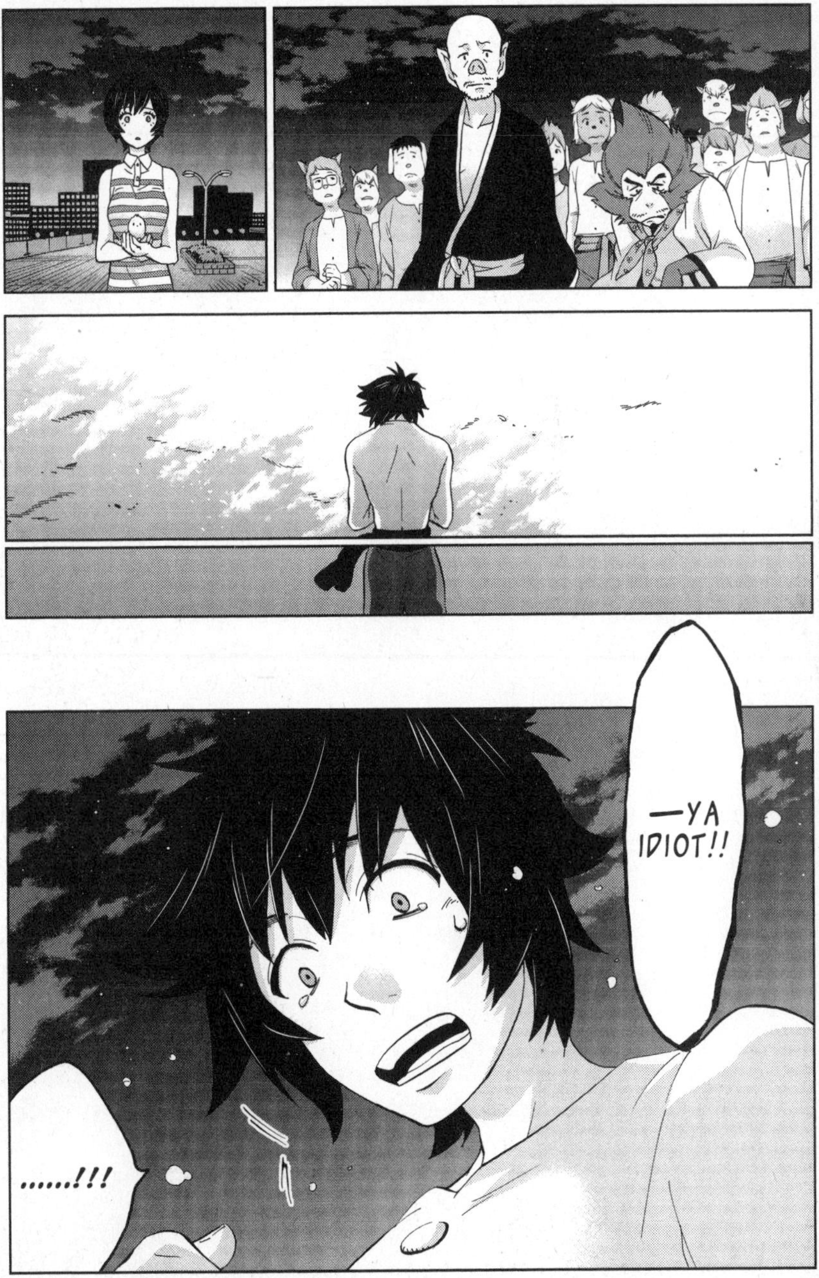
—YA IDIOT!!
......!!!

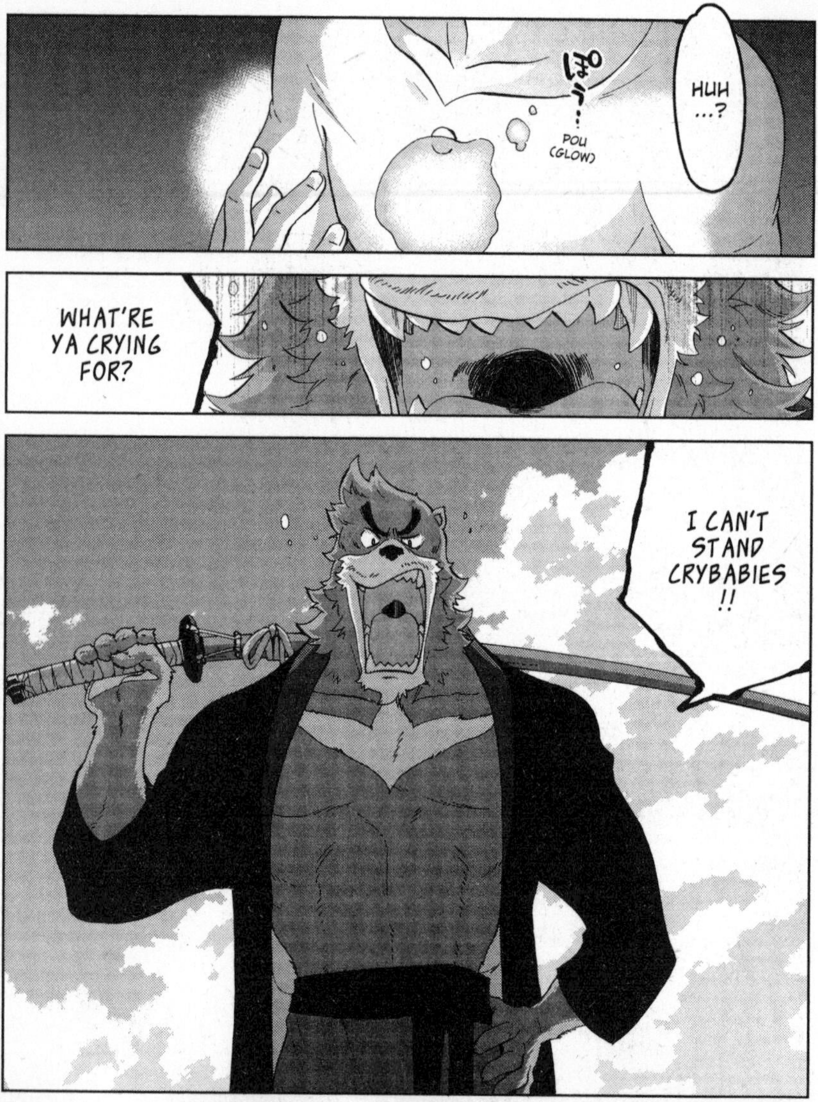

...
HUH ...?
ぽぅ…
POU (GLOW)
WHAT'RE YA CRYING FOR?
I CAN'T STAND CRYBABIES !!
.........!!!

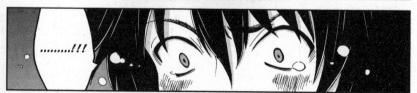

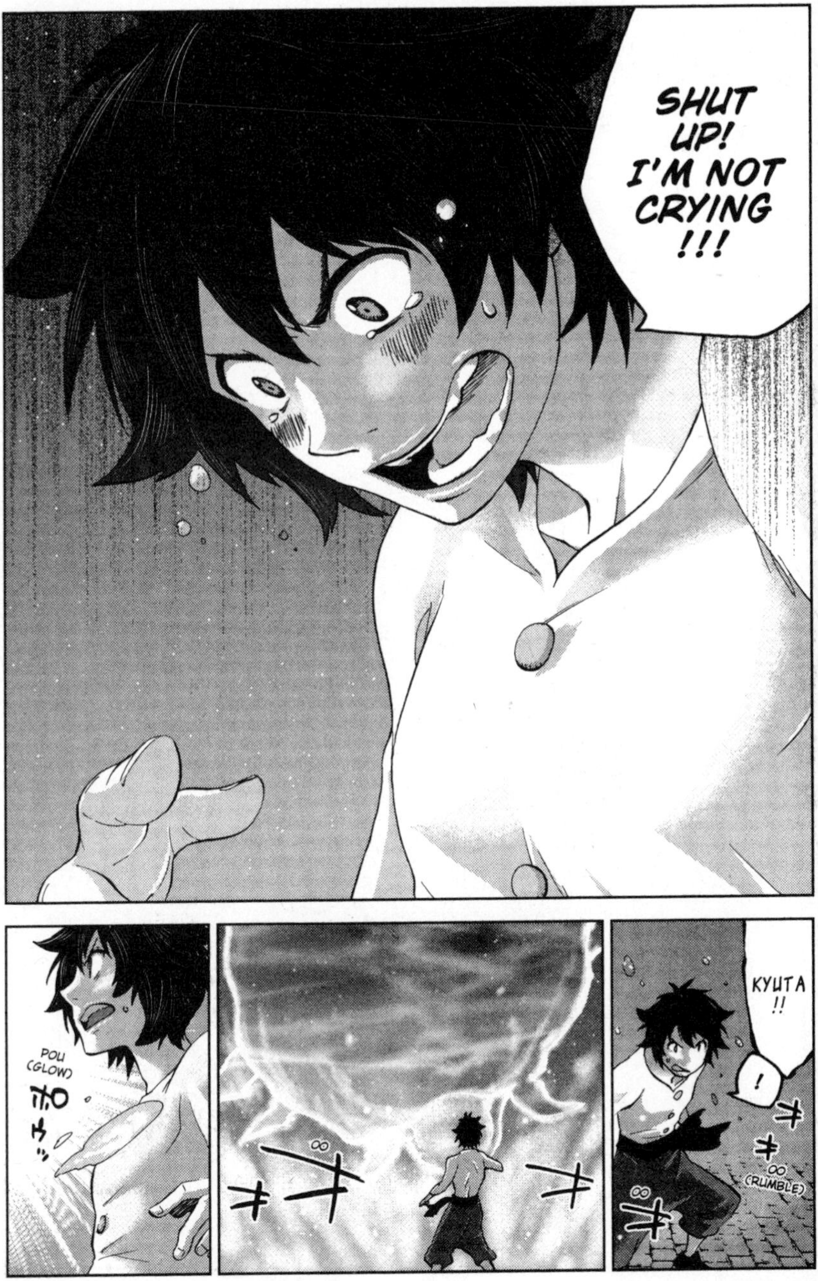
SHUT UP! I'M NOT CRYING !!!
KYUTA !!
!
(RUMBLE)
POU (GLOW)

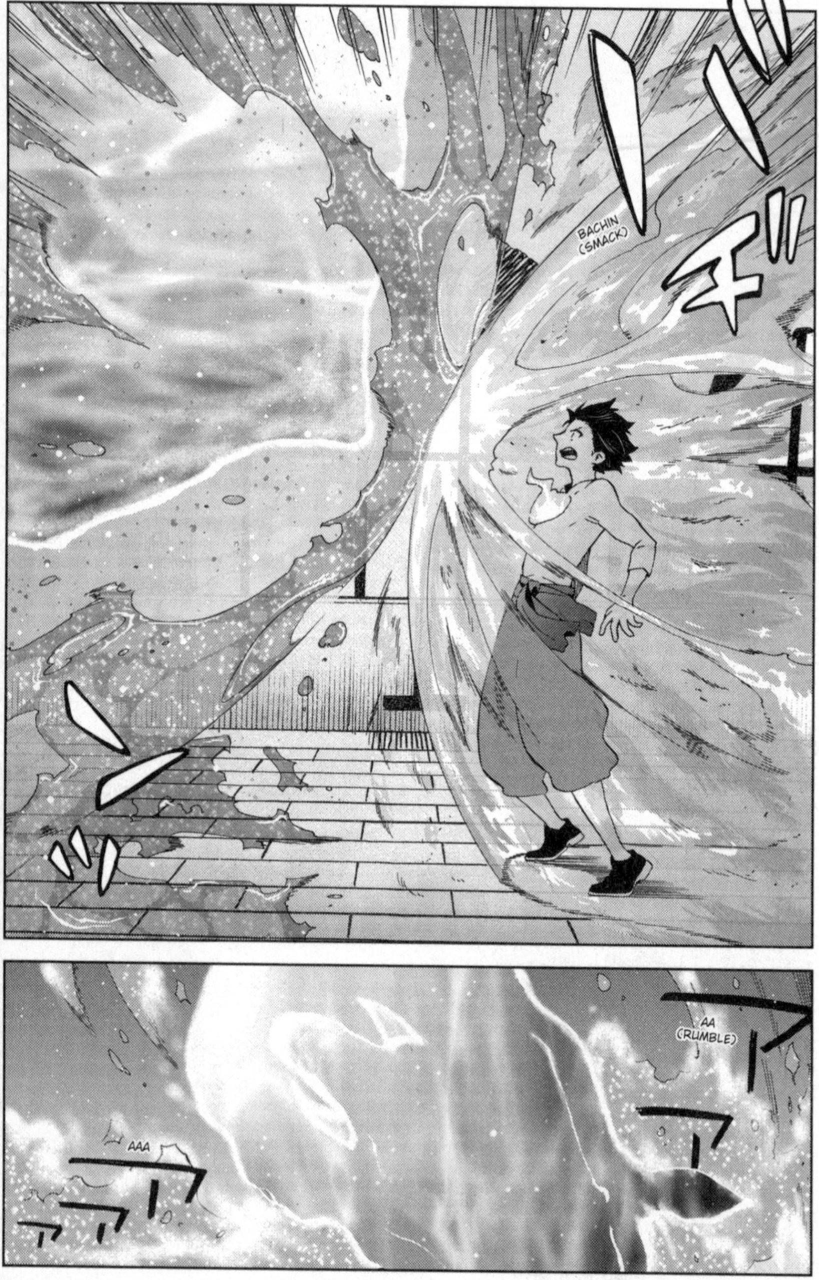
BACHIN
(SMACK)
AA
(RUMBLE)
AAA

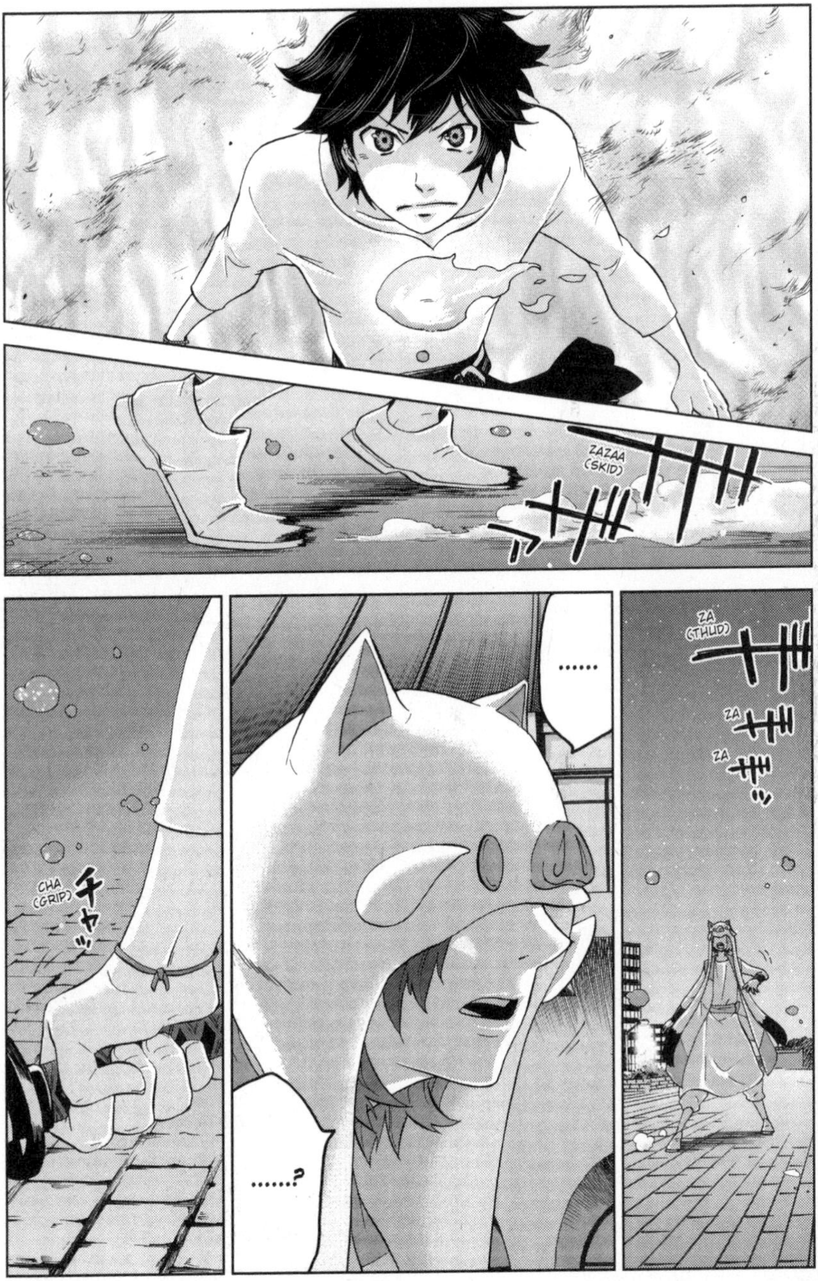
ZAZAA (SKID)
ZA (THUD)
ZA
ZA
......
......?
CHA (GRIP)

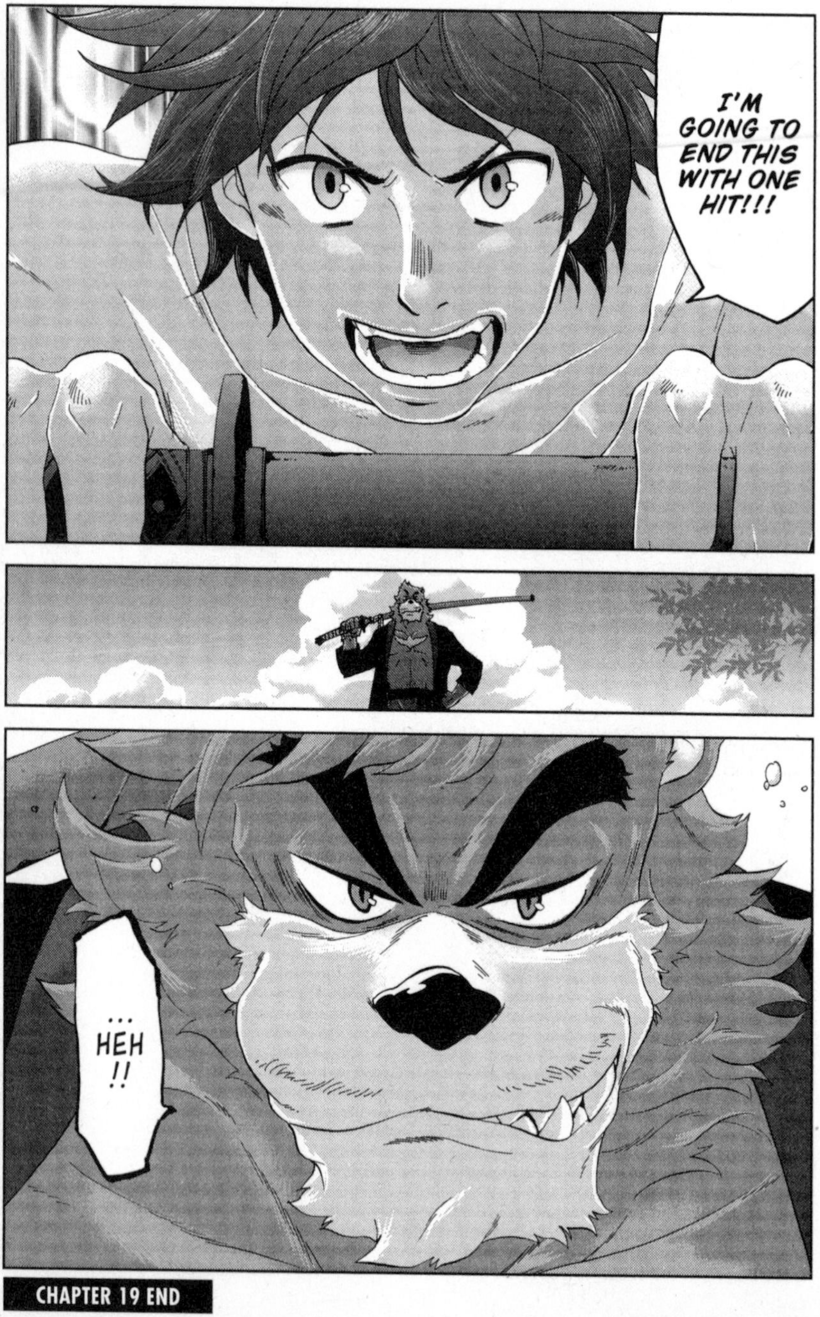
I'M GOING TO END THIS WITH ONE HIT!!!
... HEH !!

CHAPTER 19 END

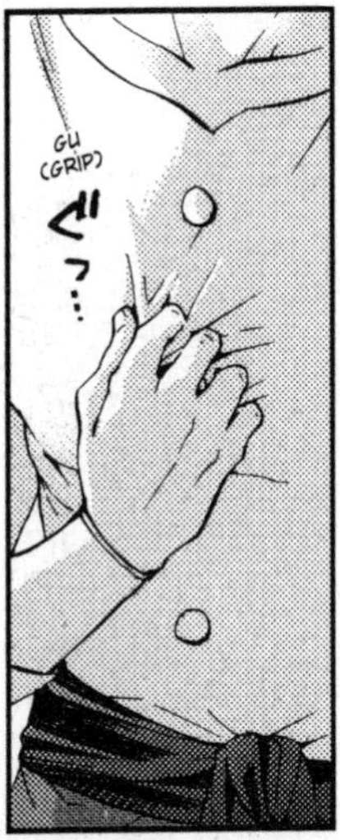
GU
(GRIP)
グッ…

THE BOY & THE BEAST

FINAL CHAPTER TO THE FUTURE!

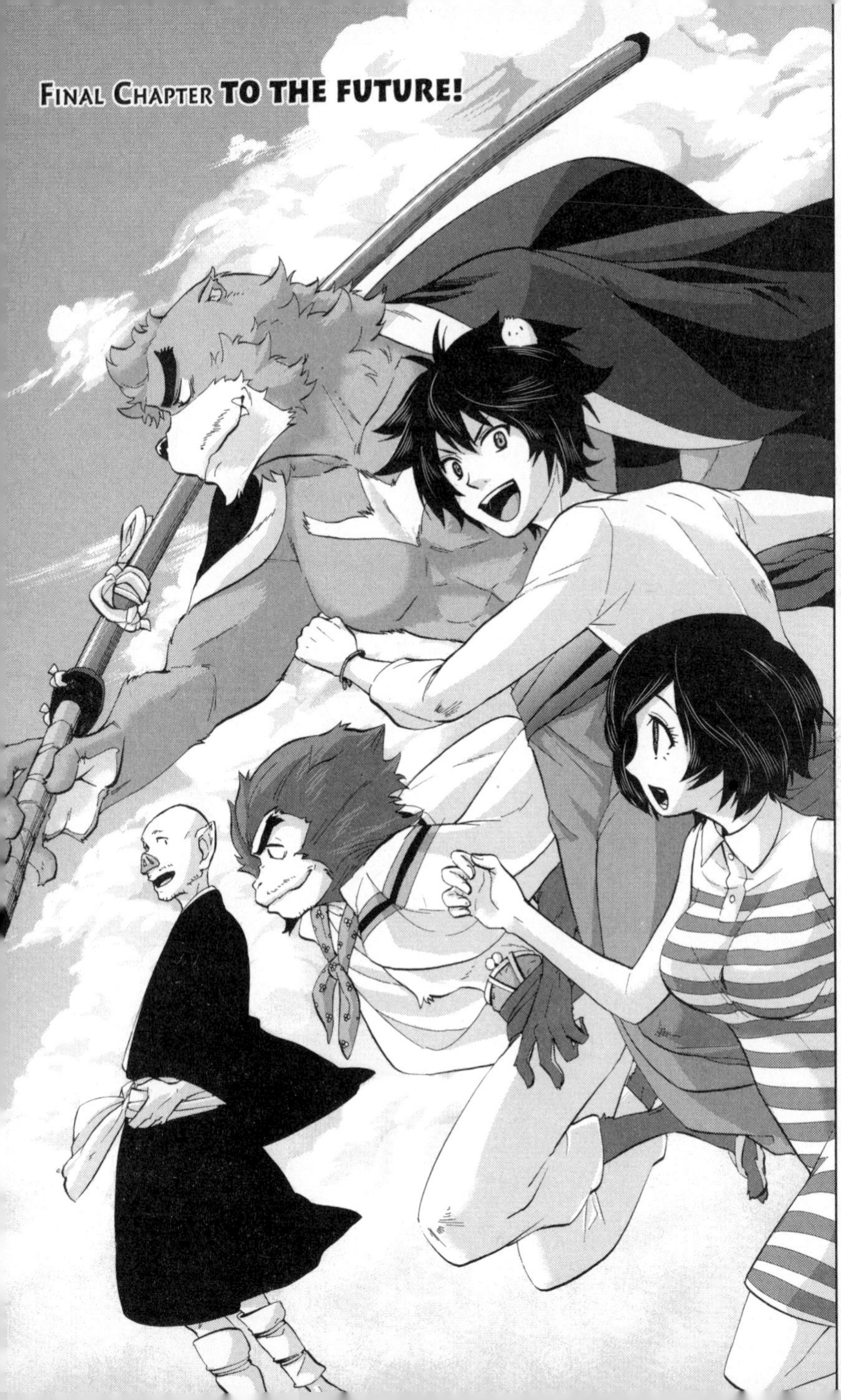

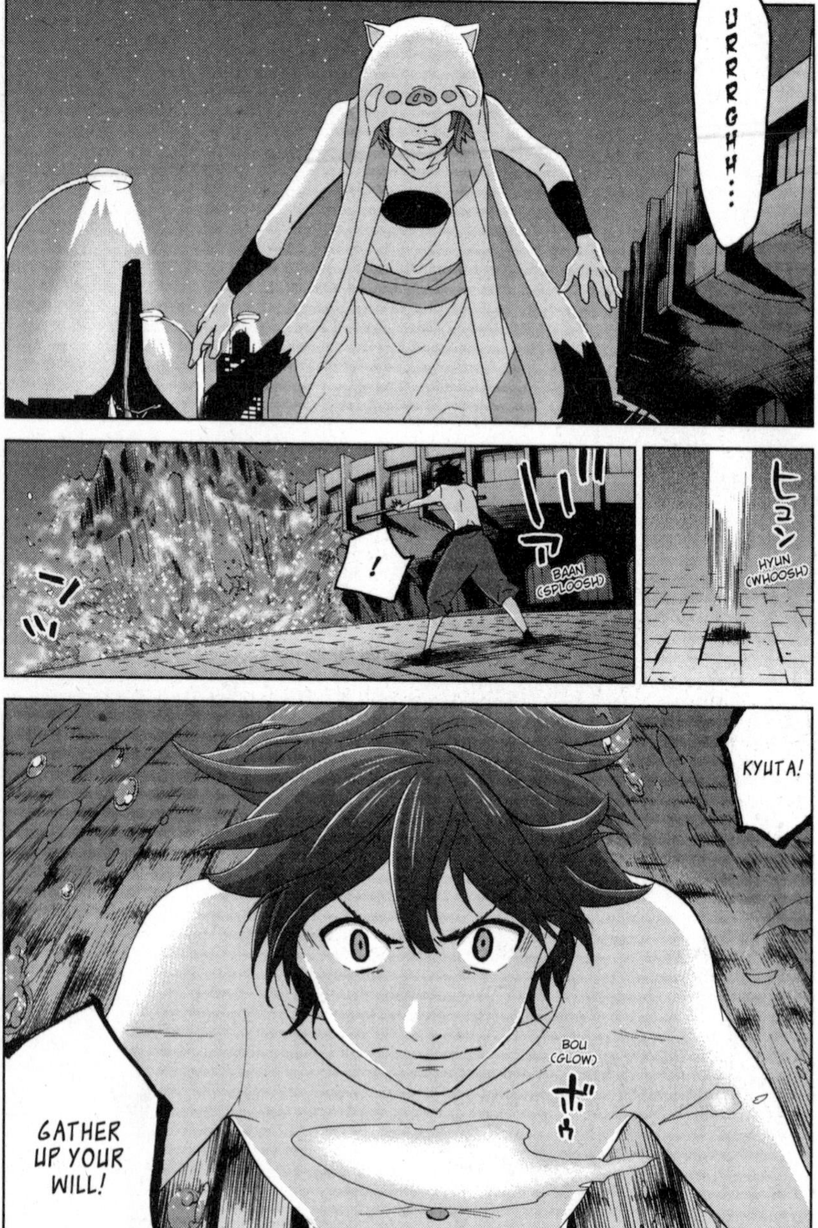
URRRGHH...
ヒュン
HYUN (WHOOSH)
BAAN (SPLOOSH)
!
KYUTA!
BOU (GLOW)
ボゥ
GATHER UP YOUR WILL!

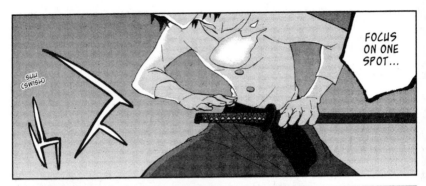

FOCUS ON ONE SPOT...

SUU
(SWISH)

...AND AIM AT YOUR TARGET!!!

GO
(RUMBLE)

DOOOO
(WHOOSH)

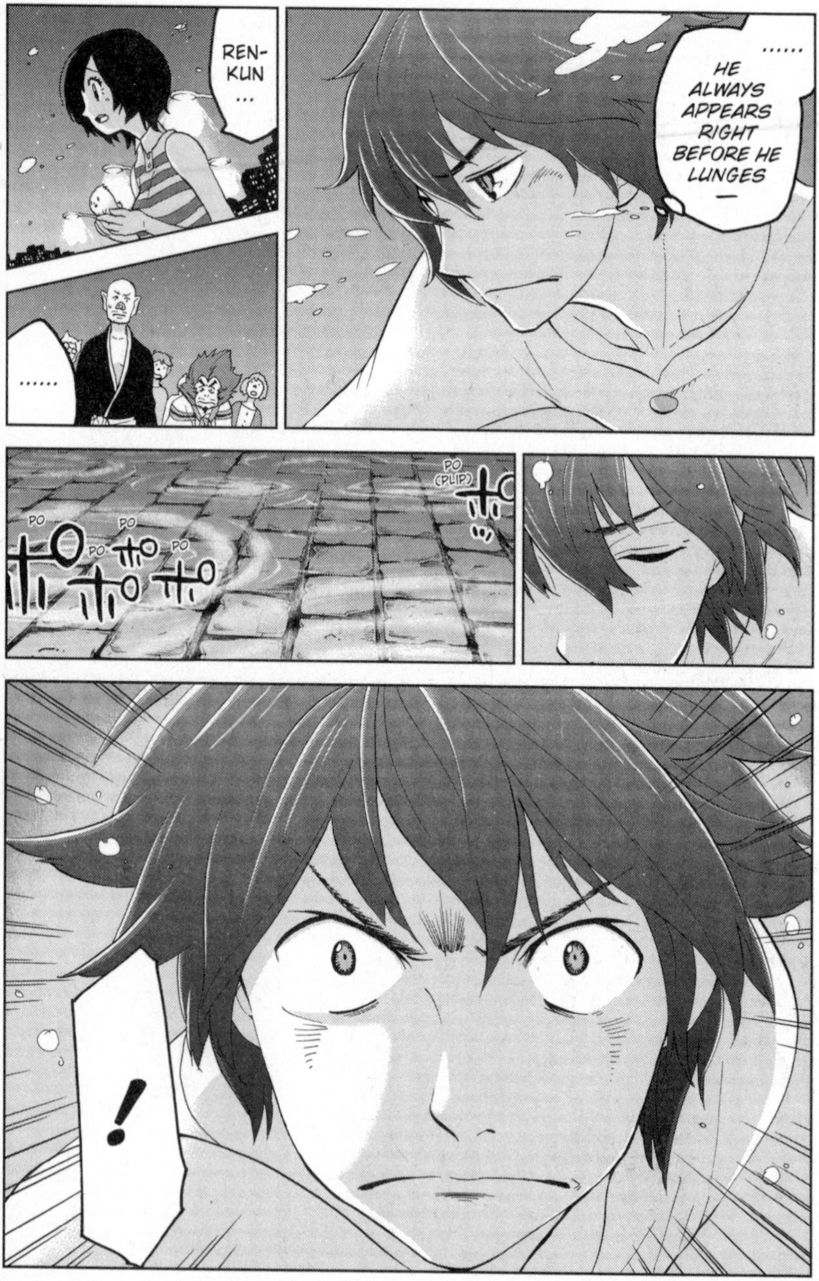
......
HE ALWAYS APPEARS RIGHT BEFORE HE LUNGES —
REN-KUN ...
......
PO (PLIP)
PO PO PO PO
!

NOW
!!!

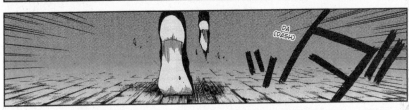

DA
(DASH)

SHUN
(SWISH)

!!??

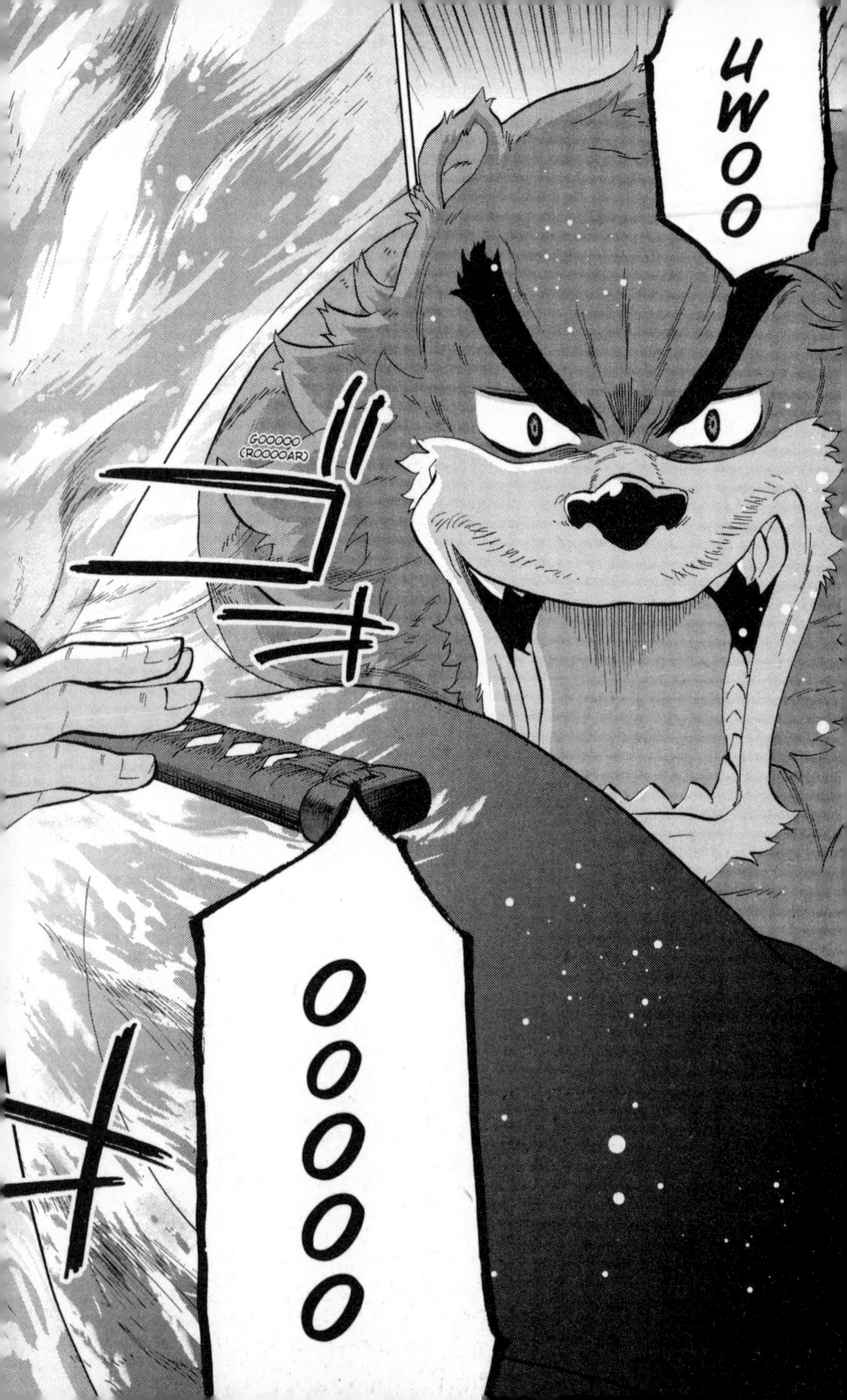
UWOO
GOOOOO (ROOOOAR)
OOOOOO

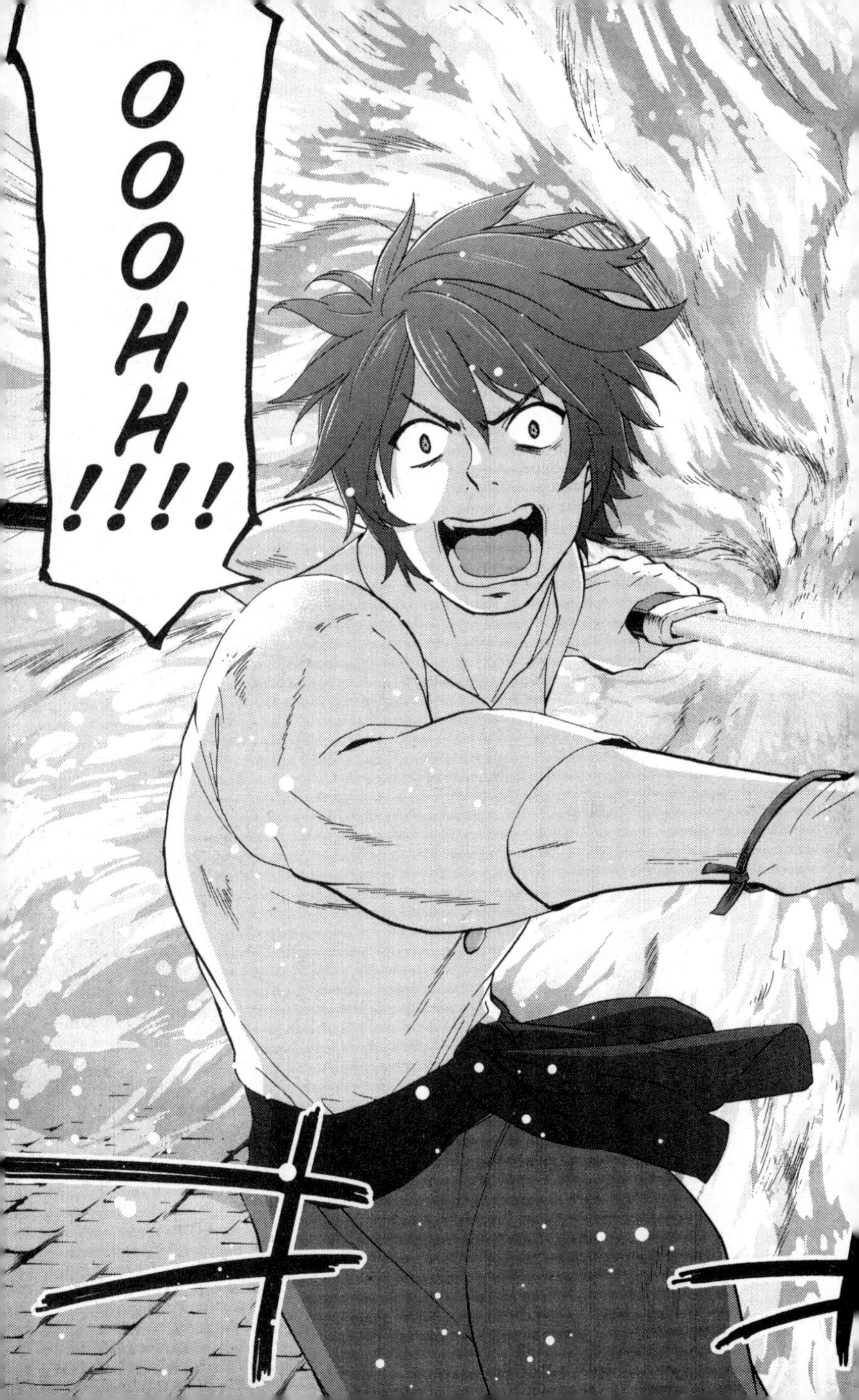
OOOHH!!!!

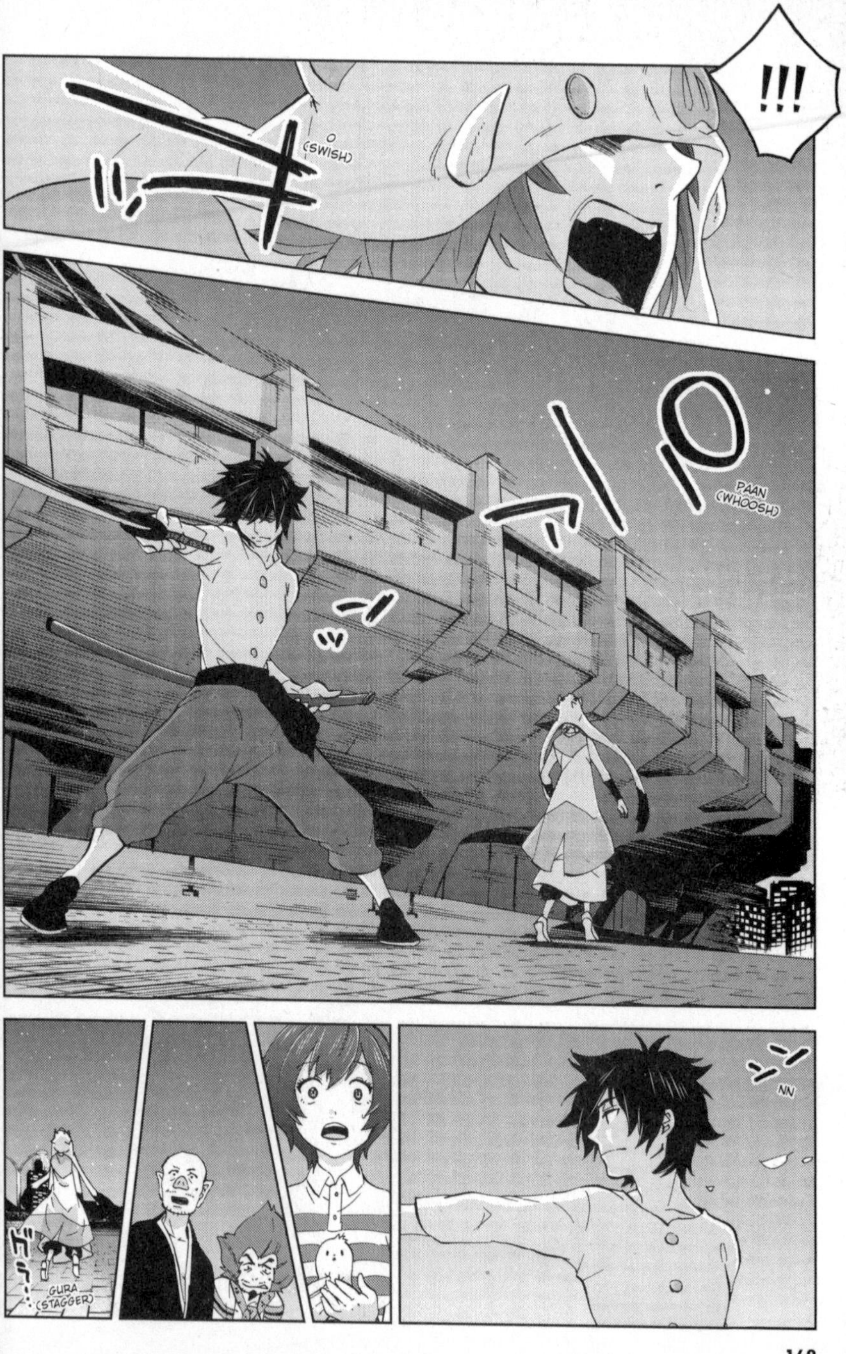
!!!
O (SWISH)
PAAN (WHOOSH)
NN
GURA (STAGGER)

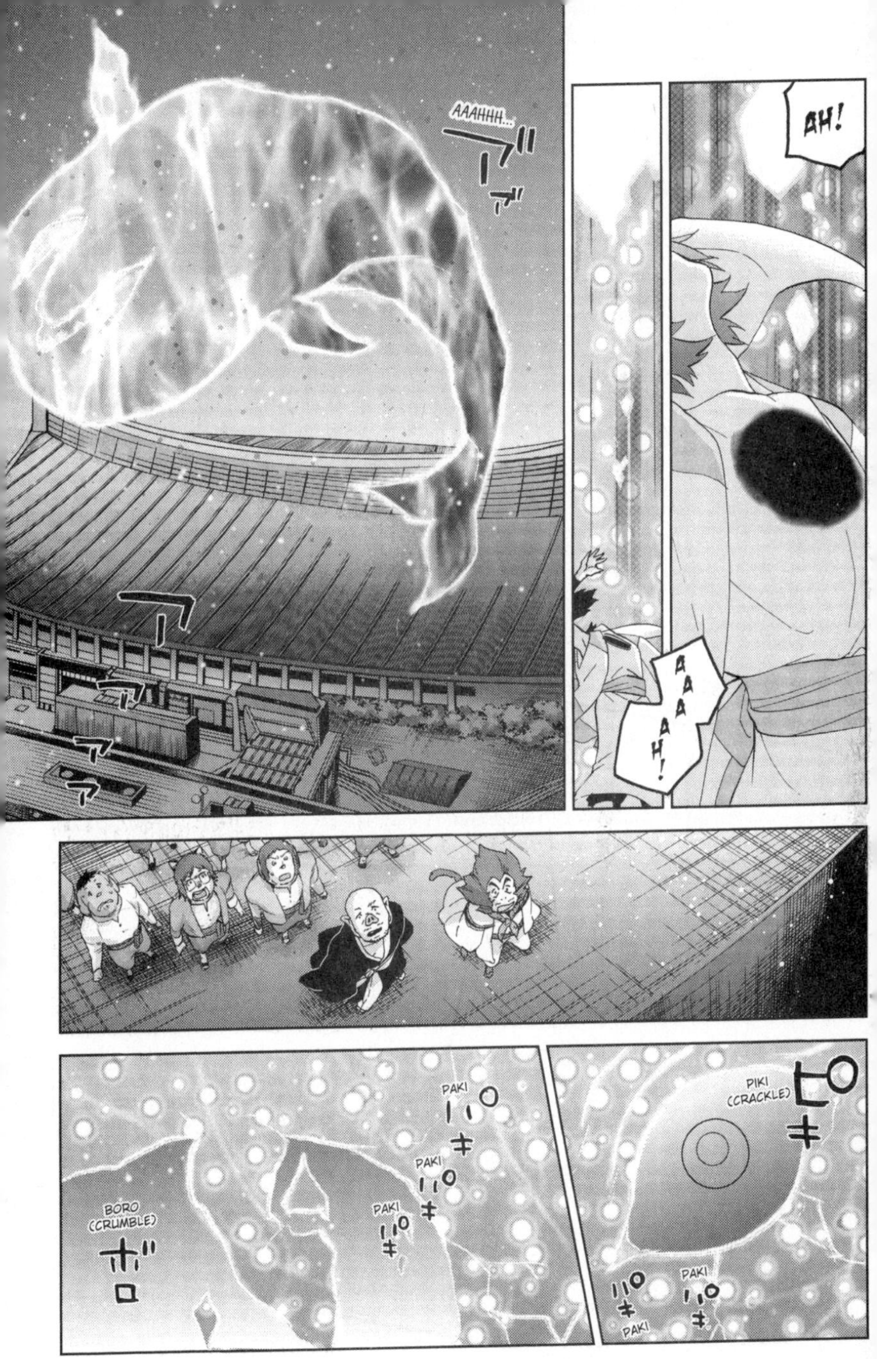
AH!
AAAAH!
AAAHHH...
PIKI (CRACKLE)
ピキ
PAKI
パキ
PAKI
パキ
PAKI
パキ
PAKI
パキ
PAKI
パキ
BORO (CRUMBLE)
ボロ

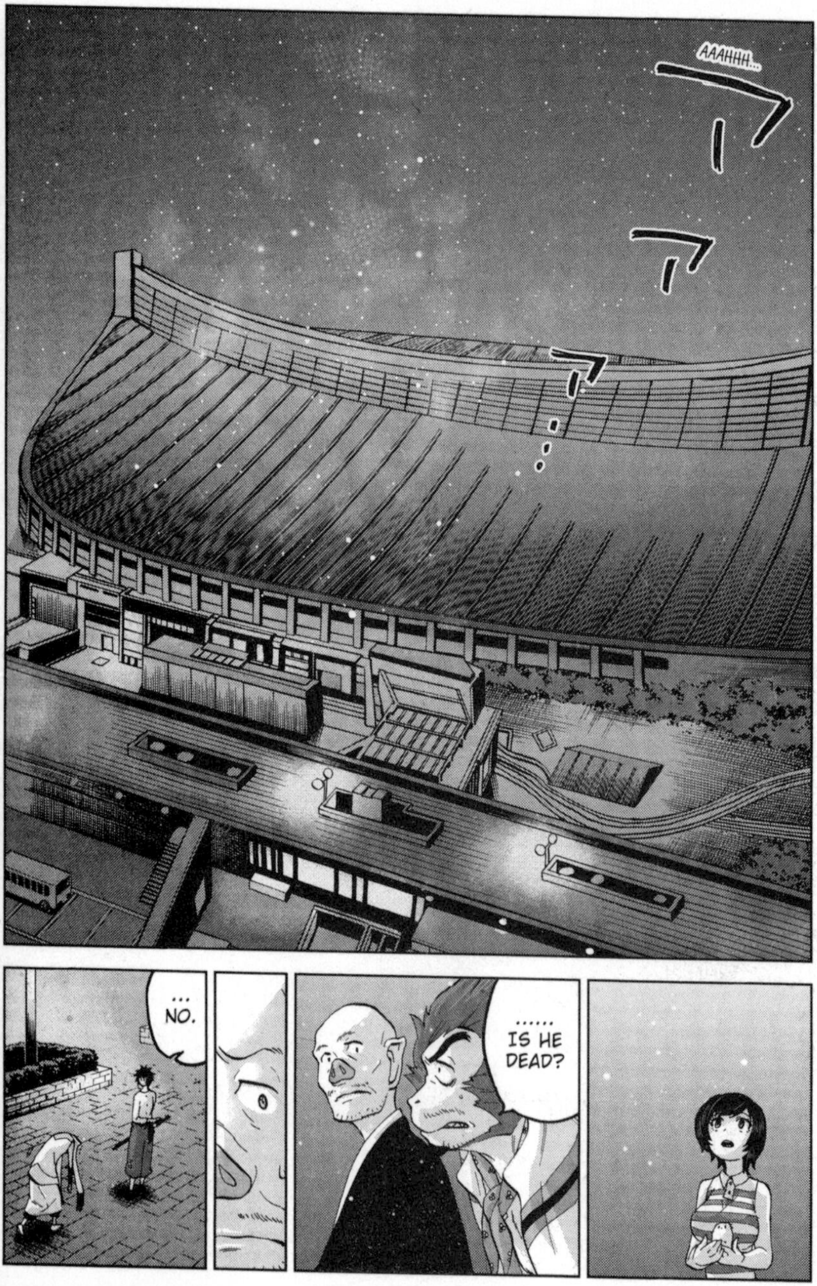
AAAHHH...
アーアア…
...... IS HE DEAD?
... NO.

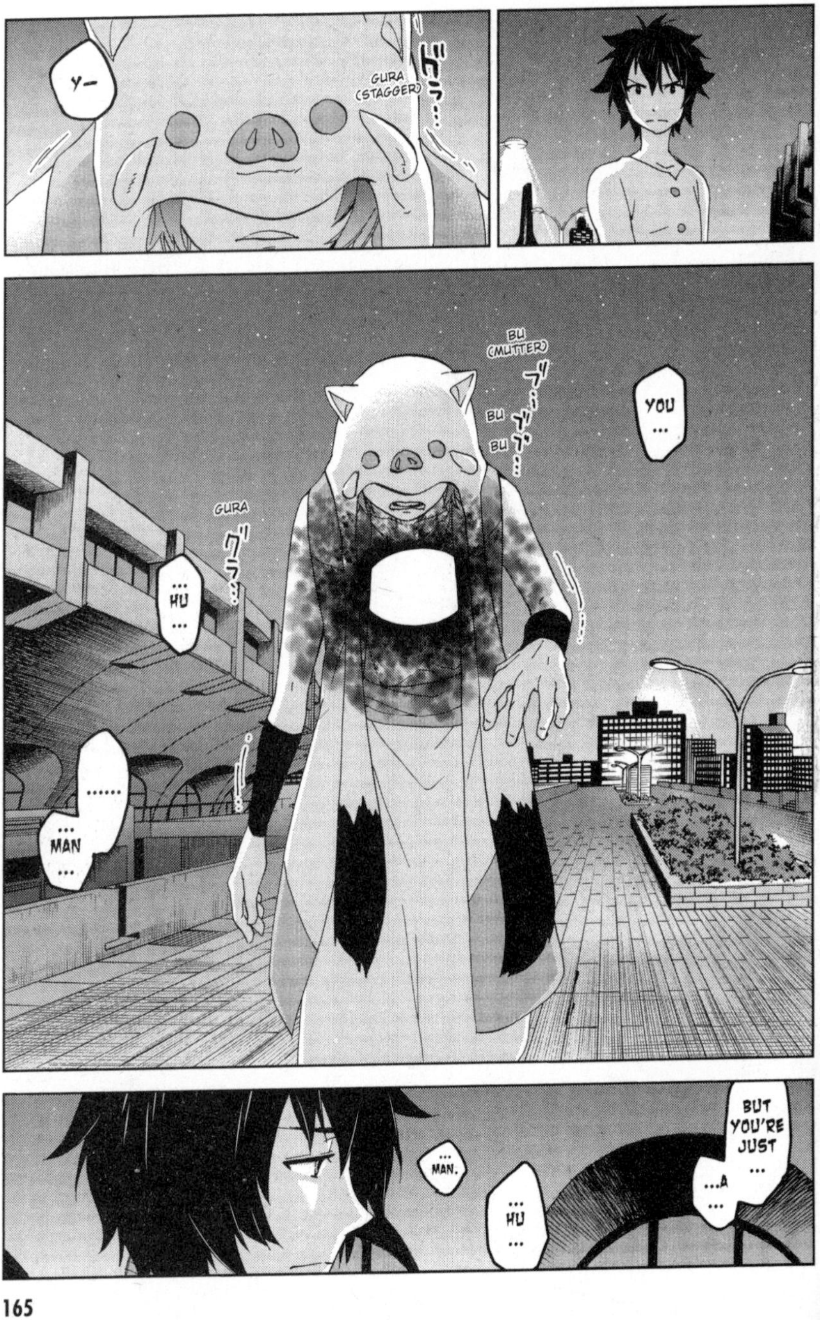
Y–
GURA (STAGGER)
グラ…
YOU …
BU (MUTTER)
ブ…ブブ…
BU BU
GURA
グラ…
… HU …
……
… MAN …
BUT YOU'RE JUST …
…A …
… HU …
… MAN.

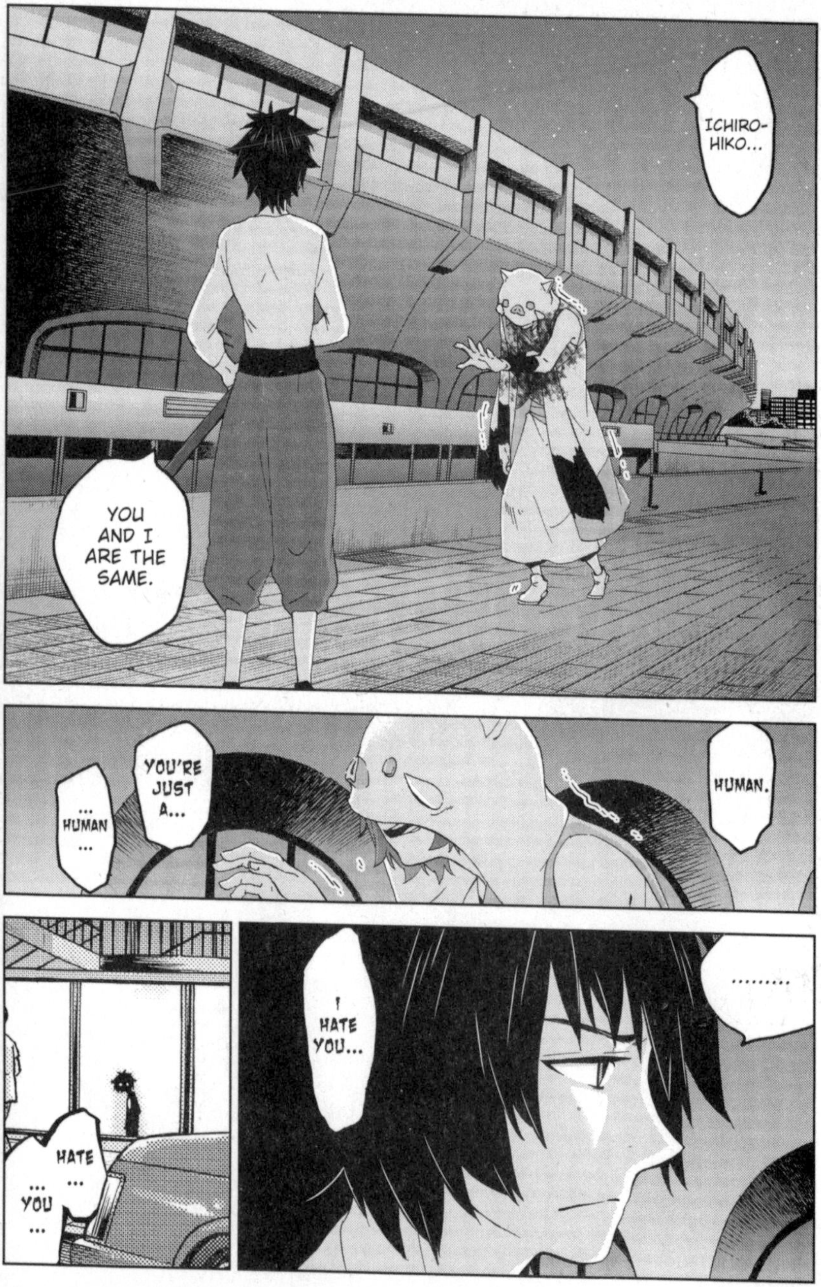
ICHIRO-HIKO...
YOU AND I ARE THE SAME.
HUMAN.
YOU'RE JUST A...
...HUMAN...
....
I HATE YOU...
HATE... ...YOU...

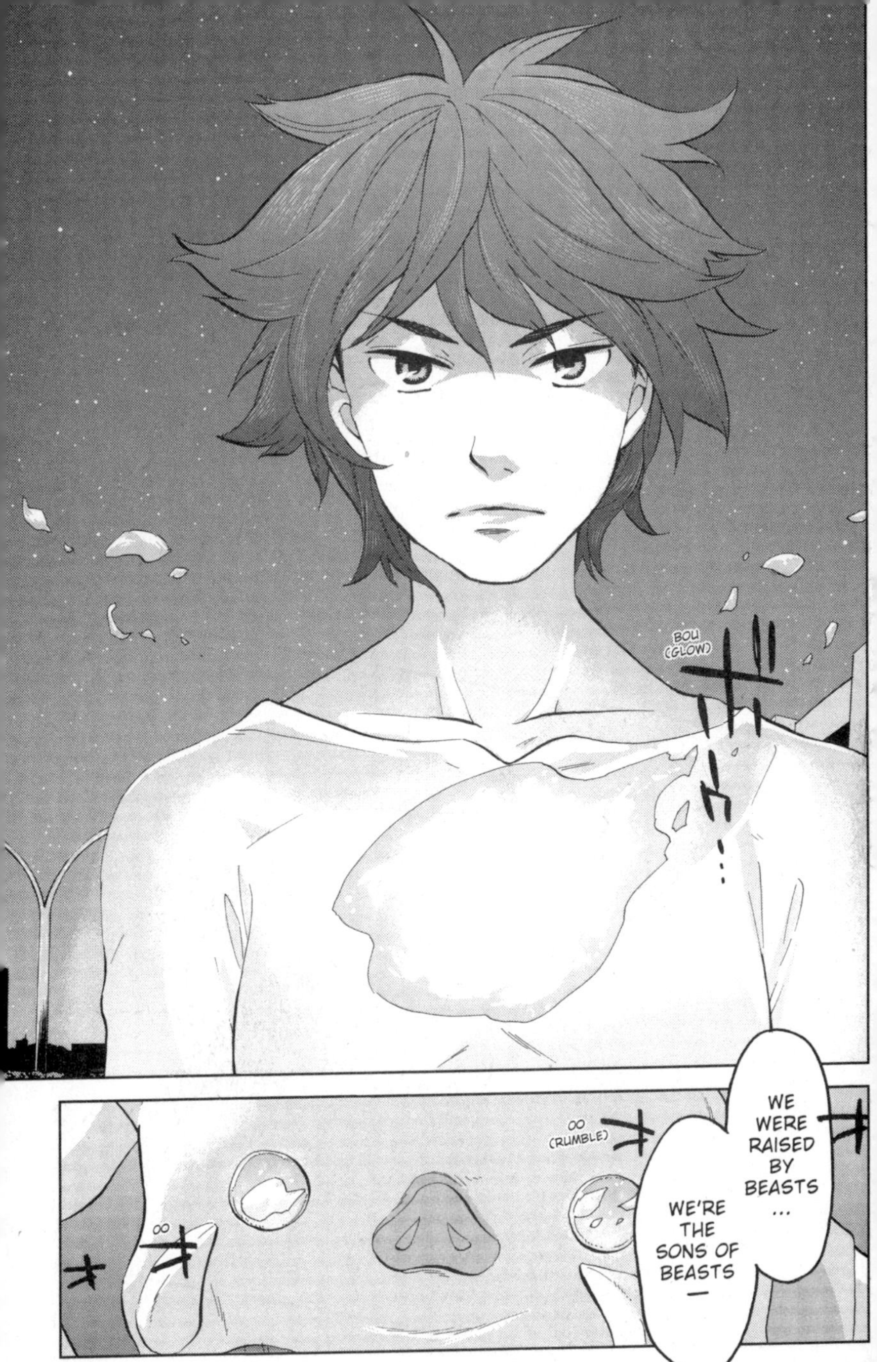
BOU (GLOW)
WE WERE RAISED BY BEASTS...
WE'RE THE SONS OF BEASTS—
OO (RUMBLE)
OO

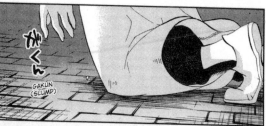

GAKUN
(SLUMP)

DOSA
(THUD)

SU
(SWISH)

YOU'RE
JUST
A...

...HU...

...MAN.

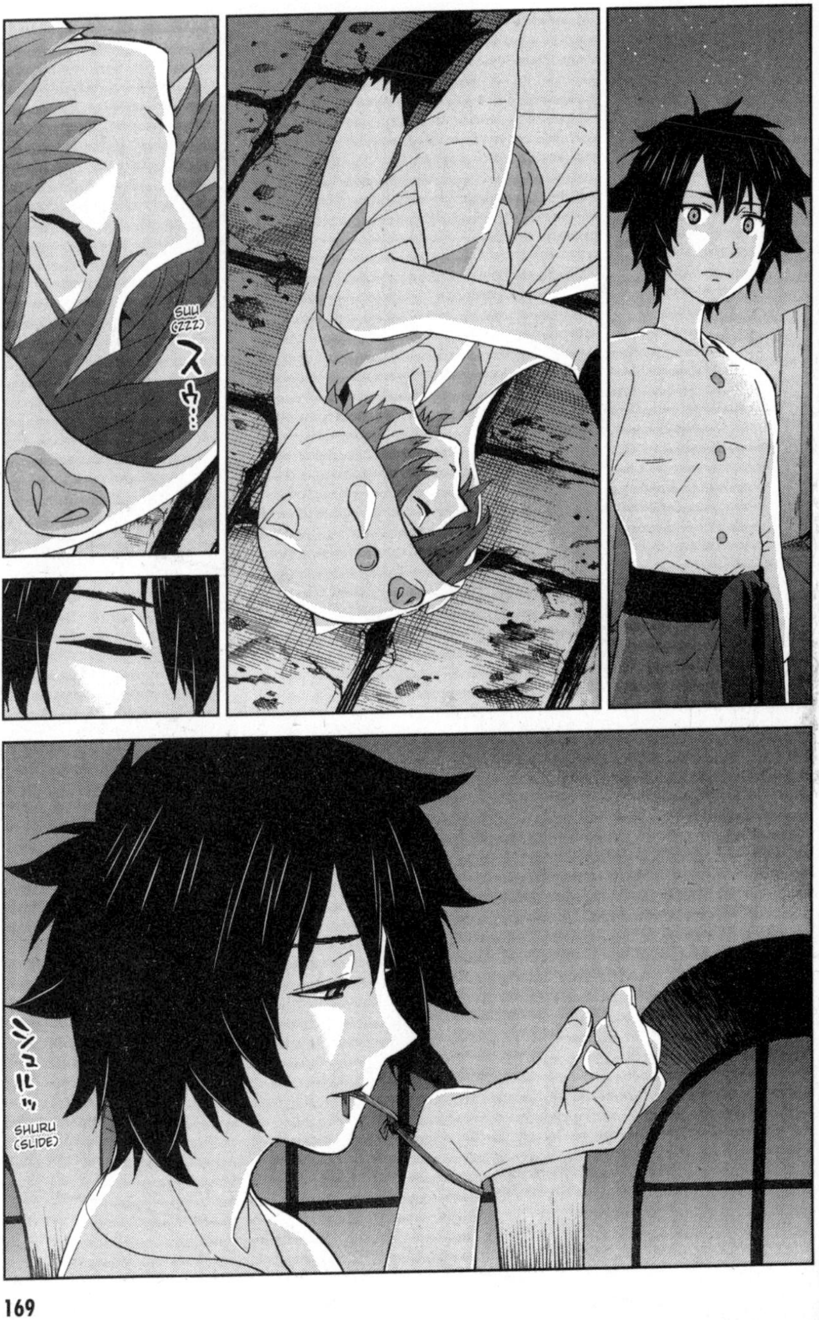
SUU (ZZZ)
スゥ…
シュルッ
SHURU (SLIDE)

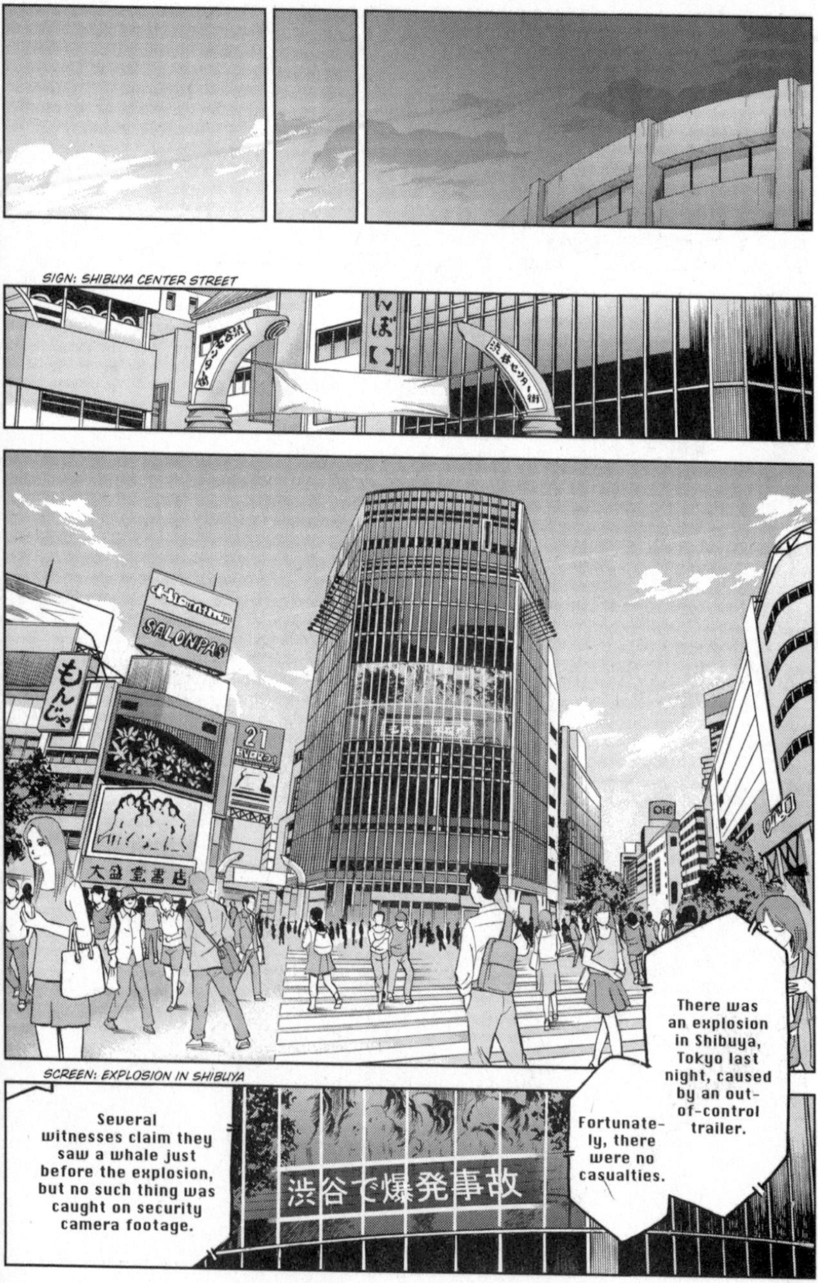
SIGN: SHIBUYA CENTER STREET
渋谷センター街
SALONPAS
もんじゃ
21
大盛堂書店
SCREEN: EXPLOSION IN SHIBUYA
There was an explosion in Shibuya, Tokyo last night, caused by an out-of-control trailer.
Fortunate-ly, there were no casualties.
渋谷で爆発事故
Several witnesses claim they saw a whale just before the explosion, but no such thing was caught on security camera footage.

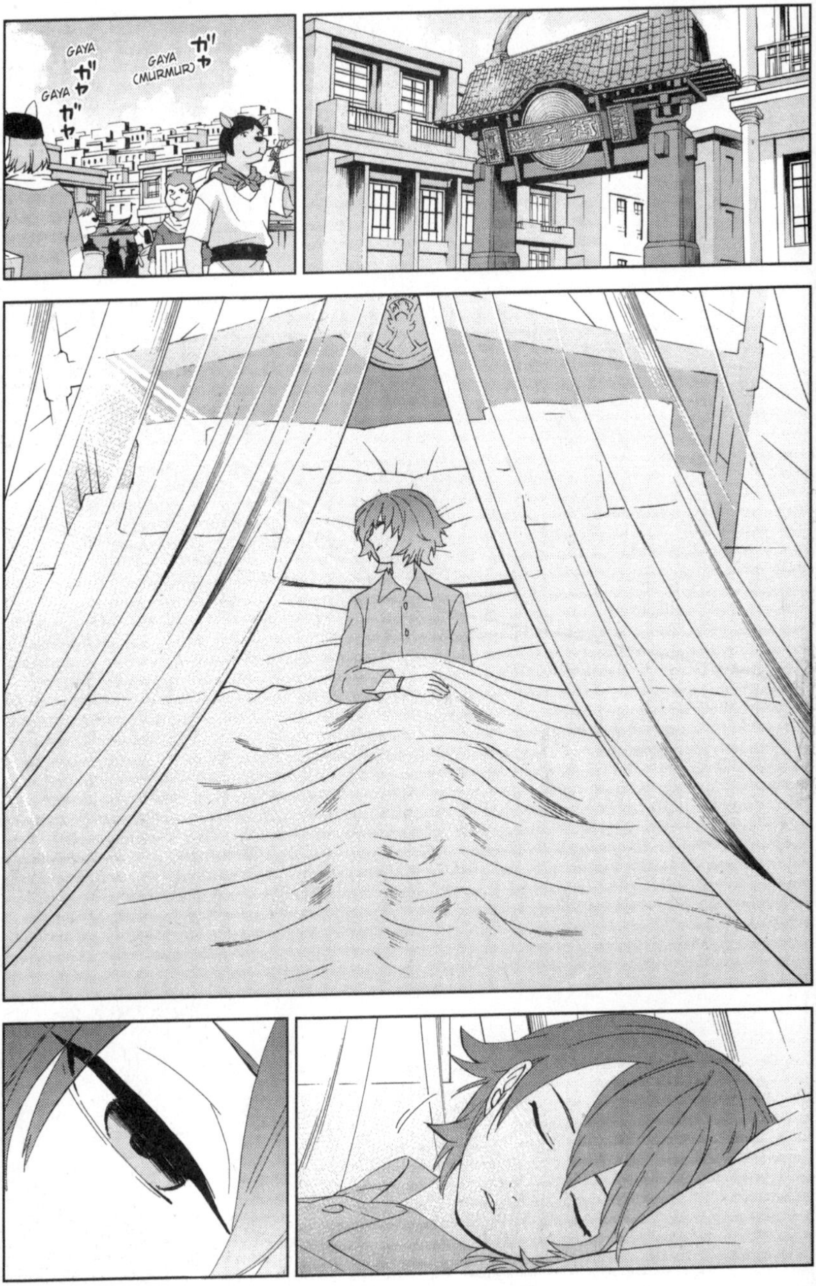
ガヤ
GAYA (MURMUR)
GAYA
ガヤ
GAYA
ガヤ

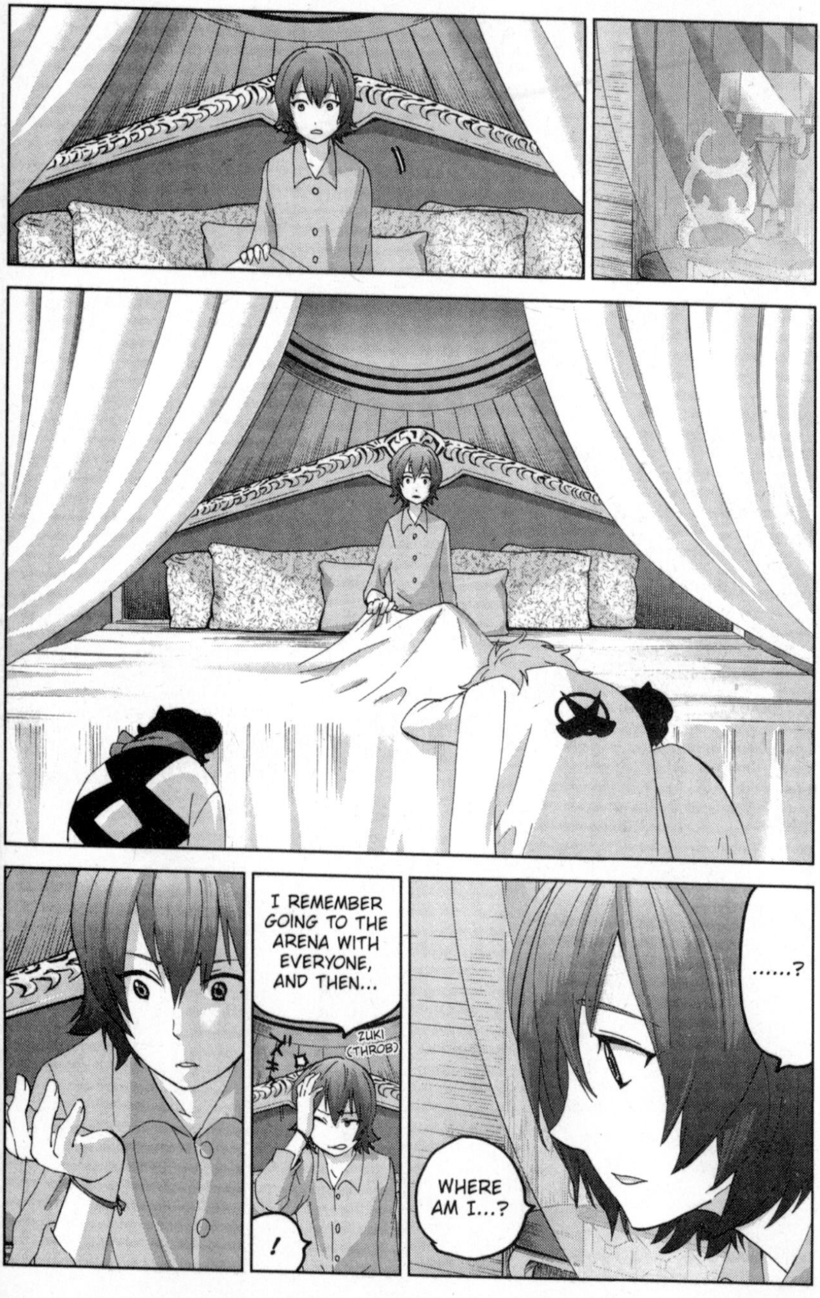

......?
WHERE AM I...?
I REMEMBER GOING TO THE ARENA WITH EVERYONE, AND THEN...
ZUKI (THROB)
!

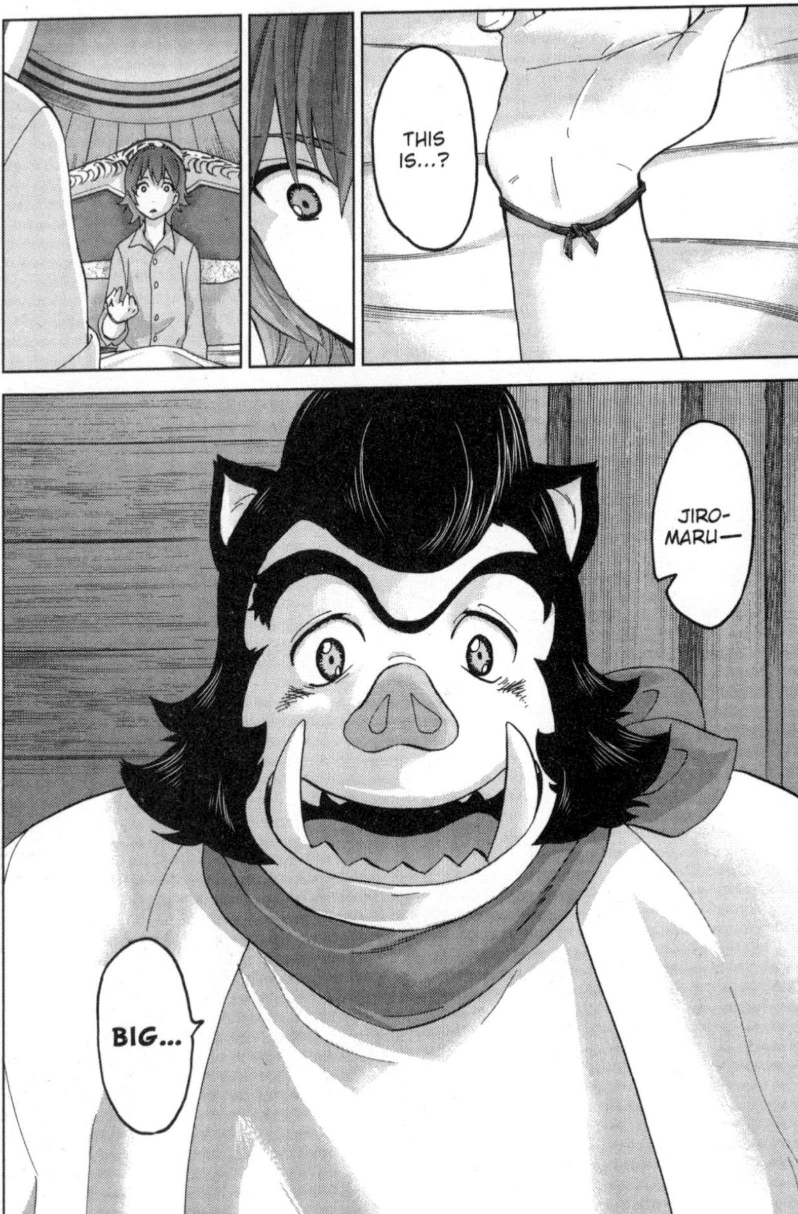
THIS IS...?
JIRO-MARU—
BIG...

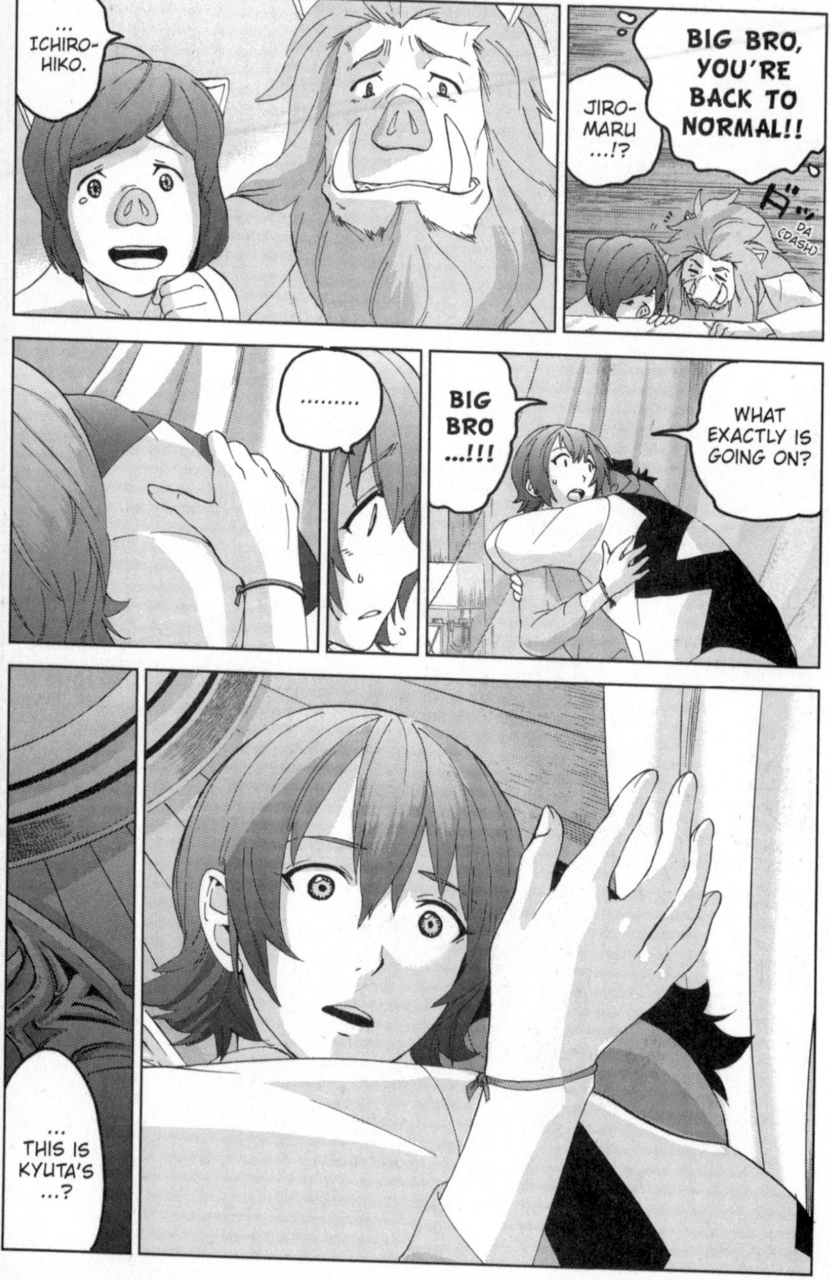
BIG BRO, YOU'RE BACK TO NORMAL!!
JIRO-MARU ...!?
DA (DASH)
... ICHIRO-HIKO.
WHAT EXACTLY IS GOING ON?
BIG BRO ...!!!
....
... THIS IS KYUTA'S ...?

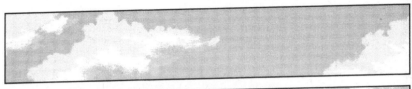

KYUTA.

...HA. I KNOW THAT.

I'M NOT THE SORT OF GUY WHO WAVERS ONCE I'VE DECIDED WHAT I'M GONNA DO.

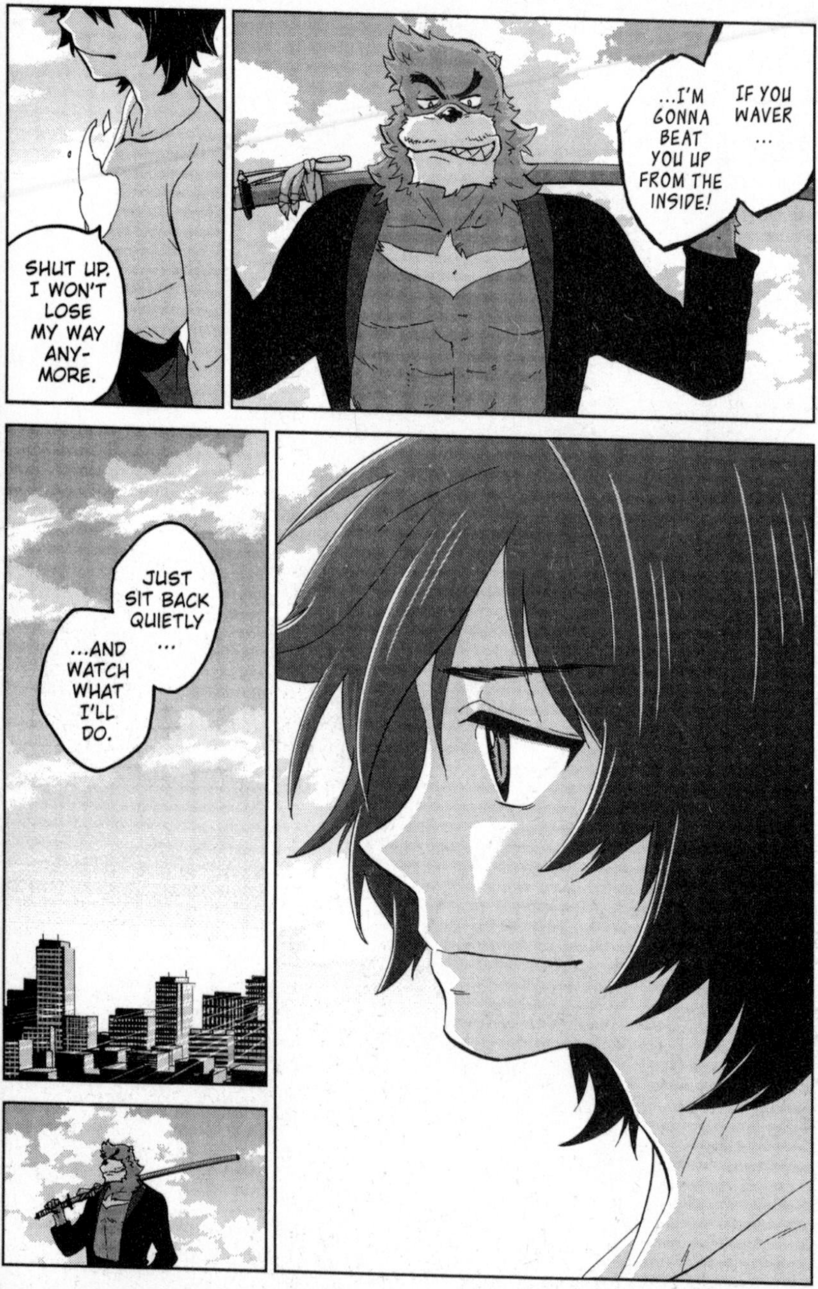
IF YOU WAVER ...
...I'M GONNA BEAT YOU UP FROM THE INSIDE!
SHUT UP. I WON'T LOSE MY WAY ANY-MORE.
JUST SIT BACK QUIETLY ...
...AND WATCH WHAT I'LL DO.

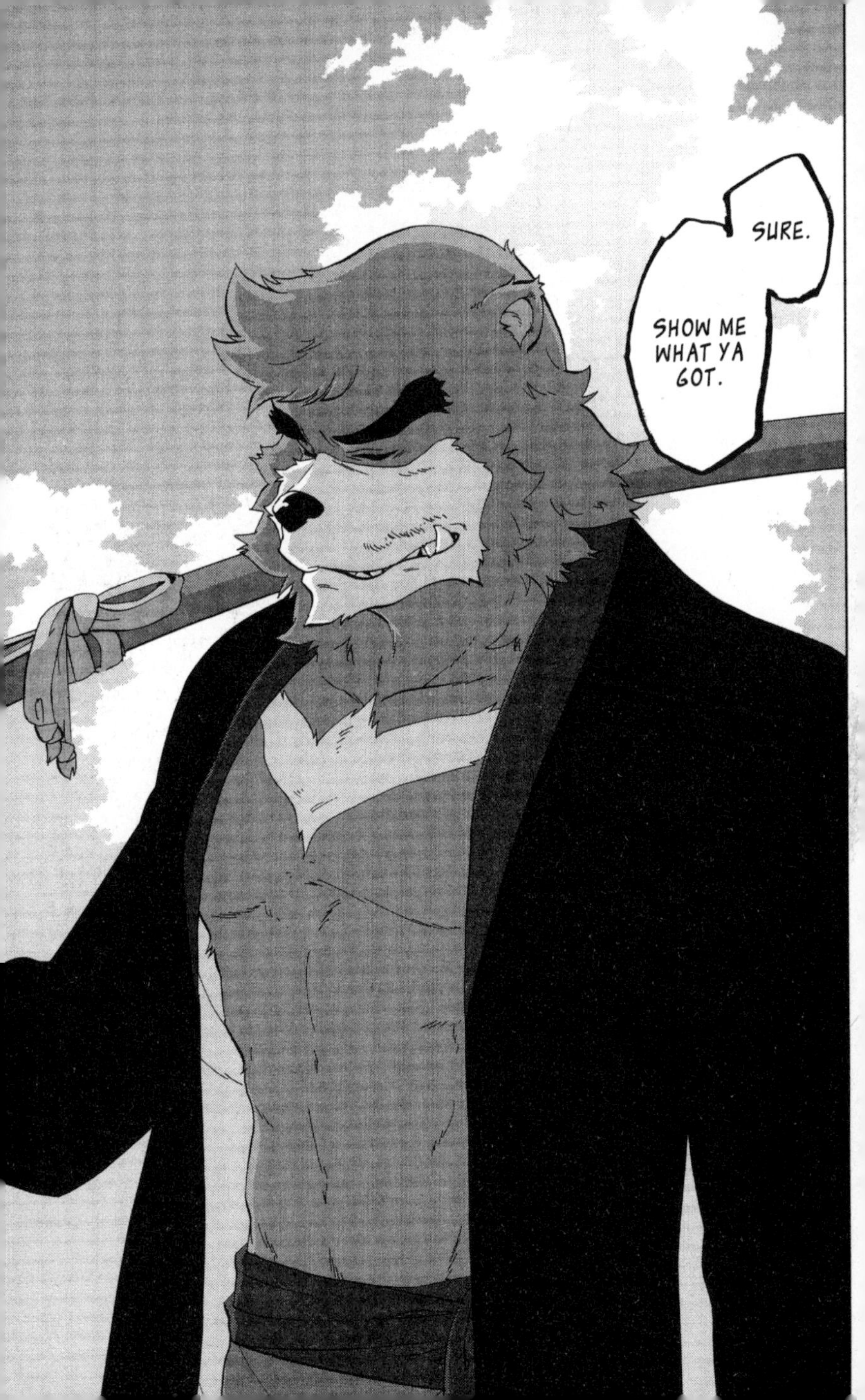
SURE.
SHOW ME WHAT YA GOT.

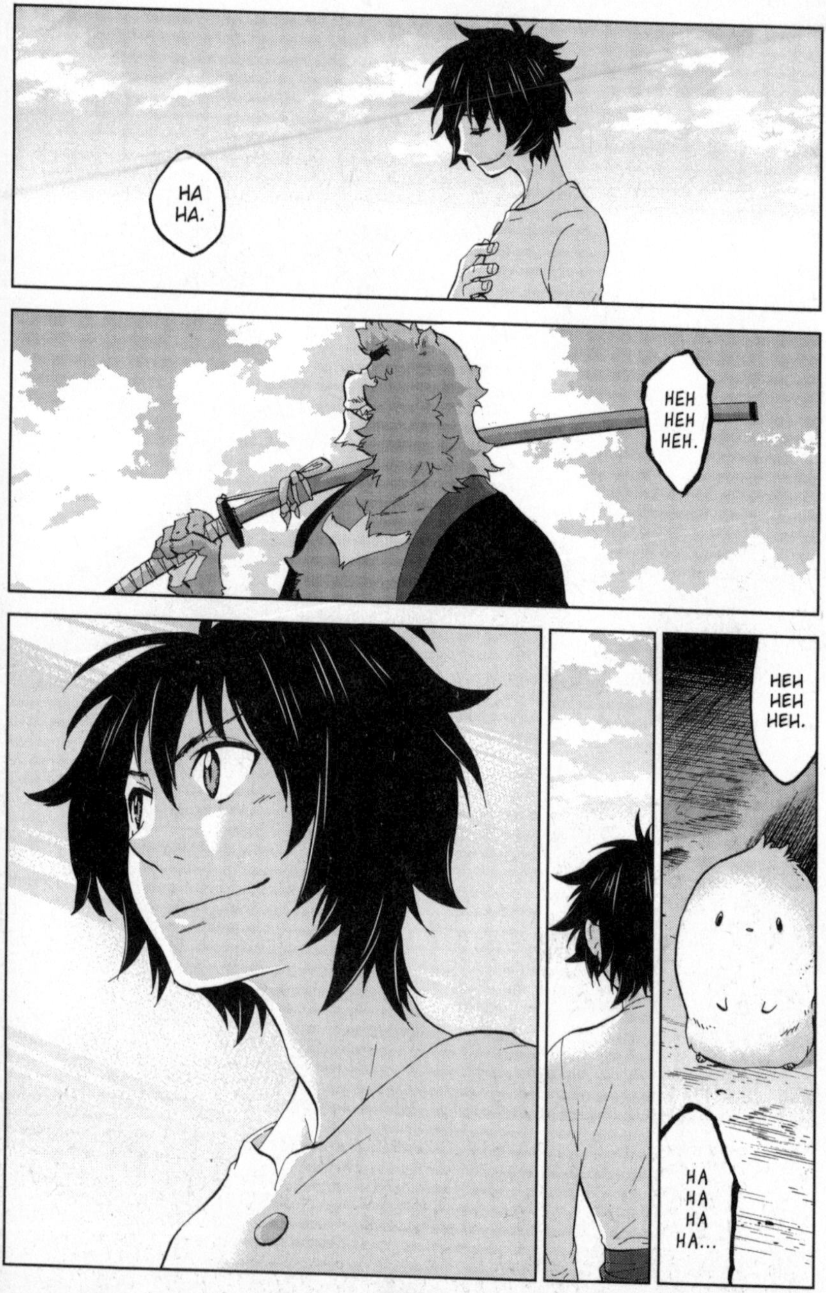
HA HA.
HEH HEH HEH.
HEH HEH HEH.
HA HA HA HA...

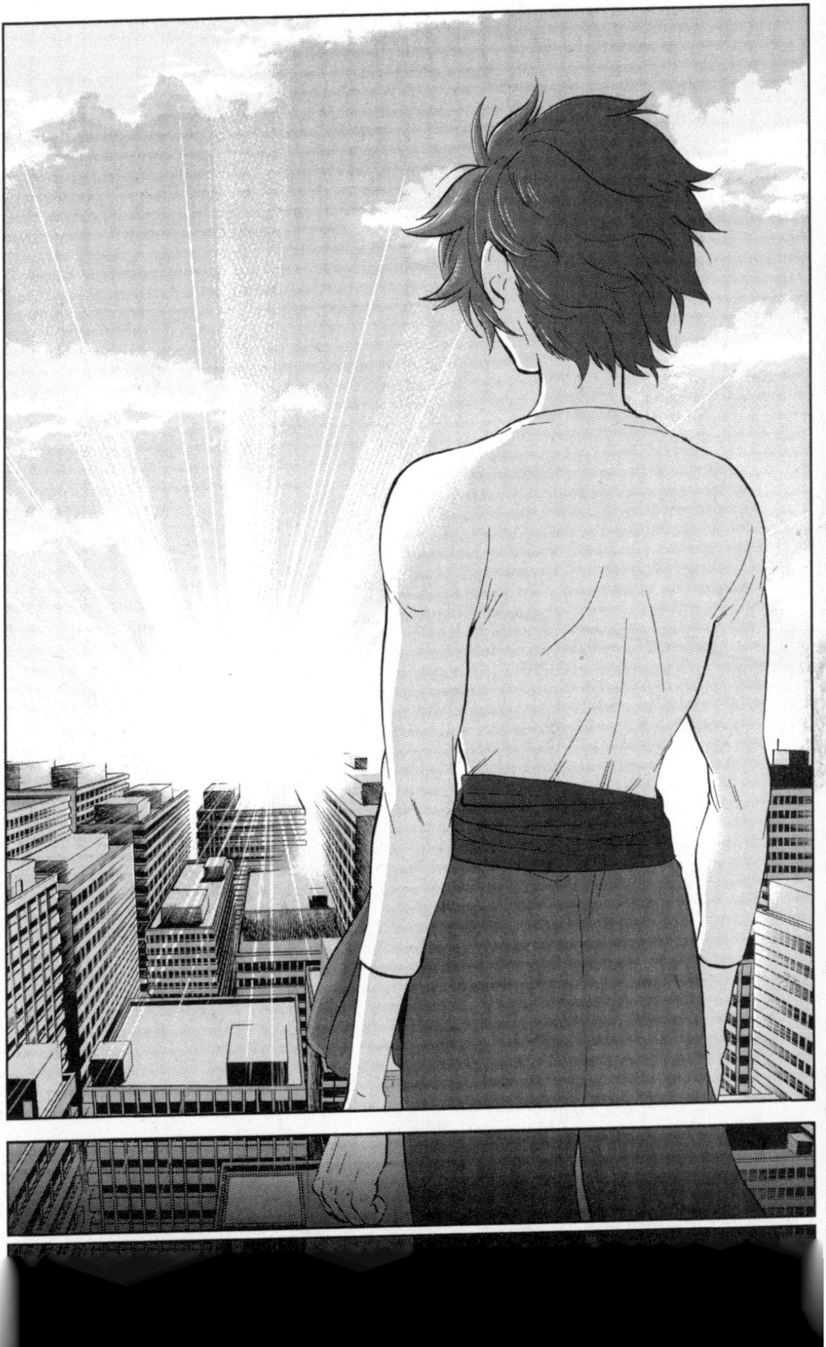

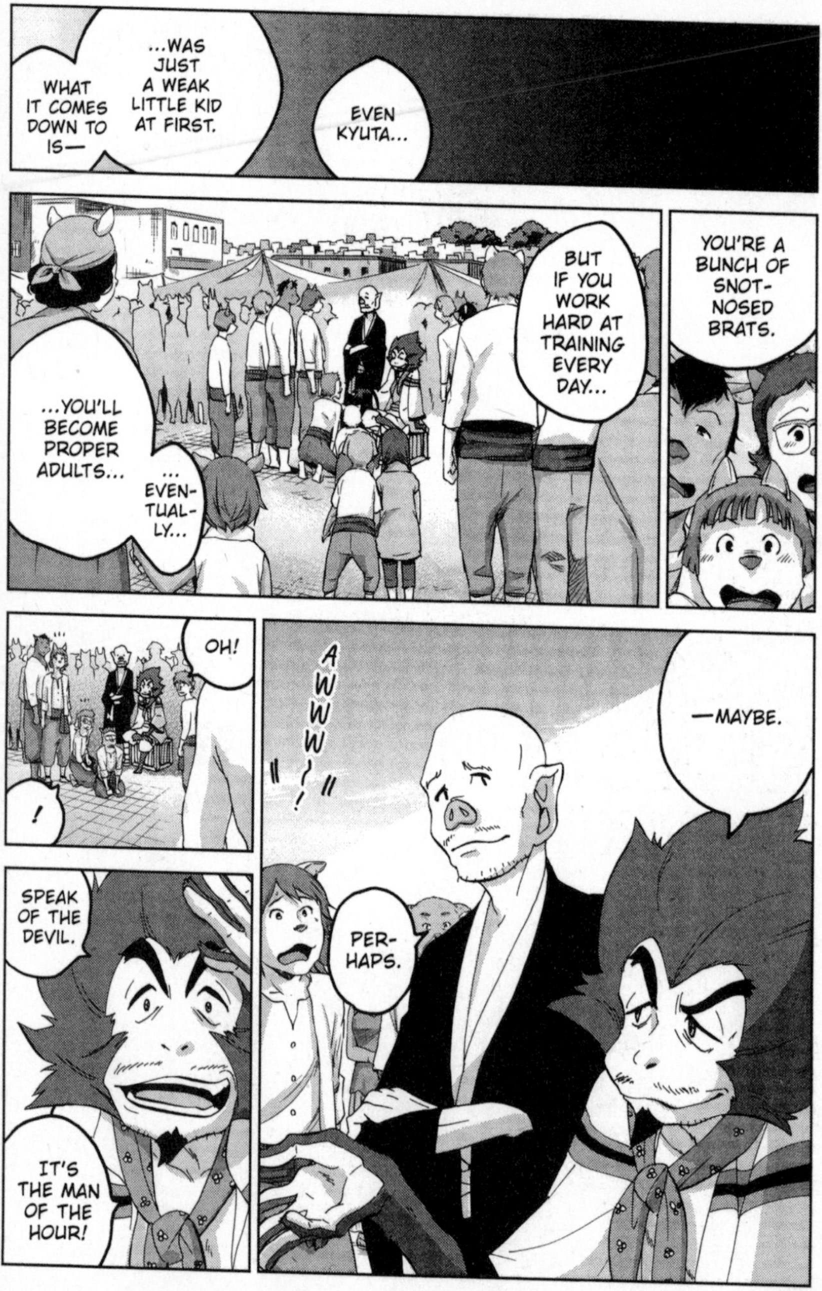
EVEN KYUTA...
...WAS JUST A WEAK LITTLE KID AT FIRST.
WHAT IT COMES DOWN TO IS—
YOU'RE A BUNCH OF SNOT-NOSED BRATS.
BUT IF YOU WORK HARD AT TRAINING EVERY DAY...
...YOU'LL BECOME PROPER ADULTS...
...EVENTUALLY...
—MAYBE.
AWWWW~!
PERHAPS.
OH!
!
SPEAK OF THE DEVIL.
IT'S THE MAN OF THE HOUR!

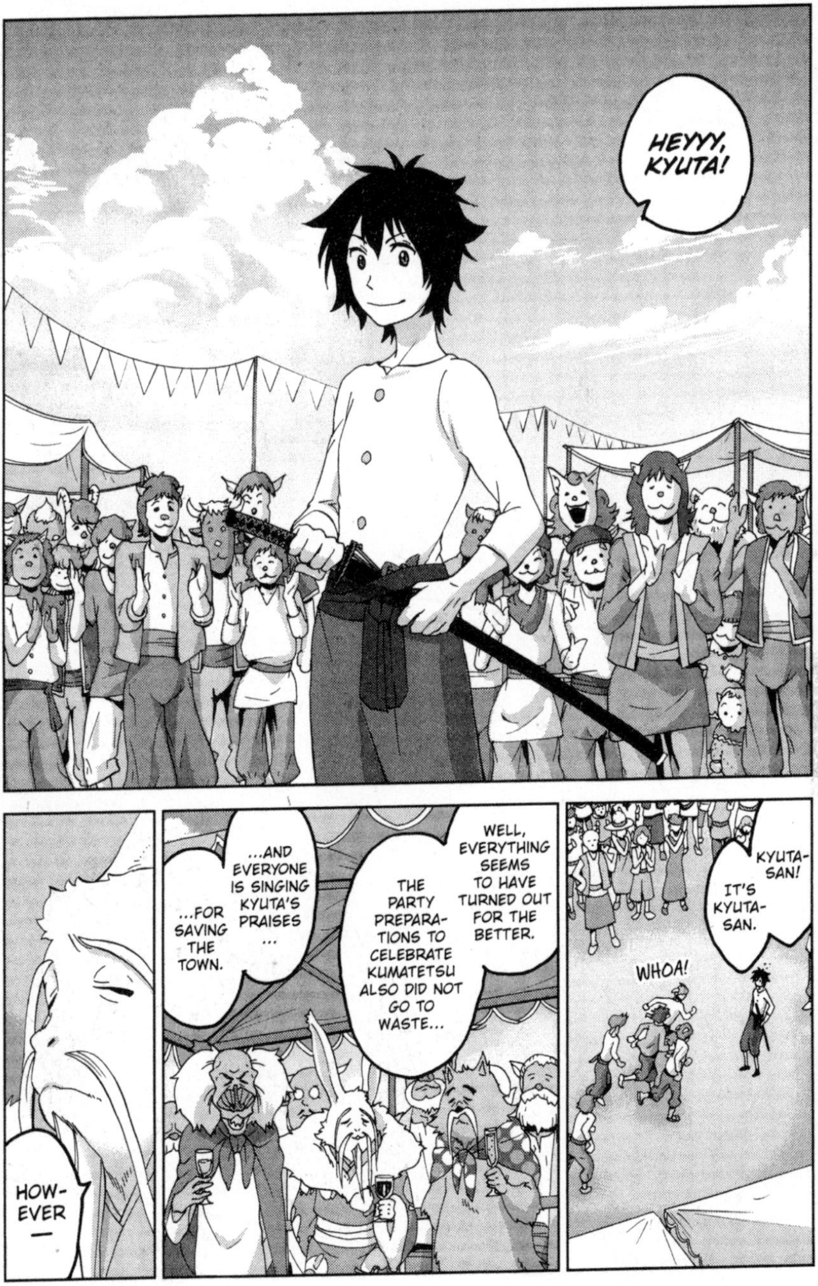
HEYYY, KYUTA!
KYUTA-SAN!
IT'S KYUTA-SAN.
WHOA!
WELL, EVERYTHING SEEMS TO HAVE TURNED OUT FOR THE BETTER.
THE PARTY PREPARATIONS TO CELEBRATE KUMATETSU ALSO DID NOT GO TO WASTE...
...AND EVERYONE IS SINGING KYUTA'S PRAISES...
...FOR SAVING THE TOWN.
HOWEVER—

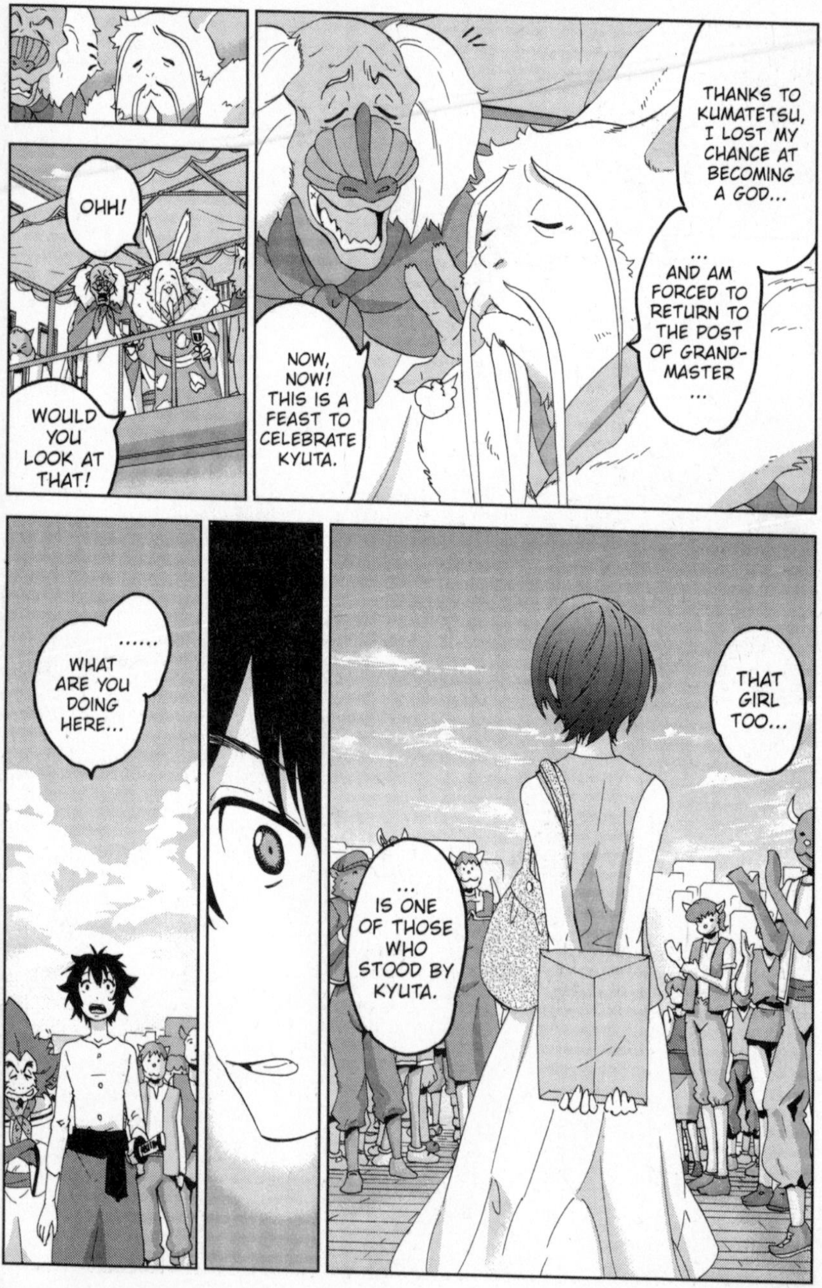
THANKS TO KUMATETSU, I LOST MY CHANCE AT BECOMING A GOD...
... AND AM FORCED TO RETURN TO THE POST OF GRAND-MASTER ...
NOW, NOW! THIS IS A FEAST TO CELEBRATE KYUTA.
OHH!
WOULD YOU LOOK AT THAT!
THAT GIRL TOO...
... IS ONE OF THOSE WHO STOOD BY KYUTA.
...... WHAT ARE YOU DOING HERE...

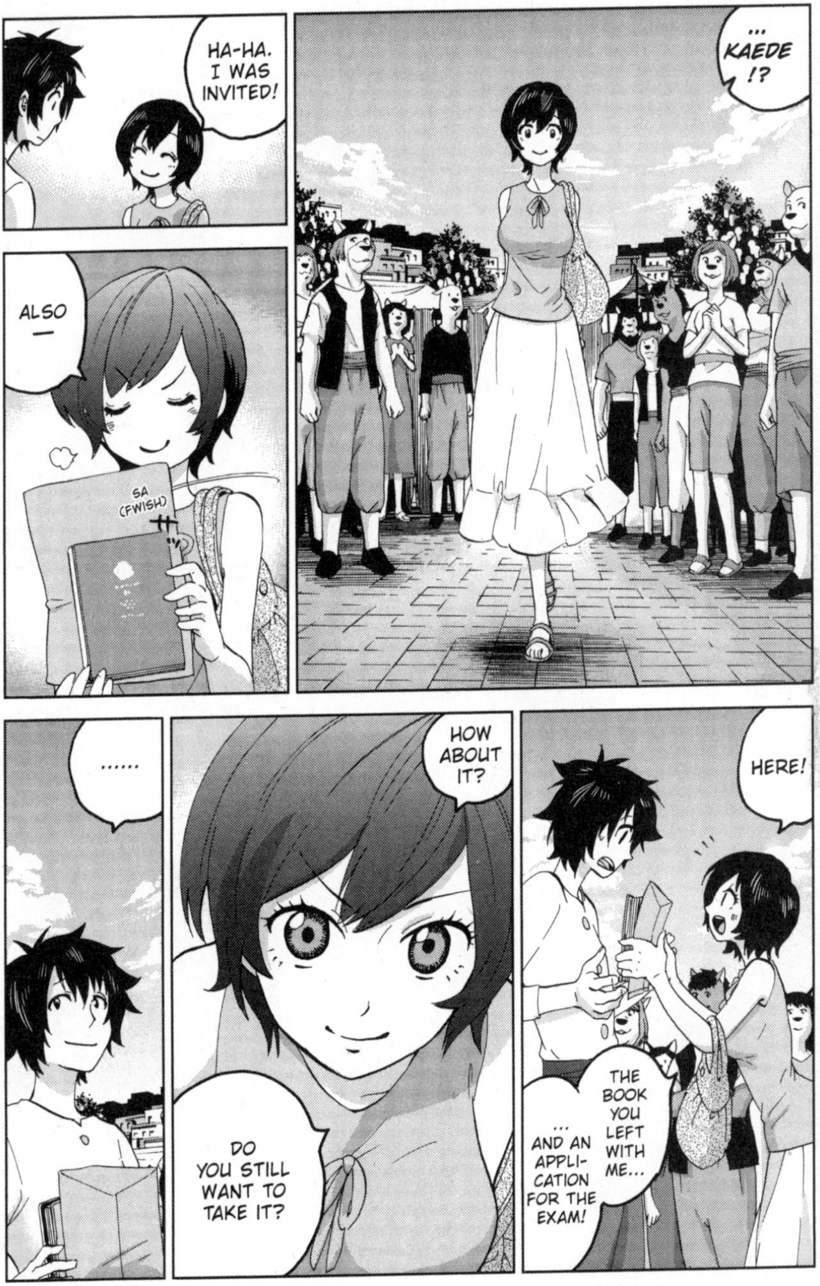
...KAEDE!?
HA-HA. I WAS INVITED!
ALSO —
SA (FWISH)
HERE!
THE BOOK YOU LEFT WITH ME...
...AND AN APPLICATION FOR THE EXAM!
HOW ABOUT IT?
DO YOU STILL WANT TO TAKE IT?
......

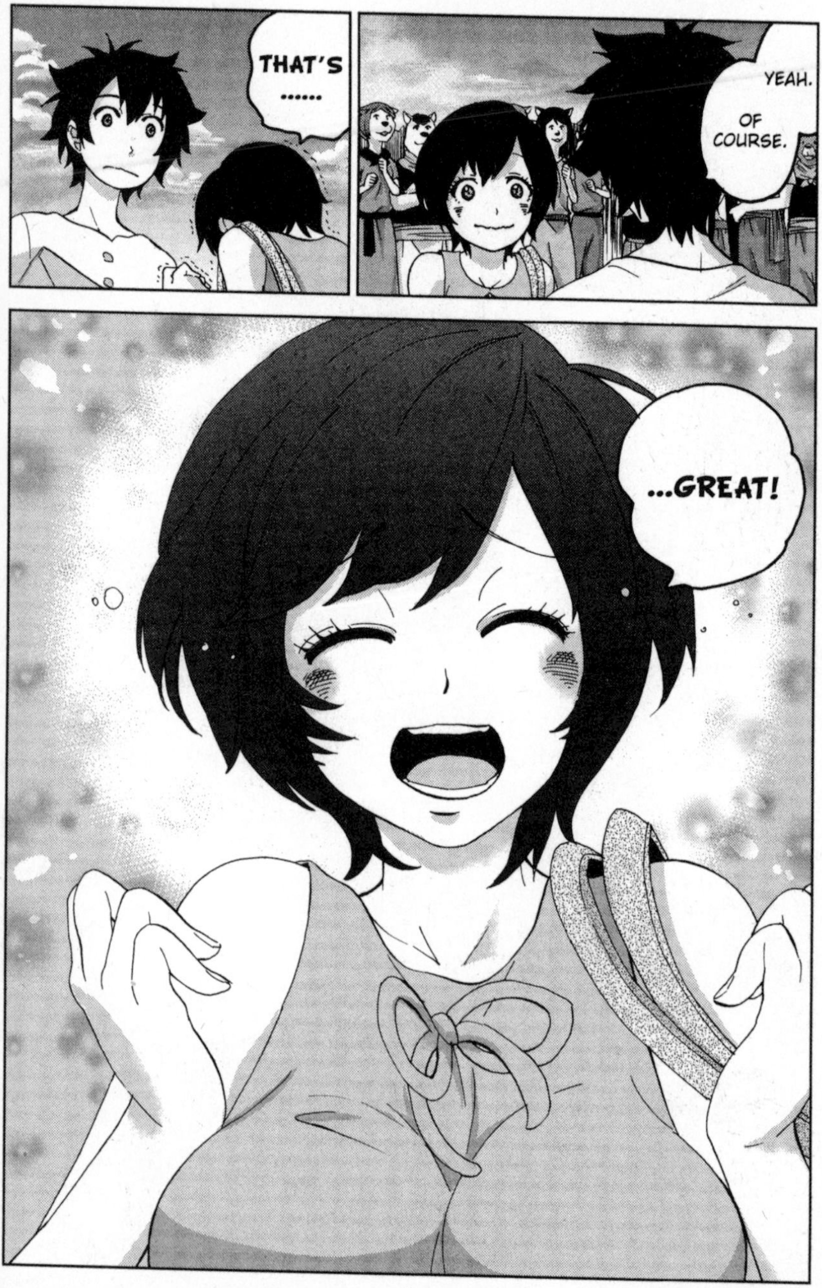
YEAH.
OF COURSE.
THAT'S ......
...GREAT!

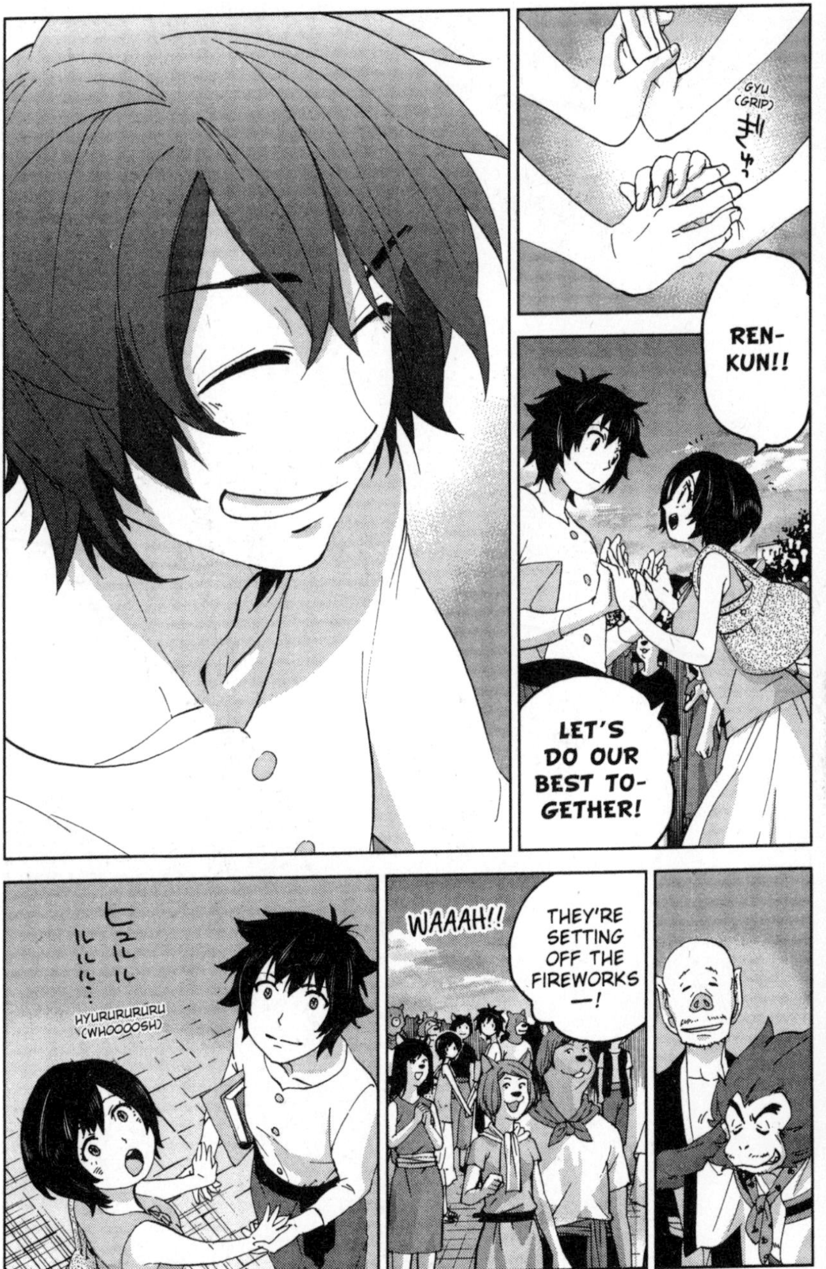
GYU (GRIP)
ぎゅ
REN-KUN!!
LET'S DO OUR BEST TO-GETHER!
WAAAH!!
THEY'RE SETTING OFF THE FIREWORKS—!
ヒュルルルルル…
HYURURURURU (WHOOOOSH)

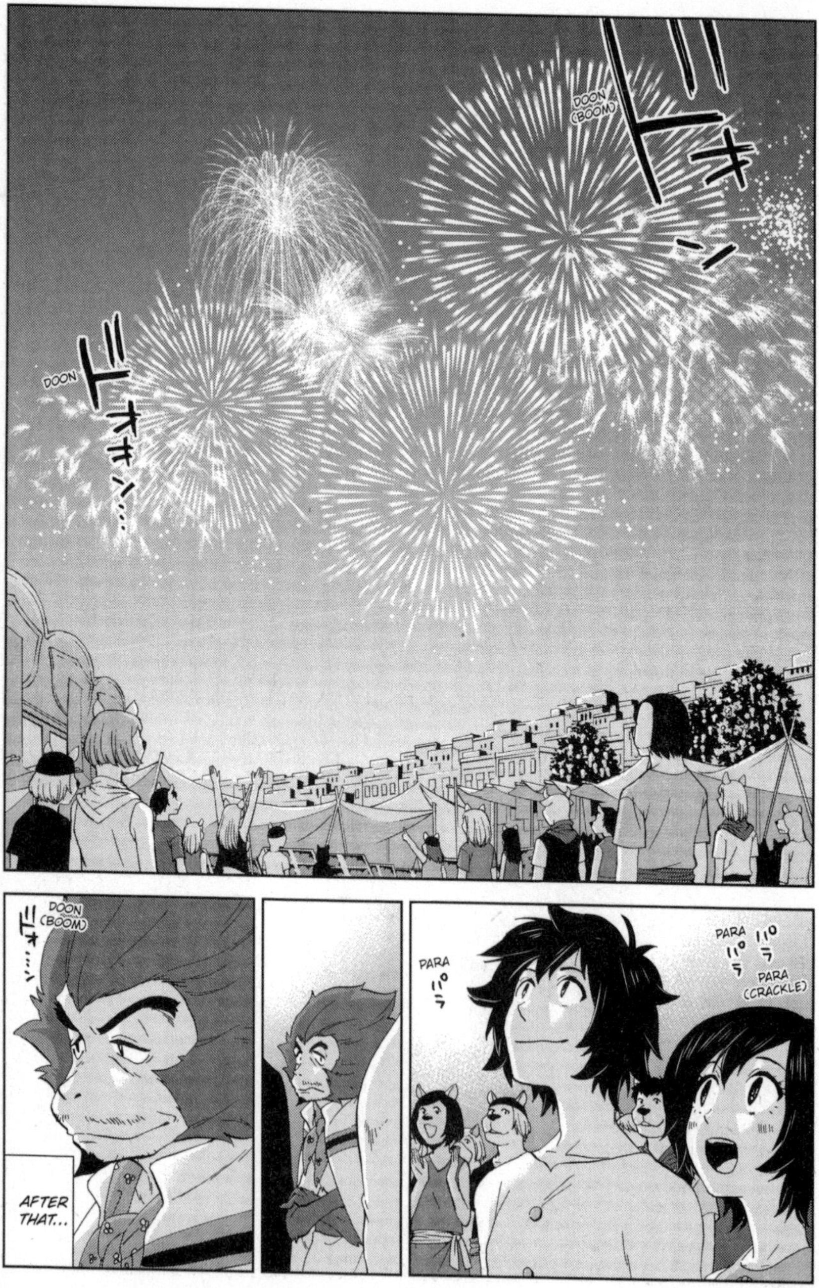
DOON (BOOM)
DOON
PARA
PARA
PARA (CRACKLE)
DOON (BOOM)
AFTER THAT...

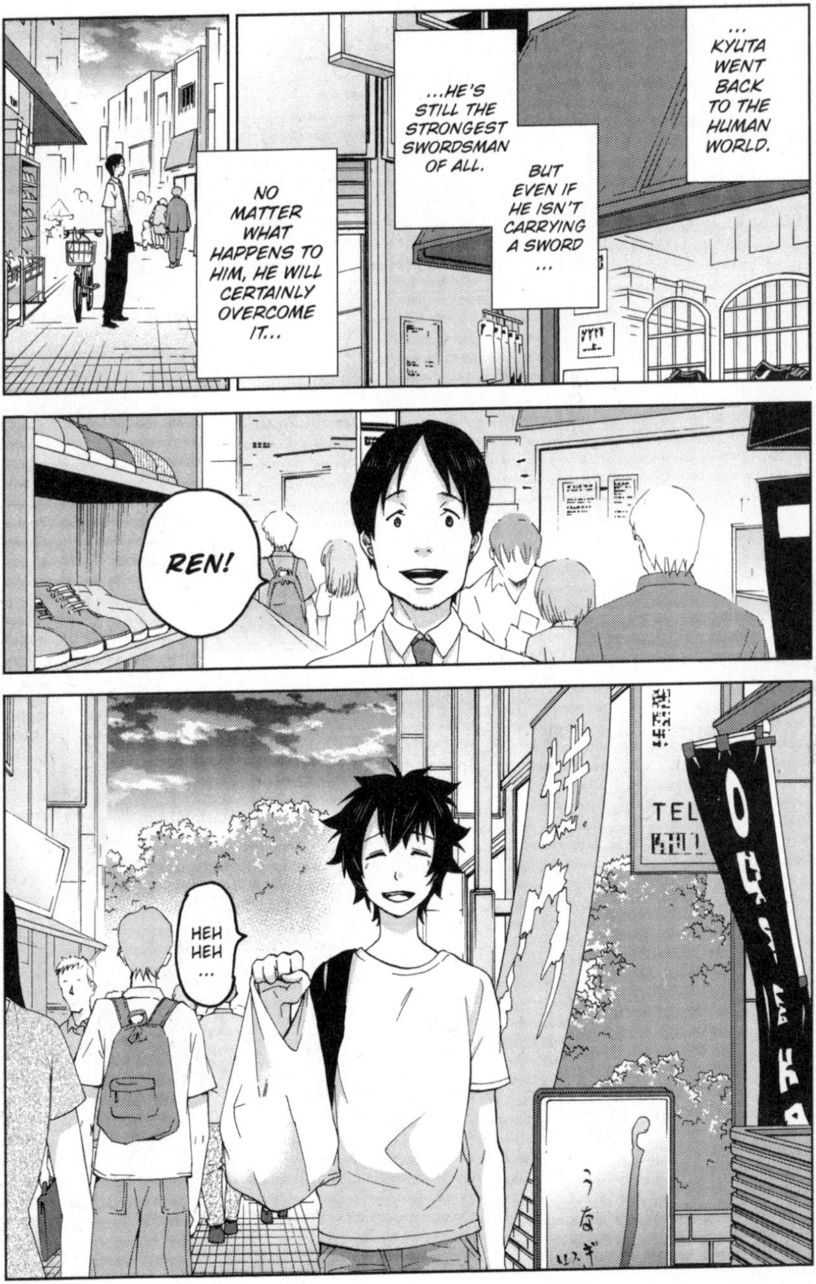
...KYUTA WENT BACK TO THE HUMAN WORLD.
BUT EVEN IF HE ISN'T CARRYING A SWORD...
...HE'S STILL THE STRONGEST SWORDSMAN OF ALL.
NO MATTER WHAT HAPPENS TO HIM, HE WILL CERTAINLY OVERCOME IT...
REN!
TEL
HEH HEH...

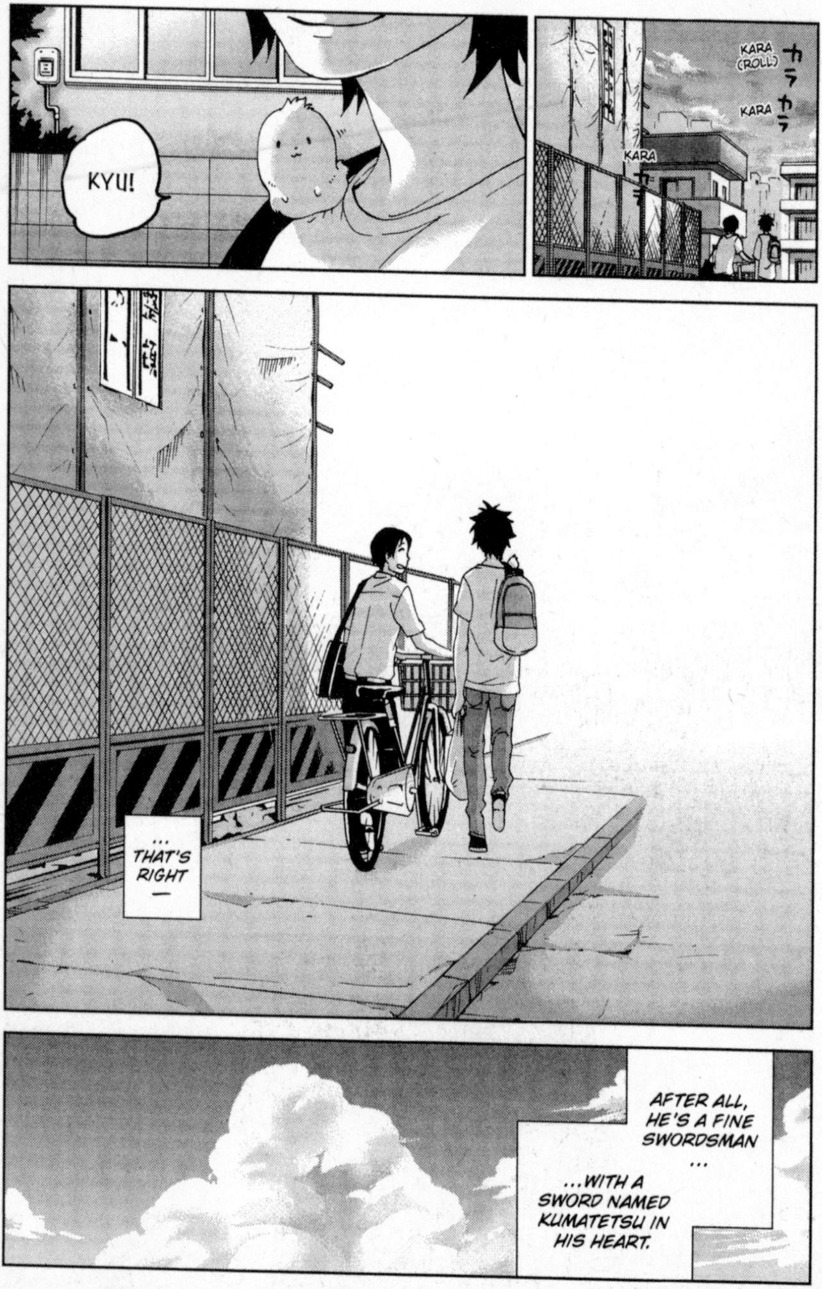
KARA (ROLL)
カラ
KARA
カラ
KARA
KYU!
...THAT'S RIGHT—
AFTER ALL, HE'S A FINE SWORDSMAN...
...WITH A SWORD NAMED KUMATETSU IN HIS HEART.

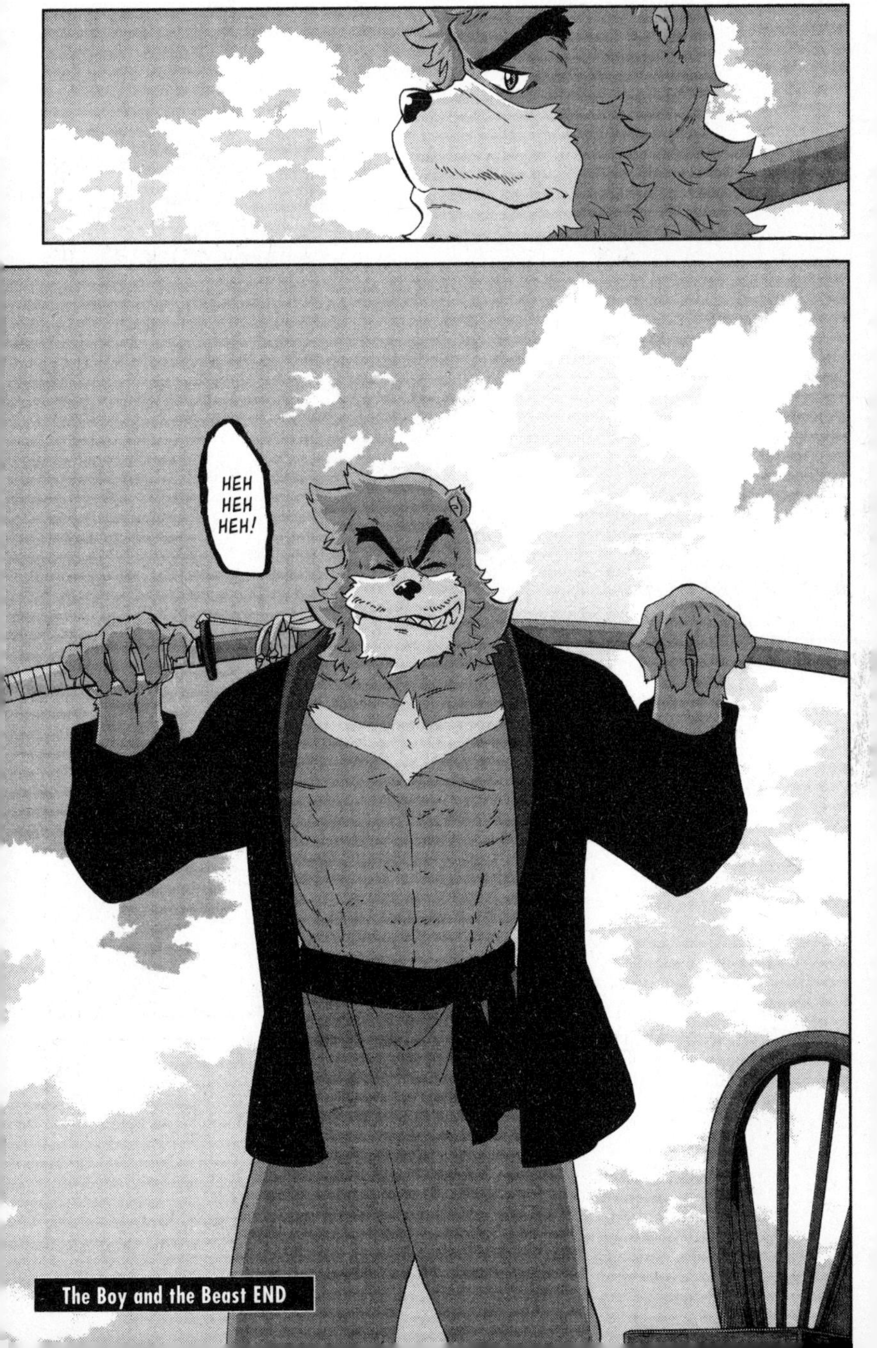
HEH HEH HEH!
The Boy and the Beast END

THANK YOU VERY MUCH FOR READING *THE BOY AND THE BEAST* VOLUME 4!

THIS IS RENJI ASAI. THANK YOU VERY MUCH FOR READING ALL THE WAY TO THE END! TO ME, THE MOVIE *THE BOY AND THE BEAST* WAS AN INCREDIBLY WARM FILM THAT WRAPPED ME IN A FEELING OF KINDNESS. IT TEACHES JUST HOW MUCH A WEAK LITTLE BOY, ALL ALONE, NEEDED THE POWER AND HELP OF SO MANY PEOPLE TO BECOME "STRONG." IT TEACHES THAT YOU ARE NEVER ALONE.

I WONDER WHAT EVERYONE THOUGHT AFTER SEEING THE MOVIE AND READING THE MANGA. I IMAGINE SOME PEOPLE WANT TO BE COOL AND STRONG LIKE KYUTA. AND SOME MAY SEE IT FROM A TEACHER OR PARENT'S POSITION, LIKE KUMATETSU, AND WANT TO SEE BOTH PARENT AND CHILD GROW TOGETHER. AND I'M SURE THERE ARE MANY, MANY MORE THINGS THAT PEOPLE FELT. I THINK THERE ARE ALWAYS SEVERAL WAYS THAT PEOPLE WILL INTERPRET THE MESSAGE OF A WORK, BUT I JUST HOPE THAT YOU ALWAYS TREASURE WHATEVER YOU FELT UPON ENCOUNTERING *THE BOY AND THE BEAST*.

DIRECTOR HOSODA, AND EVERYONE FROM STUDIO CHIZU, THANK YOU FOR ALLOWING ME THE PRECIOUS EXPERIENCE OF BEING INVOLVED IN THE COMIC ADAPTATION OF THIS MOVIE. I EAGERLY AWAIT THE ANNOUNCEMENT OF YOUR NEXT PROJECT!

SPECIAL THANKS!
YUHO UEJI-SENSEI, YAMAUCHI-SAN, OOSAKO-SAN, KAMIYA-SAN, NAGASHIMA-SAN, AKABANE-SAN, OOHASHI-SHI, NAOKI, MY EDITOR KOUSUKE KINOSHITA-SAN.

TRANSLATION NOTES

Many of the character and place names in *The Boy and the Beast* carry special significance.

-san: The Japanese equivalent of Mr./Mrs./Miss. This honorific is used as the fail-safe form of polite address.

-kun: Used most often when referring to boys, this honorific is usually used among peers and indicates familiarity or affection.

Jutengai taken literally, means "rough heavens town." However, the Japanese character for *ju* in *jutengai* corresponds to the character for *shibu* in Shibuya, so it is also meant to imply a sort of Shibuya for beasts.

Kumatetsu, appropriately enough, comes from the Japanese characters for "bear" and "strike."

Kyuta means "ninth boy." Kumatetsu gives Kyuta this name upon learning that he is nine years old. Kyuta's name in the human world, ***Ren***, means "lotus," which connotes holiness and enlightenment in the Buddhist tradition.

Iozen is derived from "boar," "king," and "mountain." Quite fitting for such a regal mountain of a boar. His two sons, meanwhile, are ***Ichirohiko*** ("first boy") and ***Jiromaru*** ("second boy").

PAGE 75
Ichirohiko picks up the copy of *Moby Dick* that Kaede has dropped. The novel often refers to Moby Dick as "the white whale," the two being synonymous.

PAGE 138
Tsukumogami are a type of *youkai*, or spirits in Japanese folklore. They are produced from tools or other objects that have been used and beloved by their owners for one hundred years. The suffix *-gami* means "god," and since Kumatetsu can decide what kind of god he would like to reincarnate as, he chooses to become the *tsukumogami* of his sword in order to literally become the sword in Kyuta's heart.

The Boy and the Beast ❹

Original Story **Mamoru Hosoda** · *Art* **Renji Asai**

Translation: Leighann Harvey · Lettering: Bianca Pistillo

THE BOY AND THE BEAST
©Renji ASAI 2016
©2015 THE BOY AND THE BEAST FILM PARTNERS
First published in Japan in 2016 by KADOKAWA CORPORATION, Tokyo. English translation rights arranged with KADOKAWA CORPORATION, Tokyo, through TUTTLE-MORI AGENCY, INC., Tokyo.

English translation © 2018 by Yen Press, LLC

Yen Press
1290 Avenue of the Americas
New York, NY 10104

Visit us at yenpress.com
facebook.com/yenpress
twitter.com/yenpress
yenpress.tumblr.com
instagram.com/yenpress

First Yen Press Edition: December 2018

Yen Press is an imprint of Yen Press, LLC.
The Yen Press name and logo are trademarks of Yen Press, LLC.

The publisher is not responsible for websites (or their content) that are not owned by the publisher.

Library of Congress Control Number: 2015955216

ISBN: 978-1-9753-2621-0

10 9 8 7 6 5 4 3 2 1

WOR

Printed in the United States of America